Essays on Secularism and Multiculturalism

ECPR Press

ECPR Press is an imprint of the European Consortium for Political Research in partnership with Rowman & Littlefield International. It publishes original research from leading political scientists and the best among early career researchers in the discipline. Its scope extends to all fields of political science, international relations and political thought, without restriction in either approach or regional focus. It is also open to interdisciplinary work with a predominant political dimension.

ECPR Press Editors

Editors

Ian O'Flynn is Senior Lecturer in Political Theory at Newcastle University, UK.

Laura Sudulich is Senior Lecturer in Politics and International Relations at the University of Kent, UK. She is also affiliated to Cevipol (Centre d'Étude de la vie Politique) at the Université libre de Bruxelles, Belgium.

Associate Editors

Andrew Glencross is Senior Lecturer in the Department of Politics and International Relations at Aston University, UK.

Liam Weeks is Lecturer in the Department of Government and Politics, University College Cork, Ireland, and Honorary Senior Research Fellow, Department of Politics and International Relations, Macquarie University, Australia.

Essays on Secularism and Multiculturalism

Tariq Modood

ROWMAN &
LITTLEFIELD
───── INTERNATIONAL
London • New York

Published by Rowman & Littlefield International, Ltd.
6 Tinworth Street, London SE11 5AL
www.rowmaninternational.com

In partnership with the European Consortium for Political Research, Harbour House, 6-8 Hythe Quay, Colchester, CO2 8JF, United Kingdom

Rowman & Littlefield International, Ltd. is an affiliate of
Rowman & Littlefield
4501 Forbes Boulevard, Suite 200, Lanham, Maryland 20706, USA
With additional offices in Boulder, New York, Toronto (Canada), and London (UK)
www.rowman.com

Copyright © 2019 by Tariq Modood

All rights reserved. No part of this book may be reproduced in any form or by any electronic or mechanical means, including information storage and retrieval systems, without written permission from the publisher, except by a reviewer who may quote passages in a review.

British Library Cataloguing in Publication Information
A catalogue record for this book is available from the British Library

ISBN: HB 978-1-78552-318-2
ISBN: PB 978-1-78552-319-9

Library of Congress Cataloging-in-Publication Data Available

ISBN: 978-1-78552-318-2 (cloth)
ISBN: 978-1-78552-319-9 (pbk.)
ISBN: 978-1-78552-317-5 (electronic)

For Bhikhu Parekh and the rest of the Bristol School of Multiculturalism, and for Geoff Levey for noticing.

Contents

Acknowledgements	ix
Introduction: Rethinking Political Secularism: The Multiculturalist Challenge	1
I: The Racialisation of Muslims / Muslims as 'Race Relations' Actors	**31**
1 Racism, Culturalism and Cultural Racism	33
2 Ethno-Religious Assertiveness Out of Racial Equality	47
3 Maintaining Civility and the Feelings of the Hated	61
4 Islamophobia and the Struggle for Recognition	75
5 Pointing to a Multicultural Future: Rethinking Race, Ethnicity, Religion and Britishness	89
II: Multiculturalism and Secularism	**115**
6 Muslims, Religious Equality and Secularism	117
7 Multicultural Citizenship and the Shari'a Controversy in Britain	135
8 Moderate Secularism, Religion as Identity and Respect for Religion	145
9 Multiculturalism and the 'Crisis of Secularism'	163
10 State-Religion Connexions and Multicultural Citizenship	179
11 Multiculturalizing Secularism	195
12 Intercultural Public Intellectual Engagement	215
Index	235

About the Author 249

Acknowledgements

The following chapters are republished with the kind permission of the publishers of the original essays.

Part I:
The Racialisation of Muslims / Muslims as 'Race Relations' Actors

1. *Multicultural Politics: Racism, Ethnicity, and Muslims in Britain*. Minneapolis: University of Minnesota Press and Edinburgh: Edinburgh University Press, pp. 6–21 (2005).

2. 'Ethno-Religious Assertiveness Out of Racial Equality'. In Llewellyn, D. and Sharma, S. (eds.), *Religion, Equalities, and Inequalities*, pp. 38–48. Farnham, UK: Ashgate (2016).

3. 'Hate Speech: The Feelings and Beliefs of the Hated'. In 'Understanding and Regulating Hate Speech: A Symposium on Jeremy Waldron's *The Harm in Hate Speech*'. *Contemporary Political Theory*, 13, pp. 104–109 (2014); and 'Censor or Censure: Maintaining Civility'. In Griffith-Jones, R. (ed.), *Islam and English Law: Rights, Responsibilities and the Place of Shari'a*, pp. 216–224. Cambridge: Cambridge University Press (2013).

4. This chapter is expanded from my 'Islamophobia and the Struggle for Recognition'. In Elahi, F. and Khan, O. (eds.), *Islamophobia: Still a Challenge for Us All*. London: Runnymede Trust, pp. 66–68 (2017) and my Submission to the All-Party Parliamentary Group on British Muslims in response to the call for evidence on 'Working Definition of Islamophobia', 1 June, 2018: https://www.academia.edu/36775691/Islamophobia_A_Form_of_Cultural_Racism.

5. 'Pointing to a Multicultural Future: Rethinking Race, Ethnicity, Religion and Britishness'. In Foblets, M.-C. and Alidadi, K. (eds.), *Public Commissions on Cultural and Religious Diversity: Vol. 2, Internal Dialogues,*

Critical Compromises and Real-Life Impact, pp. 23–46. Farnham, UK: Ashgate (2018).

Part II:
Multiculturalism and Secularism

6. 'Muslims, Religious Equality and Secularism'. In Levey, G. B. and Modood, T. (eds.), *Secularism, Religion and Multicultural Citizenship*, pp. 164–185. Cambridge: Cambridge University Press (2009).

7. Modood, T. (2010). 'Multicultural Nicholas Citizenship and the Shari'a Controversy in Britain'. In Ahdar, Rex J. and Aroney, Nicholas (eds.), *Shari'a in the West*, pp. 33–42. Oxford: Oxford University Press (2010).

8. 'Moderate Secularism, Religion as Identity and Respect for Religion'. *Political Quarterly*, *81*(1): 4–14 (2010).

9. '2011 Paul Hanly Furfey Lecture: "Is There a Crisis of Secularism in Western Europe?"'. *Sociology of Religion*, *73*(2), pp. 130–149 (2012).

10. 'State-Religion Connections and Multicultural Citizenship'. In Cohen, J. L. and Laborde, C. (eds.), *Religion, Secularism, and Constitutional Democracy*, pp. 182–203. New York: Columbia University Press (2016).

11. 'Multiculturalizing Secularism'. In Shook, J. and Zuckerman, P. (eds.), *Oxford Handbook on Secularism*, pp. 354–368. Oxford: Oxford University Press (2017).

12. 'Intercultural Public Intellectual Engagement'. In Mansouri, F. (ed.), *Interculturalism at the Crossroads*, pp. 83–103. Paris: UNESCO (2017).

I am also thankful for the funding which has provided me with the time to write the above essays:

Leverhulme Trust Bristol-UCL Programme on Population Movements (2002–2008);

AHRC Fellowship, 'Political Secularism and the Accommodation of Muslims in Western Europe' (2010–2011);

Visiting Professor, Institute of Human Sciences (IWM), Vienna (2011);

EU FP7 'Tolerance, Pluralism and Social Cohesion' (ACCEPT) Project (PI: Anna Triandafyllidou, EUI) (2010–2013);

Robert Schuman Fellow, Robert Schuman Centre for Advanced Studies, European University Institute, Florence (2013–2015);

University of Bristol Research Fellowship (2014–2015);

Thinker in Residence, Programme on Multiculturality, Royal Academy of Flanders, Brussels (2017);

EU H2020, 'Radicalisation, Secularism and the Governance of Religious Diversity: Bringing together European and Asian Perspectives (GREASE)' project (PI: Anna Triandafyllidou, EUI) (2018–2021).

Finally, I am grateful for the many invitations I have had – too numerous to mention – to present my work in progress and engage with a variety of scholars, students and publics.

Introduction

*Rethinking Political Secularism:
The Multiculturalist Challenge*[1]

There may be various reasons to rethink political secularism, but in my view the most significant today, certainly in Western Europe, is the one I present in this book and which I understand as the multiculturalist challenge. It is clear West European states are now highly exercised by the challenges posed by post-immigration ethno-religious diversity and that the new Muslim settlements of the last fifty years or so are at the centre of it. This forces new thinking, not only about questions of social integration but also about the role of religion in relation to the state and citizenship. Accordingly, a fundamental issue that many thought had long been settled re-emerges with new vitality and controversy – namely, political secularism, especially as it articulates with questions of tolerance, recognition, and governance. My own contribution to the climate of 're-thinking secularism' has been to argue that what is sometimes talked about as the 'post-secular' or a 'crisis of secularism' is, in Western Europe, quite crucially to do with the reality of *multiculturalism*. By which I mean not just the fact of new ethno-religious diversity but the presence of a multiculturalist approach to this diversity. That is to say, the idea that equality must be extended from uniformity of treatment to include respect for difference; recognition of public/private interdependence rather than dichotomized as in classical liberalism; the public recognition and institutional accommodation of minorities; the reversal of marginalisation and a remaking of national citizenship so that all can have a sense of belonging to it. This multiculturalist challenge, at one time seen to go with the flow of liberalism – of human rights, racial equality, decomposition of collectivities such as the nation – is properly understood as requiring not just the reform and extension of liberal democratic institutions, but also a re-thinking of liberalism. Equally, the question arises, with greater and greater force, what implication does the emergence of this ethno-religious sociopolitical complex have for political secularism (indeed for secular institutions such as workplaces, schools, hospitals, universities, etc., more generally).

This collection of essays published during 2005–2018 explains the racialisation of Muslims in Western Europe, especially Britain, by reference to issues such as discrimination, free speech and incitement to hatred, identity assertiveness, institutional accommodation and the re-making of national identity and argues that the result is that political secularism is once again a live issue in Europe. This time it is not to do with the power of a dominant church or two rival Christian denominations but religious minorities that centre on their religious identity in ways that most Europeans have ceased to do. To insist that, notably, Muslims should also not prioritise their religious identity – or if they do they should not expect equal citizenship or full membership of the national community – is to pit a religion-marginalising radical secularism, most visible in France, against the kind of diversity-based inclusion that is being practiced in relation to ethnic/racial minorities, not to mention women, LGBT communities or sub-state nations.

If the first step of my argument is to show that Islamophobia is a form of cultural racism, the next step is to show that anti-racism, whether in terms of difference-blind neutral liberal state or in terms of active de-othering, is not enough. We need a conception of equal citizenship that brings together the equality of same treatment with the equality of respect for difference – in short, a multiculturalism. Combining a sociology of cultural racism, an analysis of a number of West European political controversies involving Muslims and a political theory of multiculturalism the essays here show that equal citizenship requires a difference-sensitive accommodation of Muslim and other religious identities and that this means revisiting and rethinking the concept of political secularism. I distinguish between the U.S. religious-freedom based separation of church and state, a French-style marginalisation of organised religion in the public space and what I argue is the dominant mode of political secularism in Western Europe. I call this 'moderate secularism' and I elaborate its norms in the way of a Weberian ideal type or contextualised political theory (as explained below), demonstrating that it does not consist of a separation of religion and the state. It in fact includes state recognition of and state support for religion (e.g., all the states of the European Union, including France, fund specific faith schools or instruct specific Christian faiths in state schools: Stepan 2011, 117) but insists that religious authority must not control political authority. In giving primacy to liberal democratic constitutionalism it marries a conception of religious freedom with an understanding that religion can be a public good and that the state may need to assist it in achieving that good (see chapter 8). I argue that

Muslims can be and should be accommodated within moderate secularism; and to do so is to achieve an egalitarian integration, a multiculturalized secularism.

ANTI-RACISM, IDENTITY ASSERTIVENESS AND MULTICULTURAL ACCOMMODATION

When I began to write on these topics, following interventions during 'the Rushdie affair' in the 1990s, religion and secularism were marginal topics in both sociology and political theory, yet they have become highly prominent in both. This movement has had many strands. Contrary to many I do not believe that the central issue is the passing away of enlightenment ideologies, an intellectualised 'crisis of secularism' or 'post-secularism' but the emergence of religion in the field of 'the politics of difference'. These essays, then, are a multiculturalist interrogation of political secularism in the West, specifically Western Europe. In this region there are two main movements/reactions. While one approach, in which Britain has been a pathfinder, is to extend and reconceptualise multiculturalism; the other, most evident in France is to use or radical secularism to refuse the accommodation of Muslims and Islam and to reinforce a rejection of multiculturalism (see chapter 9).[2]

How in Western Europe groups and controversies defined in terms of race or foreignness came to be redefined in terms of religion and how the accommodation of Muslims came to be the dominant issue in relation to multiculturalism has now been well established (Modood 2005 and 2007/2013). Part I probes further this trajectory of racialisation in relation to issues such as Islamophobia, hate speech and Muslim assertiveness and I will not add to that aspect of the book here. I will devote this introduction to how these controversies have a multiculturalist aspect and as such have stimulated debates about what was thought to be the dead topic of secularism; and also reflect a little on the modes of analysis I deploy. The last section of the introduction will summarise what is to be found in each chapter.

A good entry point into thinking about these themes is to consider how we have travelled from the racial equality of what we might call basic liberalism – say, the civil rights movement of the Reverend Martin Luther King – to the multicultural accommodation of assertive religious minorities. King's basic plea was that the United States live up to the pledge of its constitution that all men are equal and recognise African Americans as full U.S. citizens with the same – no more, no less – rights as white Americans. Implicit in his deeply Christian political mobilisation and the African American struggle for dignity more generally was to get black Americans to think of themselves as a group, as a people, as black Americans and to invest their time, energy, passion and hope in that identity; and be willing to make, where necessary, substantial self-sacrifices for the dignity of that identity. The younger radicals, such as Malcolm X (who changed his name to El-Hajj Malik El-Shabazz after his conversion to Islam), extended this logic further – not just in terms of a political radicalism, but also in the new emergent black identity – and argued African Americans should not just invest in this emergent identity politically but invest in it as much of their being as possible. This 'black and proud' identity – however alien to basic liberalism – came to be at the centre of, perhaps even to define, American anti-racism. This powerful movement found resonance among people of African descent and others living in white-dominated societies, including Britain, where its appeal extended to some newly arrived postcolonials from South Asia. What this movement achieved was to turn what until then was perceived as a negative identity – namely, 'black' (such that the BBC could not use that word on air but referred to 'coloured people') – into a positive identity. Black people had appropriated the term for themselves, not to describe a condition of inferiority but of hope and struggle for equality. An equality not of abstract, colour-blind individuals but of colour-self-defining collectivities as well as individuals.

The long-term effect of this identarian anti-racism was not just in the creation of one powerful identity movement but also in making self-chosen identity movements central to equality and majority-minority relations. In Britain, one of these was the refusing of a racialised identity for an ethnic identity. While the American case of turning a negative racialised identity (black) into a positive identity (black) was emulated by British anti-racists in the 1970s and 1980s, the minorities themselves followed the spirit rather than the letter of the U.S. case. British Asians – more numerous than people of African descent or African Caribbeans in Britain by the 1980s – began to think of themselves as British Asian or as British Indians, Pakistanis, Bangladeshis, and so on and to request that British society attend to them as such. This development was initially allied with and later overtaken by the refusal of a racialised identity for a religious identity. Initially led by the Sikh campaign for the right of Sikh men to wear turbans in schools and workplaces (recognised in English law in 1982 through a victory in the courts), it came to be most identified by the demand of some Muslims that they wanted British society to primarily recognise them and include them as Muslims rather than or not just by reference to a colour identity or their non-European origins.

This identarian thrust of anti-racism, besides showing the religious roots of anti-racism in the United States in the third quarter of the twentieth century, and the influence of that movement in Britain is critical to the emergence and development of multiculturalism. While Canada's state multiculturalism and the contribution of its illustrious political theorists such as Charles Taylor, Will Kymlicka, James Tully and Joe Carens is, with good reason, often cited as a beacon of multiculturalism, in Britain the African American influence is stronger. It gave to British multiculturalism its bottoms-up and anti-racist character which is not so evident in, say, Canada or Australia, where multiculturalism was largely led by European ethnic minority lobbies and elite policymakers (Uberoi 2009 and 2016, Levey 2008).[3]

As a result of the way that a politics of equality focused on religious identity emerges as one legitimate development of anti-racism as explained above, one is tempted to say we must treat religious identity in the same way as other equality-seeking multiculturalist identities. There is something right here but only when it is married to an understanding that the identities that are the primary object of multiculturalism form a 'multi' (Modood 2007/2013). That is to say they are not uniform. As we have just seen in the above account of identarian anti-racism, not all ethnic identities are of the same kind. While some groups perceive their liberation or want to recognise themselves or be recognised by others in terms of a racial/colour identity, others turn to a continental or national-origin identity and yet others – or the same groups at a later moment, such is the fluidity of these identities – a religious identity. When to an appreciation of this phenomenon, we also consider how different again are gender and sexuality from the identities I have been considering, we realise that in the field of identity group–based equality we cannot be restricted to a single sociological or policy template. So, while egalitarians must not exceptionalise religion because it does not conform to racial or gender-equality policy templates, nor must we deny that religious equality will have its own distinctive character. For example, there is no racial or non-religious aspect of the Sikh turban or halal meat, but that does not mean that accommodation of the latter cases are not features of religious equality in, say, schools or workplaces. Yet this should not generate a difficulty for those egalitarians who do not understand equality simply in terms of sameness but also in terms of attending to differential needs where they are relevant (Dworkin 1977).

Group identities are not just a 'multi' but groups can shift from, say, a race to a religion focus, or fuse foci – for example by combining ethnicity and religion. Religion itself is of course a multi-dimensional activity. For example, there is scripture, doctrine, worship, organisation, codes of living, community, art, architecture and so on. The multiculturalist interest is centred on an ethno-religious-identity group that needs to be protected against racism and whose practices and symbols need to be accommodated in a respectful way in the public culture and institutions of a country in which currently they are marginalised or not recognised as part of that country. A good example of such an ethno-religious group which has been subject to racialisation are the Jews. Jews could be understood to be followers of a religion, Judaism, but 'follow' here clearly cannot mean to believe in and strictly adhere to its rules. Many proud, self-defined Jews who are recognised as Jews by fellow Jews, as well as non-Jews, are atheists and/or do not participate in approved collective worship and/or do not follow the rules of living, such as keeping a kosher kitchen or covering their heads appropriately. Indeed, it is perhaps better to think of Jews as a people with a religion, such that peoplehood and religion mutually inform each other, with religion a characteristic or a possession of a people, not of individuals per se. So, while Jews would not be the people that they are without Judaism, not every individual Jew has to be religious in order to be a Jew. Moreover, there can be sources of Jewish identity other than those that are the strictly religious, such as the Holocaust as a memory of a people or a collective commitment to the state of Israel. I hasten to add, as will probably be obvious to the reader, I am talking of a sociopolitical understanding of Jews, including the self-understanding of many Jews, not an understanding internal to Judaism. I am aware that different branches of Judaism have their own and differing criteria for defining who is a Jew and that the differing criteria are a matter of great religious and – in so far as it pertains to the state of Israel – political dispute, both among different branches of Judaism and between them and non-religious Jews.

As with Jews, so similarly with Muslims (and Hindus and Sikhs, etc., albeit not discussed here). Various Islamic schools and sects have their own view on what is expected of a Muslim and while they have some influence on how Muslims will decide who is and is not a fellow Muslim, as in the Jewish case, that is not decisive. Muslims also relate to each other as family members, as a community, as a political unity against Islamophobia or for justice for Palestinians, where non-religious Muslims, as long as they are not conspicuously anti-Islam, are taken to be Muslims. Muslims, in these essays, are primarily understood in this way – namely, as a people or ethnic groups with a religion, Islam, without any assumption that all individuals are religious or that the unity of the group is exclusively religious. In recognising they are a group or a people we do not need to assume an exaggerated unity, just as in talking of black people in Britain or as an Atlantic diaspora we do not. Indeed, in thinking with my chosen category, 'ethno-religious', we not only make explicit that we are talking about people, not simply doctrines or organised religion, these just being a feature of the people (as in my example of the Jews) and not exhaustive of the category. We also have a tool for recognising internal variation, especially in terms of ethnic group aspects. For example, many British Muslim parents have a strong preference that their children marry a Muslim. In communicating this to their offspring, whether they are aware or not, they are likely to assume 'Muslim' means a specific ethnicity: for example, Pakistani parents may feel that their offspring have not understood them if one of them introduces a Somali Muslim as a prospective partner. The parents' image of a Muslim – at least in a context like this – is likely to be an ethno-religious one – namely, of a Pakistani Muslim. This ethnic dimension can be found at the very heart of the religion. Of the more than 1,100 mosques in Britain for which data are available, the large majority are mainly mono-ethnic and fewer than 5 per cent have a multi-ethnic management committee (Naqshbandi 2017).

Thinking of groups such as Jews and Muslims as ethno-religious has another advantage in that these terms do not just describe religiosity or people in terms of religion. They are groups who are racialised as a homogeneous, single group with uniform characteristics (sometimes this refers to a biological appearance but it does not have to [Modood 2005; and chapters 1 and 4]). This is done because the group in question is perceived to be a threat or inferior or simply exotic; and each of these can be the basis for discrimination and unfavourable treatment of members of the group. Moreover, groups such as Jews and Muslims may also valorise their religious identity as a group over other features of group formations, rather than, say, shared socio-economic circumstances, at least in relation to, say, non-Jews and non-Muslims.

The processes of group identity formation, then, can be from the outside in (racialisation) or from the inside out (an intersubjective sense of having a group identity). We, therefore, have to be careful here to not simply see the group as constituted by racialisation or 'othering' – that is, from the pressures and the discriminatory treatment acting upon the group from the outside. This is a theme discussed in chapter 1 and also in 4 and 11, where I argue that authors exclusively focused on the aspect of racialisation or 'othering' such as Islamophobia or analysts of secularism such as Cécile Laborde legitimise state action in relation to the 'vulnerability' of this group but not the recognition and institutional accommodation (Laborde 2017). The view seems to be that liberal equality has done its work if religious freedom and protection from vulnerability is in place. Yet, this is in effect to reduce group identity to those aspects that are in need of protection, non-discrimination, non-othering by not making institutional provision for an element of ethnic identity that goes beyond race/othering and requires 'recognition' (Taylor 1994) – for example, Jewishness beyond anti-Semitism. For multiculturalists the challenge of group identities is not simply about eliminating discrimination and related obstacles to an individual's opportunities; it is also about positive recognition, sharing the public space which is structured by certain dominant identities. Minority identities may be of importance to liberals in terms of state neutrality towards cultural and religious identities while protecting those who experience discrimination or worse. For multiculturalists, there is an issue of relations between identity groups and between individuals as bearers of different and indeed multiple identities. This means, as just stated, that recognition is central; it also means facilitating dialogue between groups and emphasising that the integration of minorities is a two-way process and not just about the possession of rights or assimilation.

Another implication of the above discussion that I would like to make explicit is that identities are relational. One's identity only makes sense and has the significance it has due to its relations with the other identities that are present. In so far as identities are about distinguishing oneself from others, any sensible politics, let alone an egalitarian one, must also emphasise and cultivate commonalities. For most self-labelled multiculturalists, including myself, this has taken the form of a common national citizenship. This leads one to think about the imaginative power of national identities to support a citizenship. Here one is bound to think of ways in which existing national identities marginalise minorities or are in need of updating, but one also begins to think about the role of majority identities within the field of public identity relations in general and specifically within the national identity. For in both situations of domination and of attempts at inclusivity, the majority identities will be doing most of the work. Accordingly, multiculturalists are at one level or another engaged with aspects of majority identities. Yet, often this can simply take the form of focusing on the ways in which the latter dominate. However, in recent years I have started paying more explicit attention to majority identities, not merely as a problem but as objects of attention in their own right and of their potential contribution to a common multiculturalist national identity (Modood 2017a and 2019 forthcoming). This has been partly the result of the rise of majority anxiety in parts of the West (Gest 2016, Mann and Fenton 2017), and on the other hand, liberal nationalism in political theory (Miller 1995, Kymlicka 2001a, Levey 2008, Soutphommasane 2012 and Orgad 2015), with Bouchard (2011) and Goodhart (2013) uniting the theoretical and the practical. Yet – and this may be just of biographical interest – the significance of the majority and its place in the national identity seemed to be more striking when I thought of religion: if one was to accommodate, say, Muslims and Hindus, the question arose, How were Christians currently accommodated? Moreover, how was that being adjusted as nominal, rather than believing Christians, or 'Nones' were trending towards a majority and expected society to reflect their emergent or newfound majority status? This forced the issue of majority identity upon me in the way that, say, dismantling colour-racism or thinking of ethnic minority languages in England did not.

In any case, without 'majority', 'minority' is meaningless. This is not just a semantic point. The multiculturalist interest in 'difference' is in extending equality to those identities that have not been positively incorporated into the majority matrix. Of course the idea of a (cultural) majority does not imply a homogeneity or a monistic group. The majority may be a composite, especially from the perspective of majority-minority relations, as in 'Anglo-Celtic' in Australia or Anglo-French in Canada. Or take the case of Switzerland: the majority are German speakers but when it comes to issues of post-immigration minority formations, difference and integration, all of the speakers of the four official languages see themselves as and are seen by the minorities as the majority. A similar situation prevails in Belgium, where, say, those with origins in Turkey or Morocco clearly do feel a minority and are regarded as such by Francophones, regardless of the fact that only about 40 per cent of Belgians are native French speakers. Groups like the Turks are a minority in Belgium and Switzerland, and not simply because of their experience of discrimination but because in each of those countries there is indeed a cultural majority, albeit a composite one, and the Turks are not a part of it. Composite cultural majorities do not just describe an emergent phenomenon in the light of current demographic trends (e.g., white people are no longer a majority in California) but may be the best way to understand most cultural majorities per se.

RELIGION AND SECULARIST ACCOMMODATION

The emergence of the non-racial forms of minority-identity assertiveness that I mentioned in the last section was not anticipated or welcomed by British (or European) politicians or sociology. Similarly, just as the sociology of race for some time had a poor and distorted understanding of the identities of Muslims and the kinds of exclusion they experience in the West – a 'misrecognition' of an ethno-religious group in terms of race and class – political theory, including political theory of multiculturalism, has been slow to rise to the occasion (Parekh 1990 and 2000, Modood 2007). If we have to think normatively of the place of religion in a polity and, ultimately, a multicultural citizenship, then existing political theory is not a good place to start because it has too limited traction with actual liberal democratic secular polities in which the challenge of a multicultural citizenship is being exercised. Standardly, theories of political secularism assume that it consists of separation of state and religion and/or state neutrality in relation to religion. Yet, even a cursory glance at what we might take to be secular states shows this to be false. Nearly a third of all Western democracies have an official religion and more than half of all 47 democracies in the Polity data set officially or unofficially give preference to one religion. Indeed, most of the others give preference to more than one religion (Perez and Fox 2018). So, let us seek greater empirical traction than political theorists usually do by beginning with a minimalist understanding of secularism – namely, the view that there are two significant modes of authority, political and religious, and each must be allowed to enjoy a certain autonomy within their own spheres of concern. Each actual political instantiation or normative concept will be more than this but by beginning with this minimalist concept, we will not take a particular interpretation or set of institutions to exhaust the possibilities that exist. Rather, it enables us to work with the full range of empirical cases without normatively excluding them or misdescribing them empirically (chapter 6).

Even 'autonomy' of spheres is perhaps too strong to cover all the cases we observe in the world, and it is best to just recognise there are two sets of institutions and activities, the political and the religious, each to some extent – sometimes to a limited extent – organises itself in its own way, with its own conception and practice of authority. Specifically, political secularism is the claim that religious authority should not control political authority in the sphere of government, law and citizenship. Note that this understanding of secularism does not give automatic priority to religious freedom, conscience, toleration or democracy. Of course all these are important but for me they are constituent features of liberal democracy and so become features of secularism in a liberal democracy. One such version of secularism, which I identify by a grounded, empirical-normative focus on the institutions and practices of countries like Britain, is what I call 'moderate secularism', and it does indeed give an important place to freedom of religion (chapter 8). Yet, at the same time when one considers the former Soviet Union, the People's Republic of China, the Republic of Turkey and even aspects of *laïcité*, one sees that there is no necessary connexion between religious freedom and secularism, and secularists in certain times and places prize secularism above freedom of religion (as in France, see chapters 6 and 9).

Nor should we attribute liberals' concern to not treat religion as special to secularism (Eisgruber and Sager 2009). For secularists religion *is* special; their concern to delimit the sphere of religion is not extended to economics, science, the arts and so on but is singularly targeted on religion. Moreover, moderate secularism is characterised by an additional specialness as regards religion. It recognises that religion has a public good dimension and this may be supported by the state if it is judged by the state that it assists in bringing out the good. It does not promote the idea of political authority/autonomy in an anti-religious way; rather, it allows organised religion and religious motives to play their part in contributing to the public good (chapter 8). This may be taken to be a form of privileging religion and of course it is. What must be borne in mind is that few, if any, states uniquely privilege religion. Whether our criteria is the expenditure of tax revenues, management by the government or symbolic status as 'national' or teaching in state schools, most states privilege various sectors of the economy (the British socialist Tony Benn, when defending state ownership of various industries, use to refer to the Church of England as the first example of 'nationalisation'), science and universities, museums, areas of natural beauty, the arts and sport and so on – all matters strictly outside the sphere of political authority (chapter 10). So apart from extreme libertarians and anarchists, most of us rightly have no problem with the idea of state privileging various social activities and judge each case on its merits – what I call 'multiplex privileging' (chapter 10). It may be that we think that religion is unworthy of privileging in some or all of the above ways. Yet that is not the existing political contexts in which multiculturalists are seeking egalitarian inclusion. You could say that, in the way my idea of 'multi' above applies to groups, multiplex privileging applies to activities and social spheres. For similar reasons I argue that the liberal goal of state neutrality about culture or religion is impossible (Modood 2007/ 2013; chapters 6 and 10 below).[4] Indeed, there is a sense in which the separation of religion and state is not a neutral view about religion; it is a very definite view that favours some religions and attitudes to religion while disfavouring religions that want a partnership with the state. Or, to put it another way, if non-separation of religion and the state is reflective of an ethical-cultural perspective – what, following Rawls, is referred to as 'a conception of the good', then so is its negation, the separation of religion and politics. There may be good arguments for separation but they describe few contemporary states and to pursue separation is not an ethically neutral position. Most liberal democratic states may not choose multiculturalism or to accommodate ethno-religious groups but they are not prevented by doing so by their existing form of political secularism.

If state neutrality about culture is impossible and 'privileging' certain activities and language(s), historical narratives and perspectives on religion are inevitable, it does not mean that the state has to endorse everything it supports or funds. I have been careful to stress that multiculturalist recognition of ethno-religious identities does not consist of such endorsement (Modood 2007/2013) – identity recognition as a form of equal citizenship and inclusion but without any strong evaluation or endorsement of any identities or ways of life. Peter Jones has argued that identity recognition as understood by Charles Taylor and Anna Galeotti amounts to endorsing the beliefs of 'recognised' religious groups if we are being asked to recognise, say, Muslims *as* Muslims, rather than just as equal citizens (Jones 2006). While it is true that in Taylor's account of recognition it gets connected to an evaluation of someone's culture, this is not the case for Galeotti, whose reading I follow (Modood 2007/2013, 65–66/60–61). For Galeotti and I, differences should be publicly recognised not because they are important or significant, per se, but because they are important for their bearers (Galeotti 2002). And 'the bearers' may be important to us because they are co-citizens. Jones refers to this as 'mediated' recognition because Muslims are being recognised as citizens. The point I am stressing, however, is that they are not just being recognised as abstract individuals or as citizens in the abstract but as groups with identities. So, to recognise them as citizens is – contrary to standard liberal or civic individualism – to recognise their group identities. Hence, in so far as there is an endorsement, it is an endorsement of co-membership, including the identities of the groups endorsed as belonging, not endorsement of beliefs or practices. For example, the Prime Minister attending an iftar, the eating of a meal to break the daily fast in Ramadan, is not endorsing Islam in preference to non-Islam or raising those who fast above those who do not. She is endorsing that Islam is part of Britain, not asking anyone to follow it or uncritically endorsing any and every belief or practice that someone says is Islamic. The impossibility of neutrality argument, then, is not an argument within moderate secularism but comes from multiculturalism and is related to the argument that civic recognition must go beyond non-discrimination or difference-blindness; equal citizenship requires positive inclusivity through identity recognition and accommodation. It is this argument that multiculturalism uses to engage with secularism – in my case, with moderate secularism.

I would like to conclude this section, in a way which I hope explains further my view of neutrality, endorsement and recognition, by considering an argument about how state recognition – even simply symbolic recognition of a religion or a certain number of religions – necessarily alienates all those who do not identify with that religion or religions. The argument appears in Cécile Laborde's *Liberalism's Religion* (2017). In the very short period of time since that book appeared it has already placed itself at the centre of political theory discussions about the place of religion and takes the discussion forward on that theme. In my essays here I state various disagreements with Laborde's previous publications: it is not the case that the United Kingdom has only a symbolic establishment and so that is not the ground for calling it secular (see pp. 182–184 and p. 206); religion is special albeit within what I have above explained as multiplex privileging (see pp. 188–189); equal citizenship does not just require state action on anti-racism/othering but also positive accommodation of cultural and religious needs (see pp. 204–205); and on whether groups such as British Muslims are alienated by state recognition of a Christian church or churches (see pp. 206–207). It seems, however, that I may have misunderstood her position on alienation or she may have developed it so I would like to revisit the disagreement here.[5] She argues that '[s]ymbolic religious establishment is wrong when it communicates to its citizens that a religious identity is a component of civic identity. . . . [It] thereby denies civic status to those who do not endorse that identity, who are then treated as second-class citizens' (Laborde 2017, 135). To an earlier version of this argument I had responded by saying that in the case of the Church of England establishment, Laborde had not provided any evidence of British Muslims being alienated and indeed there was no evidence (see pp. 206–207 below).[6] It seems that I had misunderstood her argument. She now states clearly that '[w]hat matters is not the subjective feeling of alienation but, rather, whether the social meaning of particular displays can be objectively construed as disparaging [of civic/insider status]. Objective social meaning is context-dependent but not individual-dependent;

it turns on how a reasonable (and reasonably well-informed) member of a community would understand the actions of public officials who undertake to display material that has religious content' (ibid., 85).

Yet, what if there is not a consensus on the social meaning of establishment among, say, British citizens? The reference to the reasonable person being reasonably informed suggests that (s)he needs to take into account some empirical data, and presumably it would be reasonable that this should include the view of Muslims (and others). We know that at any one time there can be disagreement on, for example, what counts as sexual and racial harassment, and women and minorities sometimes have to educate others (cf. my parallel argument about hate speech in chapter 3). Giving voice to minorities and encouraging the majority to be genuinely dialogically open is certainly the multiculturalist position here (Parekh 2000; see chapter 12). Returning to the Muslim case, many people think that the niqab (the face veil) and/or the hijab (the headscarf) is oppressive of women and so state action to ban them in public places is liberating and is not alienating. But this would not be a reasonable view if it did not seek evidence from Muslim women. Indeed, given that they are the object of the analysis and that state action is being called for on their behalf, it would be reasonable to give special weight to the perspective of Muslim women, rather than to the reasonable person. So, similarly in case of the Anglican establishment and British Muslims. I therefore continue to hold the view (as in chapter 11) that the claim that British Muslims are alienated by the Anglican establishment is groundless and the introduction of the idea that the argument turns on not the views of British Muslims but 'the reasonable person' in the British political community does not save the original claim. More substantively, I would add the observation that disestablishment without some institutionalised religious pluralism would mean the general public devaluing of religion and could make groups like Muslims more alienated than the status quo. So, we should not assume that state recognition of one or some religions is the only potential source of alienation on this matter; strict state-religion separation can also make alienated those for whom their religious identity is especially important and subjectively and objectively diminish their civic standing. Which is a further reason why minority perspectives cannot be assumed to be understood by simply engaging in a 'reasonable person' exercise and without allowing the minority to speak for themselves.

MULTICULTURALIST MODERATE SECULARISM

The essays of this book elaborate various aspects of the arguments of this introduction in relation to a number of topics. I will however offer two preliminary examples of how I think multiculturalism and moderate secularism can be brought together. They are both drawn from a British or English context and to what extent they apply in detail to other places is not too important; contexts will clearly vary. They are meant to illustrate how the two 'isms' may work together, not to be an institutional blueprint to be applied everywhere, as well as different aspects of multiculturalism.[7] They also give an indication of how I think majority and minority identities can be part of a national framework.

The first example is that of the Church of England, which clearly is an institutionalised feature of England's and Britain's historical identity. This is reflected in symbolic and substantive aspects of the constitution. For example, 26 Anglican bishops sit by virtue of that status in the upper house of the U.K. legislature, the House of Lords. It is the Archbishop of Canterbury that presides over the installation of a new head of state – namely, the coronation of the monarch. I do not see the presence of a state church, such as the 'established' Church of England, as contrary to political secularism,[8] as long as it does not impinge upon political authority, is consistent with liberal democratic constitutionalism and contributes to the advancement of the public good – which in the context of religious diversity includes the promotion of multiculturalism (see chapters 10 and 11). Given the rapidity of changes that are affecting British national identity, and the way in which religion, sometimes in a divisive way, is making a political reappearance, I think it would be wise not to discard lightly this historic aspect of British identity, which continues to be of importance to many even when few attend Church of England services and when that Church may perhaps have been overtaken by Catholicism as the organised religion with the most participants in the country. Yet, in my advocacy of a multiculturalized Britain, I would like to see the Church of England share these constitutional privileges – which should perhaps be extended – with other faiths. However, multiculturalism here does not mean crude 'parity'. My expectation is that even in the context of an explicit multifaithism the Church of England would enjoy a rightful precedence in the religious representation in the House of Lords and in the coronation of the monarch, and this would not be just a crude majoritarianism but be based on its historical contribution. To this must be added the multiculturalist condition – namely, the Church of England's potential to play a leading role in the evolution of a multiculturalist national identity, state and society. Both the historical and the multiculturalist contributions to national identity have a presumptive quality, and usually they qualify each other, yet where they are complementary, the case for 'establishment' is enhanced – and most of all where there is simultaneously a process of inclusion of non-Anglican faith communities.

My second example is about religion in non-denominational state schools.[9] I think multiculturalist moderate secularism should support a compulsory religious education (RE) in which children of all faiths and none are taught about a variety of faith traditions and their past and current effects upon individuals and societies, upon the shaping of humanity, taught to classes comprising those of all religions and of none. Such classes should certainly include the contribution of humanism as well as the atheistic critique of religion and can be combined with ethics. In many countries there are advocates for RE as part of a national curriculum. The main issue in relation to majority precedence is in relation to religious instruction (RI), the induction into a specific faith. Broadly speaking there are two majoritarian possibilities. First, we have a society where there is a majority religion and that alone is allowed as RI, and minorities might be exempted from those classes but no alternative religious instruction is provided. Or second, the majority view is that there should be no RI in state schools, as in the United States or in France (except in state-funded religious schools). Is it fair to impose either of these policies on minorities that do want RI?

That is an appropriate subject for a national dialogue but if after that certain minorities want RI as well as RE, then a truly national system, certainly a multicultural system, must make an effort to accommodate minority RI. In my understanding then, under both the majoritarian possibilities, the minorities should have the right to have their religions instructed or worshipped within the national system. On the other hand, minorities do not have the right to stop the majority from including the instruction of their religion. We should not, for example, ask schools to cease Christian RI or worship or celebrating Christmas *because* of the presence of Muslims or Hindus; rather, we should extend the celebrations to include, for example, Eid and Diwali. Such separate classes and faith-specific worship needs to be balanced with an approach that brings all the children together and into dialogue; indeed, without that it would be potentially divisive of the school and of society. But where that is in place, voluntary pursuit of one's own faith or philosophical tradition completes the multiculturalist approach to the place of religion in such schools. Learning together about different faiths, including what they have in common and – separately – being instructed in or inducted into one's faith community heritage as a normal school occurrence and not something excluded from the school community are then the two mutually balancing aspects of multiculturalism.

I here draw on three principles based on my discussion of multiculturalism above:

1. Schools should promote cross-cultural understanding and nurture inclusivity so all can develop a common sense of belonging.
2. The presence of minority identities should be accommodated on an *additive*, not a subtractive, basis.

3. The needs of minorities should not simply be understood in terms of majority preferences: just because the majority does not want something (to display faith through dress or RI classes), it does not mean there should not be institutional provision for a minority if it strongly feels it needs it and it is not harming anyone.

This approach is reflected in the report of the Commission on Religion and Belief in British Public Life (CORAB 2015), of which I was a member. It recommended that religious education – not instruction in a particular religion or secular beliefs – as a multidisciplinary subject showing the nature and presence of religion and secular philosophies across time and across the world – as a focus for individuals, communities, law, society and so on – should be a compulsory subject at school. It should be taught in classes consisting of all pupils without exemptions as part of the national curriculum. This knowledge, acquired in diverse classrooms, is essential for living together in mutual understanding and respect.

On the other hand, the existing English law requiring all schools to hold assemblies of a broadly Christian character – largely honoured in the breach in secondary schools – should be repealed. Schools should be free to have no assemblies or religion/belief-specific instruction or several of them or only for those who ask for them – to be achieved through discussions among parents, teachers, pupils and governors – and could take place within the formal timetable or as extracurricular activities. An option could be all-inclusive assemblies but no single template should be imposed.

While the first recommendation emphasises the need for a common level of understanding arrived at together, the second recognises the importance of allowing and supporting a diversity achieved through dialogue and practiced on a voluntary basis.

These two examples also illustrate an important point about the national culture. The general liberal and civic nationalist approach is to say that diversity requires a 'thinning' of the national culture so that minorities may feel included and do not feel that a thick majoritarian culture is imposed on them. This is also the approach of liberal multicultural nationalists. Will Kymlicka argues that 'liberal states exhibit a much thinner conception of national identity. In order to make it possible for people from different ethnocultural backgrounds to become full and equal members of the nation. . . . In so far as liberal nation-building involves diffusing a common national culture throughout the territory of the state, it is a very thin form of culture' (Kymlicka 2001b, 55–56). Yet the two examples above are not a thinning of moderate secularism or of religion in state schools, they are a pluralistic thickening. The multiculturalism in my examples adds to the national culture by not disestablishing the national church but by bringing other faiths into relationship with it; by not taking religion out of schools but by ensuring that commonality and diversity are both accommodated. In general, a multicultural society requires more state action to not just respect the diversity but to bring it together in a common sense of national belonging, and that in many instances means adding to a sense of national culture, not hollowing it out. In the kinds of cases this book is concerned with, the bringing of minority faith communities into playing a role in aspects of the national or public culture alongside Christians and humanists requires us to think differently about the country and so may require an appropriate public narrative about the kind of country we now are. In the light of this approach and to distinguish it from some others, I have come to call it 'multicultural nationalism' (Modood 2017a and 2019 forthcoming).

HYBRIDIC METHODS AND FORMS OF ENGAGEMENT

The reader will find in this book a hybrid of normative political theory and empirical political sociology, sometimes more of one than the other. This interdisciplinarity is deployed in developing the concepts I use – such as multiculturalism and moderate secularism – and in giving empirical or historical accounts, such as the emergence of Muslim identity politics in Britain. The latter are normatively informed by my conceptual framework, which itself is developed by drawing out normative 'isms' which are partly present in the political contexts I am interested in. This can mean accentuating an aspect of a complex context – say, bringing out the multiculturalist element of what may after all be a political pragmatic compromise, reflecting mixed motives and contesting actors. This is done to highlight its normative dimension and those aspects of its normativity which might otherwise be missed – because other observers are not sensitised to look for them or do not have the conceptual tools to identify them – or that I want to claim are novel or are part of a trend and their significance is missed if that is not appreciated. Yet this is done also because my empirical analyses are informed by advocacy, by making, say, a multiculturalist case – either by arguing in favour of something that has happened (an action, policy or law), or supporting a protest or campaign or recommending a course of action or a policy programme. Sometimes this will be about the details of the case – for example, the wording of a particular law – but mostly it will be about relating it to a larger political idea or framework, such as moderate secularism. The objects of analysis are typically a political conflict or controversy and the analysis is framed in terms of a normative political theory in order to make the controversy more meaningful in terms of the ideas and discourses involved, as well as to explain why things are taking the course that they are. Yet it is most important to me to not just leave things there. In theorising about real-world cases, I am not merely 'problematising' or 'deconstructing' them, but also pointing to feasible, contextually sensitive solutions. The aim is to be constructive, not just deconstructive or analytical (Dobbernack and Modood 2015).

As for the development of the concepts I use, the method employed bears some resemblance to Weber's 'ideal types', of which he writes:

> An ideal type is formed by the one-side accentuation of one or more points of view and by the synthesis of a great many diffuse, discrete, more or less present and occasionally absent, concrete individual phenomena, which are arranged according to those one-sidedly emphasized viewpoints into a unified analytical construct. . . . In its conceptual purity, this mental construct . . . cannot be found empirically anywhere in reality. (Shils and Finch 1997, 90)

Weber insisted, however, that ideal types were not normatively ideal, indeed they had nothing to do with values. My 'moderate secularism', like Weber's 'ideal type', too is a descriptive concept rather than a concrete description, but it is not merely a description of norms but conceptualised as norms which are currently achieving worthwhile purposes. Similarly, in relation to multiculturalism I begin not just with phenomena, but phenomena characterised as 'negative', such as exclusion (and so clearly some normative standard is already at work) and which can and should be made inclusive. I point to social facts suggesting how, as it were, the positive is struggling to be born or stay alive. There are genuine processes and movement towards developments, but there are difficulties and obstacles and there is no guarantee that the positive will be achieved. In any case, achievement here will always be relative to a previous time or to another place, not an endpoint; it is the nature of a positive ideal that more progress can always be envisaged. This is beginning to drift quite a long way from Weberian ideal types but nevertheless there is a sense in which 'moderate secularism' (or 'British multiculturalism' or 'French political culture') bears similarity to them, at least as an intermediate stage between the negative and the positive.

For Weber, values enter social science simply in the choice of subject matter – say, employment rather than the family, or poverty rather than racial inequality – but they are separate from the scientific study of any of those topics. Yet, all social science presupposes frameworks/perspectives because any inquiry must have a frame. Different research programmes and frameworks can put questions of family or equality in one way or another, at the centre or not – and this is not just about adequate explanations of what *is* or the *means* of maintaining or changing it, but rather about how we are to conceptualize, say, equality. The conceptualization is not the result of knowledge or a set of explanations; it is what directs us to a productive line of inquiry or knowledge accumulation. As the inquiry builds up a dynamic, the initial framing can be reviewed and adapted and thus there will be a dialectal relationship; but debates about different frameworks, different ways of conceptualizing society, conceptual arguments, are never reducible to questions of empirical knowledge. Such frameworks however are likely to have some normative character: should equality only be about income levels or should it also be conceptualized to include questions of respect and recognition? To disfavour the latter simply because it cannot be measured is to allow methods to dictate concepts and the inquiry. Social science must, in my view, therefore encourage engagement with normative questions for the sake of the quality of science rather than draw positivist boundaries around itself and treat values as merely personal choices. In sum, there must be a bridge between social science and normative inquiry.

Another feature in which my approach differs from Weber is that I have only slowly moved in the direction that his and allied methods recommend – namely, not just the 'idealisation' or 'conceptualisation' of a contingent, specific case, such as, say, the emergence and growth of capitalism in Western Europe at a specific time, but to construct a model that could capture the character of all capitalisms. Mindful of an Oakeshottian scepticism about cross-cultural and transnational abstract modelling in relation to social and political life (Oakeshott 1962), I expect such concepts and models to obscure more than they reveal. Perhaps that scepticism is not warranted and I do not fully abide by it in practice and so it is safer to say that my interest in the essays in this book lies in developing concepts to understand specific cases, such as Britain, rather than using that as an opportunity for generalisation and greater abstraction. For these two reasons, my concept formation is perhaps less Weberian and more a form of contextualised political theory.[10]

Simon Thompson and I have tried to give an account of such a form of theory (Modood and Thompson 2018). It is an approach that is not tied to a single national context or political tradition or culture but it gives significant weight to these contexts and cultures in its theorising in at least three important ways. First, it insists that political ideas and 'isms', including the principles of academic political theory, get their meaning from the contexts they have been extrapolated out of or engaged with. The concept of liberty has a similar but different meaning in the United States, France and Britain. A theorist whose thinking was formed in one of these contexts would reflect that context. When they applied their concept to one of the other countries they would have an imperfect understanding of that context or they could productively revise their concept of liberty. Doing the latter is clearly the way forward but it means that the context has changed the concept. Indeed, every engagement with a context, every time the concept of liberty is taken on an outing, it will have to undergo some change to reflect the cross-contextual variety. Thus even abstract principles such as liberty are reflective of the contexts that have been engaged with. So the search for generality is hollow unless it is about accommodating the richness of contextual differences rather than abstracting them out.

Second, we argue that theorists should take contexts seriously as the network of norms, practices and institutions that constitute a context are ones which people have come to identify with – they are not just bits of organisational machinery but are a sociocultural ecology in which people have made and across generations developed identity investments. While this does not mean that contexts cannot be criticised, the fact of those identity investments implies a duty of care on the part of critics. While there will always be a limit to how far this can be practiced, the point applies to majority and minority practices alike.

The last point I wanted to mention from this article is how to understand the possibility of reform and deliberate change. Oakeshott argues that political traditions are 'neither fixed nor finished', have 'no changeless centre' and no part of them is 'immune from change' (Oakeshott 1962, 128). Sometimes misunderstood as a change-averse traditionalist, Oakeshott's point is the opposite: no practice is static and there is no fixed, singular direction of change or progress. Rather, he argues, every political context, gives some indication or 'intimation' of what changes are possible, appropriate, necessary and so on. These are matters of judgement, not of rational deductive solutions, but again they point to the importance of understanding the specificity of a context: reformation means a deeper understanding of the specific case and of what is problematic within it (Modood and Thompson 2017).

One of the hazards of my approach, which brings together what Weber argued should be kept apart, Weber's social-scientific imperatives and ethical imperatives, is that sociologists will find it normative and subjective, while political theorists will object that it is too descriptive of certain times and places and not sufficiently justificatory or universal, that it does not sufficiently justify what ought and ought not to exist, in the way that liberalism does.

I accept those two sets of criticisms to some degree but I think it is still of value to social inquiry and to normative analysis, including to those who think the two should be separately pursued. Regardless of their hybridic character, they can make a contribution, albeit in not a pure form, to sociology and political theory, but more importantly they can help to direct political theory to real-world, as opposed to abstract, hypothetical problems. Moreover, while it is often backgrounded, I do think most social science, certainly sociology, has a normative character. This is especially evident in sociology centred on class – say, for instance, on the social and human cost of market-generated inequalities or of migration policies. It is highly conspicuous of the sociology inspired by the new social movements of the 1960s and 1970s – for example, around gender and sexuality. So, an approach which makes explicit and offers some argument in favour of the normative frame in which empirical inquiry is taking place is, in an important sense, more – not less – scientific for not being uncritical of its normative orientation.

One of the key values for me of this explicitly interdisciplinary approach, normative sociology or contextualised political theory, is that it lends itself to public intellectual engagement, as I explain in chapter 12. There I point to how political theory, if it is to be of assistance in multiculturalist controversies, must come to understand minority claims and protests by engaging in intercultural dialogue.[11] Here not just specificity and an openness to understanding novelty, and to relate to existing norms, is important but also one's biography; one's social location can also be critical. Thus, in chapter 12, I contrast my understanding of a public intellectual, whose rootedness and commitments can be critical to giving voice to and addressing the concerns and protests of subordinate groups, with that offered by Edward Said's more romantic portrayal of a public intellectual as 'an exile'. Similar to my concern about contextualised theory, I contend that an out-and-out 'outsider' status is not a good basis for multicultural public intellectual engagement, in which one's commitment to certain peoples and society can be the basis for moderating conflict.

Reviewing my work over the last decade or two I am aware that it is sometimes marked by a certain assertive or beleaguered tone (perhaps related to what Geoffrey Levey detects as a 'muscular' strain in the Bristol School of Multiculturalism [Levey 2018]) and yet also by a thread of optimism. Let me comment on these a little.

Leaving aside the merely demographic or descriptive meaning of multiculturalism as multi-ethnic social setting, in terms of its meaning in relation to politics it can be used in at least two different ways. First, it might refer to political questions created by forms of exclusion and their contestation, newly present claims of multicultural group needs and the adaptations and stresses in relation to these. Second, it may refer to a political 'ism' of the kind pressed for in these essays – that is, a certain intellectual-political framework for addressing the questions just referred to.

To understand why someone in the latter category may feel beleaguered, one does not have to refer to the large scale discursive backlash and hostility to political multiculturalism, some of which extends to multi-ethnicity per se, or even to the anti-migration spike and English ethno-nationalism that was a feature of the Brexit vote – and which ironically is taking the most multiculturalist country out of a union in which multiculturalism has not really taken root.[12] Indeed, the sense of being beleaguered should be intelligible if we simply contrast multiculturalism and feminism in academia. What is apparent is how few scholars and researchers who work in the field of multiculturalism are supportive of political multiculturalism as an 'ism'. This is in striking contrast to the fact that nearly everybody who works in the field of gender studies or women studies is a feminist (allowing for the fact that there are different kinds of feminism as an 'ism', just as there are in relation to multiculturalism).

Between these two meanings – a field of inquiry and a political 'ism' – there is perhaps a third: what Peter Kivisto calls a 'multiculturalist sensibility' (Kivisto 2012). This intermediate meaning denotes approaching multiculturalist questions with an unspecific pro-diversity sympathy or presumption. This is perhaps the closest that multiculturalism comes to feminism – namely, that in academia there is an unspecific sympathy or presumption in relation to each, though I would add that it's a presumption that is much more easily overturned or likely to contract when certain multiculturalist issues are discussed in any detail. This may have to do with certain anti-racist challenges such as positive discrimination in employment and especially in relation to the ethno-religious accommodation issues discussed in this book, whether the accommodation has to do with the university as an institution or politics more generally. Many readers will be aware of the kinds of gender equality initiatives undertaken by European universities in the last decade or two – requirements that job interview panels have at least one woman, training initiatives to increase the number of women in senior posts and management and gender balance in disciplines where women are still under-represented and so on – and will be equally aware that they have virtually no parallel in relation to race and religion, and nor is there is much pressure among academics that it should. (For the big gulf between gender equality mainstreaming and ethnic equality mainstreaming in Western Europe, see Westerveen and Adam 2019.)

As for the optimism despite of the above? I have been around long enough to not be unaware of the progress that has been made, at least in Britain, and from which I have benefitted, having survived racist bullying and Paki-bashing at school in the 1960s, and racism from my white Welsh in-laws in the 1970s and 1980s, to witness a steady decline in racist violence (on a per capita basis) and discrimination, and a corresponding rise in in educational, social, political and economic upward mobility of Asian and black minorities. Of course such developments have not been evenly spread across all the minorities. Moreover, the relative decline in simple racism (Ford 2014) has been accompanied by a rise in Islamophobia (Adesina and Marocico 2017). The latter is marked by certain spikes (say, following a terrorist incident) but there is also a general climate of hostility to Muslims, which is becoming an acceptable form of racism. Yet these contradictory developments have made the political accommodation of Muslims a live issue in the way it would not have been in previous decades. So, progress on some fronts can be accompanied by new exclusions and divisions (Janmaat and Keating 2019). The knowledge that some progress can be made is a basis for optimism that more is possible – though of course it is in the nature of politics that we will never reach a point that no more needs to be done.

I hope I have said enough about 'where I am coming from' and the key concepts I deploy, and I turn now to the specific contents of the book.

SYNOPSIS OF THE BOOK

In chapter 1, I explain my view that Muslims are currently being racialised in the West, just as Jews have been in various periods, and so (a dominant version of) Islamophobia should be understood as a form of cultural racism. I argue against those who hold that culturalism is not a form of racism, while also distinguishing my view of cultural racism from authors who see it as a form of 'naturalising' culture; both views suffer from a physicalist or biological view of 'race'. Once we break with the latter we can see how a religious group can be, and in the case of Muslims, is being racialised. This is one of the reasons that Muslims are central to contemporary multiculturalism (and indeed, anti-multiculturalism) in Western Europe and therefore why secularism – the place of religion in public life – is being revisited in theory and practice. Initially, however, British politicians and commentators in the 1950s saw the presence of people in Britain from the non-white Commonwealth in terms of 'race' and 'colour'. No mainstream politician or institution ever desired that religion should be at the centre of majority-minority relations.

The next chapter in the collection traces this shift, which marks an ethnic minority assertiveness which, among other things, has continuously challenged group categorisations from 'below' and extended the meanings of race, racism, ethnic, multiculturalism and so on. I trace the emergence of ethno-religious assertiveness from its beginnings in Sikh turban campaigns and the Ray Honeyford Affair to today when some perceive an Islamicisation of Europe, and anti-religious discrimination legislation, reluctantly introduced fifty years after the first racial equality laws, has been upgraded to the level of all other equality legislation in Britain. The process of multicultural equality has constantly faced new challenges and had to reform new arenas and institutions.

While no religion should be protected from criticism, I develop this argument by relating it to Jeremy Waldron's argument that certain reputational attacks amount to assaults upon the dignity of the persons affected and this justifies legislation against hate speech. Dignity or recognition as social equals, however, requires paying more attention to group subjectivities than Waldron consistently holds. Examining a number of hate speech examples against Muslims, including Danish and French cartoons, I argue Waldron fails to deal with two things. First, certain feelings in members of the target group are standardly relevant to hate speech and are part of what speech laws and other hate speech measures are trying to prevent. If the victim group feels attacked then we have a prima facie case of hate. Second, hate speech can be directed at or at least utilise the beliefs of the victim groups, so that the liberal claim that the law should protect people, not belief, is right but sometimes when people are hatefully attacked or racialised through their beliefs or as people who hold certain beliefs, then the matter is not so simple. In protecting people in such cases, one will be stopping others from attacking them through their beliefs. In such cases if one ignores their beliefs then one cannot identify the hate and so *a fortiori* one cannot protect the hated. Outlawing incitement to religious hatred is essential in a society in which mutual respect and civic equality prevail over people's right to castigate, ridicule and offend. Yet, who should be the arbiter of what is offensive? I argue that we have to listen to the victim, the people who are offended. I suggest that – contrary to liberal intuitions – an illustration of that in the comparison of Salman Rushdie's novel, *The Satanic Verses*, and the most egregious of the notorious Danish cartoons (the one with a bomb in the Prophet Muhammad's turban) means that it is the novel that is more offensive. I share, however, the liberal objection to the banning or censoring of novels and conclude that this means that we have to develop norms of civility which give us a base to censure Rushdie.

The Runnymede Trust (London) launched the public career of the concept of Islamophobia in 1997. Its approach was too located in the field of religious tolerance and pluralism and I pioneered an alternative understanding of Islamophobia that defines it as anti-Muslim racism in the context of multicultural citizenship. This is emerging as the dominant interpretation of Islamophobia (having been accepted some years ago by UNESCO and recently by the Runnymede Trust itself) and the concept is establishing itself in social science and public discourse alike. Yet I have some misgivings by the direction that some Islamophobia/Muslim studies are taking. My approach sees racialised ethno-religious group identity as having an 'inside', but in much of social science it is understood as something that is 'constructed from the outside' – namely, that it is an ascribed identity, constructed as a form of 'othering'. I think that both these aspects of groupness have a real-world existence and political significance, and cannot be reduced to each other, yet a lot of social studies is focused on 'othering' alone. In chapter 4, I challenge this latter orientation by arguing that being a Muslim is an identity that is capable of being 'recognised' and so necessarily has a dimension of group inter-subjectivity. I make a multiculturalist plea for studying Islamophobia (and groups negatively perceived from the outside, generally) within a normative framework which prioritises groups fighting outsider perceptions by boosting insider identifications and the struggle for recognition.

Part I concludes with chapter 5 considering the place of religion in relation to post-immigration diversity in Britain and British national identity as reflected in three national commission reports stretching over thirty years – namely, the Swann Report (1985) and the reports of the Commission on Multi-Ethnic Britain (CMEB 2000) and the Commission on Religion and Belief in British Public Life (CORAB 2015). Swann urges the accommodation of cultural diversity within a framework of shared values and a pluralised and expanded sense of what it is to be British but is unable to accept religious equality. CMEB explicitly included religious identification within its conceptualisation of 'multi-ethnic' but left it unintegrated in the report. It had a robust concept of multiple racisms but was ambivalent about whether Britain was a plural nation or a post-nation. CORAB was affirmative of a plural, evolving Britishness yet went beyond the previous two reports by centring on religion, offering a reworking of religion based on the concepts of the 'ethno-religious' and of 'religion and belief'. It therefore connects a multiculturalist sensibility with contemporary British moderate secularism.

Part II explores and engages with moderate secularism in a number of ways. Chapter 6 explores how religious equality should be understood and develops further the argument that the appropriate response to the new Muslim challenges is pluralistic institutional integration, rather than an appeal to a radical public-private separation in the name of secularism. This implies a reconceptualisation of equality from sameness to an incorporation of a respect for difference; a reconceptualisation of secularism from the concepts of neutrality and the strict public/private divide to a moderate and evolutionary secularism based on institutional adjustments; and a pragmatic, case-by-case, negotiated approach to dealing with controversy and conflict, not an ideological, drawing a 'line in the sand' mentality.

In 2008, an intense public debate and media controversy was triggered in Britain after a lecture delivered by the Archbishop of Canterbury. The lecture raised important questions of law, state, faith and citizenship in a modern, plural society; and its bitter, polarizing aftermath equally highlights the issue of what kind of civic discourse about these questions is necessary if they are to be properly addressed. Chapter 7 responds to the debate and controversy by viewing them in the perspective of 'multicultural citizenship', a concept which allows for nuanced understanding of the inter-relationship of 'secular' and 'religious' notions in civic life.

States have a number of reasons for taking an interest in religion. In chapter 8, I adumbrate five types of reasons the state might be interested in religion: truth, danger, utility, identity and respect. The challenge facing state secularism today is whether it can be pluralized or multiculturalized – in particular, whether it can accommodate Muslims. There are grounds for optimism, including the respect that some people, especially some Muslims, have for religions other than their own. Moreover, while radical secularism or *laïcité* seems to be struggling to cope, the prominent version of secularism, far from being in crisis, offers a resource – suitably multiculturalized – for accommodating the new religious plurality of the region. This can be seen in comparing how Britain responded to 'the Rushdie affair' and France responded to '*l'affaire du foulard*', as is done in chapter 9. Some secularists, including prominent academics, such as Rajeev Bhargava, do indeed speak of a 'crisis of secularism' but that is because, as argued in chapter 10, they have an exaggerated view of the requirements of secularism or are mistaken about the kind of secularism practiced by Western European states. And/or, their idea of religious equality is too normatively modest. In chapter 11, I discuss in this respect three multiculturalist approaches, including that of Will Kymlicka, that contend that the multiculturalizing of moderate secularism is not the way forward. One excludes religious groups and secularism from the scope of multiculturalism; another largely limits itself to opposing the 'othering' of groups such as Jews and Muslims; and the third argues that moderate secularism is the problem not the solution.

The collection concludes by picking up the themes of the previous section – namely, issues around theoretical method and public intellectual engagement. I contrast the dialogical nature of multiculturalism to the more standard political theory approach based on independent reasoning. This is partly because, as I explained in the last section, multiculturalism at its best aspires to public engagement. This can take the form of explaining why a multicultural or intercultural conflict exists, of advocacy within this conflict, of re-framing current dominant understandings of the situation and of thinking within a larger – both temporal and intellectual – horizon than civic and political actors usually do. These are essential activities if minorities are to be 'recognised' as civic actors with legitimate claims, including contesting the terms of inclusion. Against accounts of public intellectuals that emphasise universality, I suggest that a public intellectual is engaged in a particular time and place, engaged with *this* public. The commitment is not just to justice here and now but to justice for *these* people. Beyond a spatial-temporal location is also the fact of an identifiable public, a polity or a group of people, and it is a concern with the well-being or moral shortcomings of such a social body or on whose behalf that the public intellectual is engaged. The chapter and the book ends with an illustration of this through an interview in which the author is asked by a political theory colleague, Simon Thompson, to explain how he has tried to engage as a public intellectual and how that relates to his sense of being a British Asian Muslim and a multiculturalist.

NOTES

1. I would like to thank Matteo Bonnoti, Jan Dobbernack, Sune Lægaard, Geoff Levey, Nasar Meer, Bhikhu Parekh, Varun Uberoi and the editorial team at ECPR Press for their helpful comments on an earlier draft of this introduction.
2. It does not follow of course that all moderate secularist states, as Western European states except France mainly are, have taken a multiculturalist path. They mainly have not or at least not very far. They are, however, not prevented in doing so by their conception of political secularism. It also follows that in so far as different states have different understandings of secularism, this may influence their understanding of integration.
3. Relatedly, it meant that British multiculturalism was built on and incorporated a prior focus on socio-economic issues, especially on racial disadvantage and social mobility. A happy consequence was that few in Britain thought socio-economic integration and ethnocultural accommodation were rival policy programmes as in the Netherlands, where the initial culturalist accommodation was abandoned in favour of socio-economic integration, as if one could only have one or the other. It has recently been argued that Norway, too, is exhibiting a bottoms up multiculturalist struggle (Stokke 2019).
4. Worth noting is how some political theorists who argue that cultural neutrality on the part of the state is impossible and so support the state endorsement of one language argue that state endorsement of any number of religions is a wrongful breach of neutrality. It is interesting that such discussions usually include reference to Quebec (Kymlicka 2001a; Bouchard and Taylor 2008).
5. Lægaard (2017) argues that Laborde is one of a number of theorists who have been ambiguous between a civic-objectivist and a psychological-subjectivist account of alienation. In her latest book she plumbs for an objectivist 'symbolic equality' position.
6. It turns out 'there is no *cross-country* empirical data demonstrating that religious minorities in states, democratic or otherwise, that support the majority religion (via various policies) grow resentful of the state or its organs' (Perez, Fox and McClure 2017, 441). The stream of work being done by these authors in empirically testing some assumptions in political theory discussions of secularism represents a most effective contribution to empirically sensitive political theory.
7. I show how my key concepts have some traction in relation to Flanders, Belgium, in Modood 2017b.
8. Laborde 2017 has also come to the view that a Church of England type of establishment – 'modest establishment' – is compatible with minimal secularism (in Laborde 2013 she argued that it was compatible with a Rawlsian liberalism but not republican liberal secularism).
9. I am not here discussing state-funded faith schools, which are common in many European countries. For discussion of such schools and why such funding should be extended to Muslim faith schools, see Meer (2007) and Tinker (2009).
10. For political theory methodological discussions of my concept of moderate secularism, see Lægaard 2008, 2009 and 2015, and my response Modood 2009.
11. We need, however, to distinguish intercultural dialogue and interculturalism. The latter is often a vehicle for an unwarranted critique of multiculturalism and promotes intercultural encounters at a micro level, while multiculturalists emphasise dialogue at macro and national levels, as explained in chapter 10 (and see Meer and Modood 2012; Meer, Modood and Zapata-Barrero 2016; and Modood 2018a).
12. I have argued that the first New Labour government (1997–2001) has so far been the most multiculturalist government that Europe has seen (Antonsich 2015).

REFERENCES

Adesina, Z. and Marocico, O. (2017). 'Is It Easier to Get a Job If You're Adam or Mohamed?'. BBC News, 6 February: https://www.bbc.co.uk/news/uk-england-london-38751307 [last accessed 20/11/2018].

Antonsich, M. (2015). 'Interculturalism versus Multiculturalism – The Cantle-Modood Debate'. *Ethnicities*, *16*(3), 470–493.
Bouchard, G. (2011). 'Qu'est ce que l'interculturalisme? / What Is Interculturalism?'. *McGill Law Journal / Revue de droit de McGill*, *56*(2), 395–468.
Bouchard, Gerard and Taylor, Charles. (2008). *Building the Future: A Time for Reconciliation, Abridged Report.* Quebec: Gouvernement du Quebec.
Commission on Multi-Ethnic Britain (CMEB/Parekh Report). (2000). *The Future of Multi-Ethnic Britain*. London: Profile Books.
Commission on Religion and Belief in British Public Life (CORAB). (2015). *Living with Difference: Community, Diversity and the Common Good*. Cambridge, UK: The Woolf Institute.
Dobbernack, J. and Modood, T. (2015). 'Tolerance in Critical and Political Theory: Coexistence or Parts of Something Bigger?'. In Brown, W., Dobbernack, J., Modood, T., Newey, G., March, A. F., Tønder, L. and Forst, R., 'What Is Important in Theorizing Tolerance Today?'. *Contemporary Political Theory*, *14*(2), 164–171.
Dworkin, R. (1977). *Equality and Preferential Treatment*. Princeton, NJ: Princeton University Press.
Eisgruber, C. L. and Sager, L. G. (2009). *Religious Freedom and the Constitution*. Cambridge, MA: Harvard University Press.
Ford, R. (2014). 'The Decline of Racial Prejudice in Britain'. *Manchester Policy Blogs: Ethnicity*: http://blog.policy.manchester.ac.uk/featured/2014/08/the-decline-of-racial-prejudice-in-britain/ [last accessed 20/11/2018].
Galeotti, A. E. (2002). *Toleration as Recognition*. Cambridge: Cambridge University Press.
Goodhart, D. (2013). *The British Dream: Successes and Failures of Post-War Immigration*. London: Atlantic Books.
Gest, J. (2016). *The New Minority: White Working Class Politics in an Age of Immigration and Inequality*. Oxford: Oxford University Press.
Iqbal, K. (2017). *A Biography of the Word 'Paki': Racist Incident in the Workplace*. Kindle Edition.
Janmaat, J. G. and Keating, A. (2019). 'Are Today's Youth More Tolerant? Trends in Tolerance among Young People in Britain'. *Ethnicities*, *19*(1), 44–65.
Jones, P. (2006). 'Toleration, Recognition and Identity'. *Journal of Political Philosophy*, *14*(2), 123–143.
Kivisto, P. (2012). 'We *Really* Are All Multiculturalists Now'. *Sociological Quarterly*, *53*(1), 1–24.
Kymlicka, W. (2001a). *Politics in the Vernacular: Nationalism, Multiculturalism, and Citizenship*. Oxford: Oxford University Press.
Kymlicka, W. (2001b). 'Western Political Theory and Ethnic Relations in Eastern Europe'. In Kymlicka, W. and Opalski, M. (eds.), *Can Liberal Pluralism Be Exported?*, 13–105. Oxford: Oxford University Press.
Laborde, C. (2013). 'Political Liberalism and Religion: On Separation and Establishment'. *Journal of Political Philosophy*, *21*(1), 67–86.
Laborde, C. (2017). *Liberalism's Religion*. Cambridge, MA: Harvard University Press.
Lægaard, S. (2008). 'Moderate Secularism and Multicultural Equality'. *Politics*, *28*(3), 160–168.
Lægaard, S. (2009). 'Moderate Secularism, Difference Sensitivity and Contextualism: A Rejoinder to Modood'. *Politics*, *29*(1), 77–81.
Lægaard, S. (2015). 'Multiculturalism and Contextualism: How Is Context Relevant for Political Theory?'. *European Journal of Political Theory*, *14*(3), 259–276.
Levey, G. B. (2008). 'Multiculturalism and Australian National identity'. In Levey, G. B. (ed.), *Political Theory and Australian Multiculturalism*, 254–276. New York: Berghahn Books.
Levey, G. B. (2018). 'The Bristol School of Multiculturalism'. *Ethnicities*, *19*(1), 200–226.
Mann, R. and Fenton, S. (2017). *Nation, Class and Resentment: The Politics of National Identity in England, Scotland and Wales*. Basingstoke, UK: Palgrave Macmillan.
Meer, N. (2007). 'Muslim Schools in Britain: Challenging Mobilisations or Logical Developments?'. *Asia Pacific Journal of Education*, *27*(1), 55–71.

Meer, N. and Modood, T. (2012). 'How Does Interculturalism Contrast with Multiculturalism?'. *Journal of Intercultural Studies*, *33*(2), 175–196.
Meer, N., Modood, T. and Zapata-Barrero, R. (2016). *Interculturalism and Multiculturalism: Debating the Dividing Lines*. Edinburgh: Edinburgh University Press.
Miller, D. (1995). *On Nationality*. Oxford: Oxford University Press.
Modood, T. (2005). *Multicultural Politics: Racism, Ethnicity, and Muslims in Britain*. Minneapolis and Edinburgh: University of Minnesota Press and University of Edinburgh Press.
Modood, T. (2007/2013). *Multiculturalism: A Civic Idea* (2nd ed., 2013). Cambridge: Polity Press.
Modood, T. (2009). 'Moderate Secularism and Multiculturalism'. *Politics*, *29*(1), 71–76.
Modood, T. (2017a). 'Majoritarian Interculturalism and Multicultural Nationalism'. In D. Tabachnick and L. Bradshaw (eds.), *Citizenship and Multiculturalism in Western Liberal Democracies*, 87–106. Lanham, MD: Rowman & Littlefield.
Modood, T. (2017b). 'Multicultural Nationalism, Political Secularism and Religious Education'. In Modood, T. and Bovenkerk, F., *Multiculturalism: How Can Society Deal with It? A Thinking Exercise in Flanders*, 13–42. Brussels: KVA Stanpunten 51.
Modood, T. (2018). 'Interculturalism: Not a New Policy Paradigm'. *Comparative Migration Studies*, *6*(1), 22.
Modood, T. (forthcoming 2019). 'Multicultural Nationalism?'. *Brown Journal of World Affairs*, Spring/Summer Issue.
Modood, T. and Thompson, S. (2018). 'Revisiting Contextualism in Political Theory: Putting Principles into Context'. *Res Publica*, *24*(3), 339–357.
Naqshbandi, M. (2017). 'UK Mosque Statistics/Masjid Statistics'. Muslims in Britain, 16 September: http://www.muslimsinbritain.org/resources/masjid_report.pdf [last accessed 18/08/2018].
Oakeshott, M. (1962). *Rationalism in Politics and Other Essays*. London: Methuen.
Orgad, L. (2015). *The Cultural Defense of Nations: A Liberal Theory of Majority Rights*. Oxford: Oxford University Press.
Parekh, B. (1990). 'The Rushdie Affair: Research Agenda for Political Philosophy'. *Political Studies*, *38*(4), 695–709.
Parekh, B. (2000/2006). *Rethinking Multiculturalism: Cultural Diversity and Political Theory* (2nd ed., 2006). Basingstoke, UK: Palgrave.
Perez, N. and Fox, J. (2018). 'Normative Theorizing and Political Data: Toward a Data-Sensitive Understanding of the Separation between Religion and State in Political Theory'. *Critical Review of International Social and Political Philosophy*, DOI:10.1080/13698230.2018.1555683.
Perez, N., Fox, J. and McClure, J. M. (2017). 'Unequal State Support of Religion: On Resentment, Equality, and the Separation of Religion and State'. *Politics, Religion & Ideology*, *18*(4), 431–448.
Shils, Edward A. and Finch, Henry A. (trans. and eds.). (1997). *Max Weber: The Methodology of the Social Sciences (1903–1917)*. New York: Free Press.
Soutphommasane, T. (2012). *The Virtuous Citizen: Patriotism in a Multicultural Society*. Cambridge: Cambridge University Press.
Stepan, A. (2011). 'The Multiple Secularisms of Modern Democratic and Non-Democratic Regimes'. In Calhoun, C., Juergensmeyer, M. and Van Antwerpen, J. (eds.), *Rethinking Secularism*, 114–144. Oxford: Oxford University Press.
Stokke, C. (2019). 'Do Antiracist Efforts and Diversity Programs Make a Difference? Assessing the Case of Norway'. In Hervik, P. (ed.), *Racialization, Racism, and Anti-Racism in the Nordic Countries*, 205–228. Cham, Switzerland: Palgrave.
Swann, Lord. (1985). *Education for All: Report of the Committee of Inquiry into the Education of Children from Ethnic Minority Groups*. London: HMSO.
Taylor, C. (1994). *Multiculturalism and 'the Politics of Recognition'*. Princeton, NJ: Princeton University Press.
Tinker, C. (2009). 'Rights, Social Cohesion and Identity: Arguments for and against State-Funded Muslim Schools in Britain'. *Race Ethnicity and Education*, *12*(4), 539–553.

Uberoi, V. (2009). 'Multiculturalism and the Canadian Charter of Rights and Freedoms'. *Political Studies*, *57*(4), 805–827.

Uberoi, V. (2016). 'Legislating Multiculturalism and Nationhood: The 1988 Canadian Multiculturalism Act'. *Canadian Journal of Political Science / Revue canadienne de science politique*, *49*(2), 267–287.

Westerveen, L. and Adam, I. (2019). 'Monitoring the Impact of Doing Nothing: New Trends in Immigrant Integration Policy'. *Ethnicities*, *19*(1), 20–43.

I

The Racialisation of Muslims / Muslims as 'Race Relations' Actors

Chapter One

Racism, Culturalism and Cultural Racism

Race relations and racism came to be a feature of British politics and sociology in the 1960s and 1970s. Yet for at least a quarter of a century, the highlighting of the British Asian and the British Muslim experience within this context suffered from a serious obstacle. Conceptualisations of race and racism, and hence also of anti-racism and racial equality, have been too narrowly defined. They are too dependent on the black-white relationship – not just the contemporary relationship but the whole Atlantic slavery triangle of Western Europe–West Africa–Americas. This Atlantocentric perspective was dominant when I entered this field in the late 1980s. Intellectually and politically it was shaped by the assumption that the key issue was colour racism, understood as white domination of non-whites. This meant a racial dualism rather than a rainbow diversity. As racial dualism has been the U.S. experience, it was assumed Britain had to learn from the United States and that where the United States was today, Britain would be tomorrow. It was also assumed that people of African descent were paradigmatic of what it meant to be non-white in Britain and elsewhere. My very first argument was that Britain could not be understood in terms of a racial-dualist framework (Modood 1988; 1992).

In this Atlantocentric version of racism, which is certainly one of the most classical and enduring versions, phenotype explains the existence of certain cultural traits (Miles 1989, 71–72). These traits are mainly negative in the case of blacks, people of African descent. As a result, racism or racial discrimination comes to be thought of as unfavourable treatment on the grounds of colour. I refer to this as colour racism. While the stereotypical physical characteristics of blacks are taken to be enough to fill out the image of them as a group, as a race – for example, strong, sensual, rhythmical and unintelligent – the racialized image of Asians is not so extensively linked to physical appearance. It very soon appeals to cultural motifs such as language, religion, family structures, exotic dress, cuisine and art forms. These are taken to be part of the meaning of 'Asian' and of why Asians – which in Britain means South Asians – are alien, backward and undesirable. Such motifs are appealed to in excluding, harassing or discriminating against Asians – both in constituting them as a group and in justifying negative treatment of them.

South Asians, then, are clearly visible as a non-white group: they are a principal object of racist victimization, of negative treatment by whites on the grounds that they are an undesirable 'other'. They suffer, therefore, from colour racism. But they also suffer from cultural racism: a certain culture is attributed to them, is vilified and is even the ground for discrimination; this culture may include, may even be dominated by (certain perceptions) of a religion, as in the case of Asian and other Muslims. Of course, black people too can be culturally vilified, and so the colour racism/cultural racism distinction is not simply a black/Asian distinction (CMEB 2000). Nevertheless, I contend that the putative defects or strengths of black culture are attributed to aspects of their physicality – such as low IQ or rhythm – or to what whites have done to them, such as deprive them of certain heritages. The perception of Asians, whether it be in some hard-core racist discourses, such as those of the British National Party, or implicit in the wider British society, is that their defects lie deep in their culture rather than in a biology that produces their culture. This means that Asians, more than blacks, suffer a double racism. This does not mean that Asians suffer more racism – such as harassment, discrimination and institutional exclusion – than do blacks in Britain. That is a complex empirical question, and one would have to be sensitive to the fact that the answer may vary by class, age, gender, geography, social arena and so on. I think that systematic research of this sort would indeed show that the racism against Asians has been underestimated since at least the 1960s. My point is that research of this kind requires a conceptualization of racism that includes cultural racism as well as colour racism and an understanding that Asians, especially Asian Muslims, suffer a double or a compound racism.

In crafting the term 'cultural racism', I am not arguing that there is some *necessary* connection between race and culture within racist discourse and practice. For quite contingent reasons, racism can become historically connected to slavery or underclass; so, similarly, with racism and culture. Racism and sexism are conceptually quite distinct but can come together in distinctive stereotyping and treatment of black women or black men; similarly, the cultural racism against Asians is a distinctive construct, not reducible to its constituent parts. Again, one can have racism without nationalism, and nationalism without racism, but their combination can be lethal.

Cultural racism in contemporary Britain is a two-step racism (or alternatively, is a second step, with colour racism being the first step), by which I mean that most of the victims of cultural racism, most notably Muslims and Asians, also suffer colour racism and that the cultural racism is built on – embedded within – that (Modood 1997). The interesting question arises whether it could be a one-step racism: could colour racism decline and fade away and yet cultural racism remain and perhaps even grow? One can certainly imagine a future in which a group such as Asians or Muslims could continue to have their culture vilified while colour racism simultaneously declined. This might mean that assimilated or hybrid Asians, those not strongly identified with Asian culture, might not experience exclusion by whites. If that were to happen, there might be a basis for not wanting to describe the anti-Asian perceptions as racism. This distinction between what might be called racism proper and culturalism is commonly held (Blum 2002; Fredrickson 2002). It seems to me that to discriminate only against those people who are perceived to be culturally different – that is, to make an absolute distinction between cultural Asians and physical Asians, might be borderline racial discrimination. Cultural essentialism and inferiorization may be involved, and it would certainly share some of the qualities of racist stereotyping and practice today, but it may be that it would be better to regard it as cultural prejudice and cultural exclusionism rather than racism per se. Certainly one can see the difference between the scenario just described and one where colour racism declines but Asians continue to be viewed as a racial group. In this case the prejudice would still be motivated by a characterization of Asian culture, but discrimination would be exercised against all people of Asian ancestry, regardless of their fit against the image of Asian culture. Similarly, Muslims may in general be discriminated against for being of Muslim descent regardless of their level of religiosity or conformity to a stereotypical Muslim (perhaps those of Muslim descent who were public critics of Muslims and Islam might be excepted) (Meer and Modood 2009). This would certainly be cultural racism, even if colour racism had receded, because all or nearly all of a group, identified by colour and descent, are being judged by an essentialized image of a group. In the previous scenario a target group is being negatively constructed, and negative treatment follows from this construction; but if persons are targeted only on the basis of their behaviour and not on the basis of their ancestry, then might we have something that we should call culturalism or religious intolerance rather than racism? I am torn, however, as this case seems to go against what we would expect from community and social dynamics.

Since cultures and cultural practices are usually internally diverse, containing and omitting various 'authentic' elements and adaptations and mixes, the culturalized or religionised targeting of Asians may be expansive rather than purist and so in one way or another will catch most, if not all, Asians or Muslims. Some children will grow up in communities that are culturally very Asian or Muslim. Most of these children will develop feelings of family, neighbourhood, community and discourses to counter anti-Asian or anti-Muslim discourses. If as adults they move away from the culture of their childhood, they may still retain communal feelings of loyalty, solidarity and self-defence. Anti-Asians or anti-Muslims are therefore likely to target them in some ways, just as atheists in Northern Ireland can be asked if they are Protestant or Catholic atheists – their repudiation of religious doctrine is not seen as enough to distance them from a targeted community. In my hypothetical scenario, a non-religious Muslim might still be targeted as a cultural Muslim/Asian, and a noncultural Asian might still be targeted as an Asian by community, which means Asian by background, which means birth and ancestry. So it is not clear that culturalism, where it is associated with distinct communities, can be really distinguished from racism in practice, even if it can be in theory.

If a movement from cultural racism to cultural exclusion without racism seems difficult to envisage in the near or medium-term future, a sense of historical perspective, of what is possible in the long run, may be helpful. Consider the movement the other way round, as in the case of anti-Semitism. Jews have been blamed by Christians for the death of Jesus since early in the Christian era, centuries before those modern ideas we have come to call 'racism'. The move from religious antipathy to racism may perhaps first be witnessed in post-Reconquista Spain, when Jews and Muslims were forced to convert to Christianity or be expelled. At this stage, the oppression can perhaps be characterized as religious (Fredrickson 2002). Soon afterward, converted Jews and Muslims and their offspring began to be suspected of not being true Christian believers, and a doctrine developed among some Spaniards that this was because their old religion was in their blood. In short, because of their biology, conversion was impossible. Centuries later, these views about blood became quite detached from religion and in Nazi and related doctrines were given a thoroughly scientific-biologic cast and constituted a paradigmatic and extreme version of modern racism. What was once a form of religious persecution became, over a long, complicated, evolving but contingent history, not just a form of cultural racism but also one with highly systematic, biological foundations.

Because of that legacy, throughout the West today anti-Semitism is without question regarded as a form of racism ('Semitic' is taken to mean only Jews, not other Semites like the Arabs). In Britain, as in most of Western Europe, discrimination against Jews is unlawful racial discrimination. While few cases are brought to the law, and Jews seem to be disproportionately overrepresented in most elite occupations, many Jews will argue that anti-Semitism is still present. By this they mean not just the existence of some neo-Nazi fringe extremists, but mainly an insidious, if latent, prejudice. Yet virtually no one except for the neo-Nazis believes that what prejudice there is against Jews – often linked to snobbery from 'old money' and envy from below – is derived from any biological discourse, latent or otherwise, or a religious doctrine.

In anti-Semitism in Britain today, we have an example of a racism that has slipped back into being a mild culturalism or communalism. While some people dispute whether contemporary anti-Muslim prejudice can properly be called cultural racism, as opposed to religious intolerance, no one, as far as I know, asks if anti-Semitism is racism. Indeed, over the last couple of decades it has become commonplace for it to be asserted that some of the views of contemporary militant Muslims, or fundamentalists, about Jews are racist. Political Muslims reply that they are opposed not to Jews but to Zionism and the colonial militarism of Israel. My purpose is not to resolve this controversy but to point out the politically selective ways in which the terms 'racism' and 'racist' are applied. If an exclusionary '-ism' without biology is not racism, then militant Muslim venom against the Jews is not racism. It is true that there are some aggressive passages about the Jews in the Qur'an (though they require far more careful interpretation than is often given them), but none of them make any reference to biological difference. Moreover, Muslims welcome converts from all faiths and ethnic groups, including Jews, and the possibility of conversion is a condition that some scholars believe rules out belief in the biological determinism that is a necessary condition of racism as a doctrine (Fredrickson 2002). So it seems that, on that view, militant Muslim discourse about Jews is more like medieval Christian vilification than racism. On my view, in contrast, prejudice and discrimination against Jews, no less than against Muslims or Asians, can be a form of cultural racism without any biology or naturalistic determinism in play.

Regardless of what one thinks about contemporary anti-Semitism/anti-Zionism, the important historical point is that religion can be the basis of racialization as long as the religion of a group can be linked to physical ancestry and descent. So race is not just about colour, and definitely not just about white and non-white (though it can be predominantly that in some contexts). Racialization has to pick on some features of a people related to physical appearance and ancestry, otherwise racism cannot be distinguished from other forms of groupism. Physical appearance or descent is central to race, but, as in the case of cultural racism, it can be a marker only and not necessarily denote a form of determinism.

DISTINGUISHING CULTURAL RACISM

I have, then, very flexible sociological concepts of race and racism. As I understand it, the term 'cultural racism' or 'new racism' has come to have a certain currency in the United States, where it is taken to mean a characterization of a racial group, typically African Americans, such that the problems and disadvantages of that group are attributed to culture and not to biology. This is similar to my meaning, though in the European context, cultural racism or culturalism directed to a racialized or racially marked group may involve an antipathy to the group because it is perceived to be an alien culture rather than merely an inferior one. In short, in Europe when the target group is Muslim or 'Eastern', the focus of cultural racism is not primarily about attributing causes for social pathologies or economic disadvantage (or even that the target group is perceived as disadvantaged).

There is an understanding of cultural racism, or new racism, that appreciates the last point. It is found in the works of certain British authors who believe this racism emerged as a distinct ideology in England in the 1970s (Barker 1981; Gilroy 1987; Solomos 1991). They argue that such a culturalist discourse is common colour racism dressed up in culturalist garb in order to avoid the charge of racism, that it is 'coded' racism (see also Miles 1989, 84–87; for a similar French view, see Wieviorka 1997). My view is that cultural racism is not a proxy for racism, but a form of racism.

Stuart Hall recognizes that cultural racism has a distinct 'logic', different from but related to biological racism (Hall 2000). He argues, however, that I fail to see that 'these two "logics" are always present' in any actual case and as a result I draw too sharp an opposition between the two and treat them as rivals in a zero-sum game (224, 239). I do believe they are connected, as in my illustrative use of British Asian Muslims and others, but I remain unpersuaded that they must both be present in every practice or set of attitudes that we might wish to call racism. The connection is contingent, not a priori. My view is that racism involves some reference to physical appearance or ancestry but does not require any form of biological determinism, only a physical identification on a group basis, attributable to descent. Moreover, it is possible to have colour racism – namely, the explanation of cultural traits by reference to biology – without cultural racism, even if the two are typically combined to some degree or other. My belief that, on the whole, colour racism is declining in Britain except where anti-Asian cultural racism is present is an empirical claim, which Hall recognizes. Others have disputed the claim because they say it creates a hierarchy of oppression in which some groups experience more hostility and exclusion than others (Cohen 1996, 19–20; Gillborn 1996, 25; Anthias 1998, 19). Yet consider two recent examples: First, for some years it has been clear that the racist and anti-immigrant British National Party (BNP) has been disproportionately targeting South Asians, and one of their successors, the English Defence League (EDL) has single-mindedly targeted Muslims. This is clear from their literature and where they choose to be politically active. Looking at their electoral results over a number of years shows that they calculate rightly as to where they can hope to stoke up racist support; their best results tend to be in towns where the principal non-whites are Asians. With the disturbances of 2001 and then with post–9/11, the BNP has increasingly begun to distinguish between Asian Muslims and other Asians, arguing that the former are violent, criminal and disloyal; fail to integrate and so on (evidence of all remarks relating to the BNP can be found on their website at www.bnp.org.uk).

My second example is the BBC TV documentary, *The Secret Policeman*. Broadcast in October 2003, it consisted of recordings, over some months by a journalist pretending to be a policeman and a friend and using hidden cameras, of some policemen on a residential training course. While there are a few recorded remarks about blacks as muggers and drug dealers and so needing 'discriminatory' policing, these are balanced by other remarks, often by the same individual, such as, 'To be honest, I don't mind blacks, proper blacks,' and 'My best mate is black'. The overwhelming bulk of bile and violence is directed at 'Pakis', who are said to be taking over the country and should all be thrown out; as Hitler did to the Jews, so should Asians have done to them in Britain; and at least one officer said he would certainly kill an innocent Asian if he was sure he would not be found out. This is only a small selection of the remarks about Asians from this documentary, and there are no friendly remarks to balance them. This documentary, together with the case of the BNP, demonstrates that most hostility is directed towards Asians/ Muslims. It may be that evidence that runs the other way has also to be taken into account. But that is to recognize that the issue is an empirical inquiry, open to different answers at different times and places, and so a hierarchy of racisms cannot be ruled out simply because it does not sound nice. It is sometimes said that prejudice against one group usually goes with prejudice against other groups. If so, how does one make sense of the policeman who says, 'I don't mind black people. Asians? No'? (For other examples of such selective racism, see Gillborn 1990; Modood 1997; and Janmaat and Keating 2019.)

It is widely claimed that cultural racism naturalizes culture, that it treats culture in a quasi-natural or biological way, as if culture inheres in a group so that it is automatically reproduced, it does not change over time and the relevant cultural traits are found in all members of the group. Lawrence Blum, for example, argues that the distinctive feature of racism is 'inherentism': that certain qualities are inherent to a group and it is a secondary issue whether these qualities are perceived to be hereditary or cultural, racial or ethnic (Blum 2002; cf. Miles 1982, 157; and Miles 1989, 74). Avtar Brah argues that 'a characteristic feature of . . . racism has been its focus on cultural difference as the primary signifier of a supposed immutable boundary; a view of the Asian as the "alien" *par excellence*; the ultimate "other"' (1996, 168). We have already noted that for Fredrickson the distinctive feature of racism is that ethnocultural differences are regarded as 'innate, indelible and unchangeable' (2002, 5). This is, of course, related to the distinction between racism and a prejudice directed only at those members of a racial group who practice a certain culture/religion, which I discussed earlier. While I think that there is something right in this characterization and that most racisms are inherentist, I would caution against taking the analogy with nature too far. If we look at, for example, the racial stereotypes that operate to exclude some people from certain kinds of employment – for example, that blacks are less intelligent than whites – it is clear that they are not applied in a uniform way. Discriminators may be biased but are open to the possibility that certain black individuals are exceptions to the rule. If there is an inherentism, it affects the generality rather than each individual; it is to be measured in averages rather than deterministic laws of nature (see chapter 4). Moreover, stereotypes are capable of accommodating change; sometimes stereotypes can change radically. Until *The Satanic Verses* affair, Asian men were stereotyped as unassertive, overdeferential and docile, not able to stand up for themselves. Within a few years, the prevalent stereotype of Muslim men (in Britain, the majority are Asian) included the idea that they were inflexible, always demanding something, fanatical and aggressive. Nowadays one of the tropes used against Muslim men, in the form of collective blame typical of racism, is terrorism, and another is gangs sexually abusing very young, mainly white, mainly working-class, women.

CULTURAL RACISM AND ASSIMILATION

Robert Miles very usefully deploys a concept of articulation to explain how different ideologies can connect and work together, such as racism and nationalism, and it may be that cultural racism is best seen as an articulation of racism and culturalism (1989, 87–90). For him, this has the advantage of preserving the analytical clarity of 'racism' while recognizing that in practice it can sometimes be mixed up with another kind of exclusionary '-ism'. But if we accept that racism does not necessarily involve inherentism, then we do not have to rule out cultural racism as an example of racism. Moreover, we can allow ourselves to be much more sensitive to contemporary meanings and new meanings if we allow that concepts can often drift from their original meanings. Fredrickson acknowledges that 'culture can be reified and essentialised to the point where it becomes the functional equivalent of race' (2002, 7) but insists that cultural intolerance and religious intolerance are not racism because they allow assimilation, and so, at worst, are forms of culturalism. In deciding whether a particular case is racism and what is culturalism, we are not determining the degree of oppression. Fredrickson, for instance, is clear that we are determining the grounds of oppression, not the scale of it. For example, he argues that in Reconquista Spain, when Muslims and Jews were forced to become Christians or be expelled, the *Moriscos* (the Muslim converts) were treated worse than the Jewish *conversos*, but since the former were more likely to live in separate communities, in their case it is difficult to distinguish between racism and culturalism (Fredrickson 2002, 34). The racism may be less clear, yet the oppression may be greater. Fredrickson also endorses the view that North African Muslims in France and Muslims in Bosnia, Palestine, India and other places where they seem to be oppressed in ethnicized ways are not victims of racism (144).

Fredrickson takes two ambiguous positions on assimilation. The first is that even where a dominant group demands total assimilation, including something as deeply humiliating as *coerced* religious conversion, as the Spanish demanded of conquered Muslims in the fifteenth and sixteenth centuries, this is not racism because it assumes that the dominated group can be changed and so can be assimilated into the dominant culture (2002). I think my view of cultural racism deals with this – namely, that a culture of a group that is already racialized can be the basis of a more elaborate racism.

Fredrickson's second position is that 'racism is not operative if members of stigmatized groups can *voluntarily* change their identities and advance to positions of prominence and prestige within the dominant group' (2002, 7; my italics). I think that even here some cultural racism is possible: for example, there can be some anti-Semitism even while assimilated Jews are allowed to and able to rise to top positions. While the possibility of voluntary assimilation is clearly better than coercion, and indeed is desirable in some ways, the issue is why assimilation is necessary. If the reason is antipathy to the culture of a racialized group, then cultural racism is present. Hence in contemporary discussions of racial and ethnic equality, assimilationism is seen as part of the problem, not part of the solution.

Against suggestions of articulation and functional equivalence, I reiterate that a group that is already racialized can suffer from cultural vilification, and in this compound prejudice it is very difficult to distinguish racism from culturalism. Crucially, the latter can *interact* with a preexisting racism to form a new '-ism' called cultural racism, which may have a worse effect than the sum of racial discrimination and, say, religious discrimination, let alone separately. Yet either can be a trigger for the other, and when both are present and interact, there is cultural racism. In these circumstances, cultural vilification can be part of an exacerbated racism or an additional dimension of racism, not merely an adjunct to it.

The idea that religions and cultures are capable of change while racial groups, as understood by racists, are not is quite misleading. This can be illustrated by my point that a discriminator at, say, a job interview may be open to the suggestion that some members of a phenotypical group are counterexamples to the stereotype associated with a racial phenotype without feeling that the stereotype is unsound. That is, racist stereotypes are more like probabilistic generalizations (i.e., they survive exceptional counterexamples). If so, this narrows the gap between racism and culturalism, for both are susceptible to exceptions and new learned behaviors. If I am told that this probabilistic stereotyping is not racism, my reply is the Wittgensteinian one that 'meaning lies in use' (Wittgenstein 1968).

Whatever historians say about classical racism, I am interested in what is racism today, and I am partly guided by what is called racism in social life today. While there is limited research that one can point to, it does seem that a person using the vocabulary of race today, and even engaging in acts of racial discrimination, does not have to hold any strictly deterministic biological ideas in order to give meaning to their discourse and practice. While Miles, in his concept of institutional racism (1989, 83–87) is concerned about when the discourse of race fades, I am concerned about when the discourse of race continues but the meaning changes. The point in relation to Fredrickson is that space for voluntary assimilation of so-called racial groups is compatible with racism. Indeed, the history of the descendants of forcibly transported and enslaved Africans has involved selective assimilation, the degree and kind determined by whites.

Conversely, the idea that religion is about belief that can be voluntarily renounced, but race is about one's immutable biology, is also too simplistic. As in Northern Ireland, the South Asia I am from is contoured by communal religious identities. It has nothing to do with belief. If you assert 'I am an atheist', people will still think it is meaningful to ask, 'Yes, but are you a Muslim? A Hindu?' Talk of giving up one's religion is likely to be seen as a form of selling out. In such a context, religion can be less a matter of individual choice than when some 'in-between'-skinned people in the United States assert their blackness rather than 'pass'. The question of choice has to do with social structure, not religion qua religion. It is clear that in some European or Western societies the group that is deemed to be most unassimilable is Muslims. In Britain and France, for example, black people are generally regarded as much more assimilable than Asian and North African Muslims. The political party in France most associated with racism, Le Front National, explicitly campaigns on the proposition that Arab Muslims are unassimilable, not because it has given up racist ideology but because it is able to racialize Arabs without appeals to biological immutability.

Racism, then, can be involved in diverse and contradictory views about assimilation, including that a group cannot assimilate because of its religion, that coercive assimilation is necessary, and even in the subtle pressures to assimilate that may coexist with a policy of voluntary assimilation but may betoken a racialized attitude towards a group and its cultural 'otherness' (cf. Jansen 2013). This latter view helps to explain why, in the late twentieth century, several societies, such as Canada, the United States and Britain, were influenced by the idea that to require minorities and migrants to assimilate as a condition of citizenship, or of inclusion more generally, is a form of inequality. These societies assume that the culture of the majority is superior to that of the minorities and is the norm, and that deviations from the norm are a sign of inferiority and not something from which the majority might learn something of value. Aspects of a culture can be so important that they are integral to a sense of self; to require that civic equality or social acceptance depends on erasing this identity is to treat people with disrespect and not allow them to be themselves in the way that other citizens are allowed (Young 1990). Where these identities are connected with race and ethnicity, the disrespect can be a form of racial inequality and racism. This can be done without a conscious policy but is nevertheless oppressive for it consists of treating people as other than who they are and making them into something they are not and do not want to be. It is to fail to recognize them, and Charles Taylor (1994) has brought out well the importance of recognition to personal and collective self-respect and equality. Misrecognition (like invisibility in other literatures on equality) can be a major social harm. In many ways, the experience of British Asians and Muslims has been a struggle against misrecognition, as they have tried to slough off the imposed identity of political blackness (see chapter 4). This has been most dramatic in the case of Asian Muslims, especially Pakistanis, who in less than a decade transformed themselves from a relatively passive element of the 'black' constituency into a highly energized, vociferous and mobilized group asserting a religious – not a colour-based or even an ethnic – identity. There I also endorse the view that the politics of recognition can be developed further to emphasize that there is an emergent ideal of equality that repudiates the need to privatize all difference in the name of a formal or civic-republican equality. Equality is interpreted as balancing the ever-present power of hegemonic identities, usually disguised as universal, with the public recognition, even celebration, of marginal or suppressed identities. This opens the space for moving beyond mere toleration towards the creation of civic/public/national/state identities that incorporate minority ethnic and religious identities, guided by the ideal that all citizens should be able to see something of themselves in the overarching, yet internally plural, public identities. In short, they should be able to feel they belong to the country or countries of which they are citizens.

MULTICULTURALISM AND SECULARISM

The above implies an active state policy of multiculturalism – that is, recognizing the country or polity as a legitimate and irreducible plurality, as a 'community of communities' (CMEB 2000) and not just as a liberal association of autonomous individuals. It means reimagining or re-forming our national identity, our Britishness for example, so that all can be part of it without having to deny or privatize other identities that are important to different Britons. However, in talking about the multicultural, it is important to bear in mind that we are talking about at least two different kinds of development. On the one hand, there is hybridity and multiple identities, the mixing of different heritages and the refusal to be defined by any one or even a limited number of core identities. This is particularly identified with popular youth culture and with some African Caribbeans but increasingly also with some second-generation Asians – especially Indians. On the other hand, there is the development of communities, especially ethnoreligious groups, who are keen to emphasize one, or at least a limited number of, core identities and are mobilizing as political actors and seeking quasi-corporate representation at local, national and perhaps even transnational levels. Muslims are a prime example of this. I argue that it is important that political multiculturalism recognizes the legitimacy of both developments – particularly in the context of an inevitable liberal, secularist bias in the intellectual, political and recreational culture in favour of the first against the second.

The bias I have in mind can be found once again in Fredrickson. Indeed, one of the reasons I have argued at length against his definition of racism is because of its secularist bias. Fredrickson's race/religion dichotomy makes it plausible to argue that policy remedies against racism and religious intolerance should be quite different from each other. Hence with little argument, Fredrickson is able to conclude that while 'persisting racial prejudices and inequalities make the complete separation of race and state counterproductive, the first line of defence against militant sectarianism would seem to be a total separation of church and state' and that this separation should be modeled on that in the United States (2002, 147–148). The ideas of a church-state separation and that religion and religious groups should not play a role in politics and democratic contests are, of course, in one form or another, extremely popular, almost universally supported by intellectuals not just in the United States but also in Western Europe and many other places in the world. It is seen by liberal democrats, socialists and republicans as one of the central tenets of their politics, to such an extent that until recently it was simply taken for granted and thought not to need discussion. A rare but influential example of an argument for secularism in twentieth-century political theory is Rawls's *Theory of Justice* (1971). Rawls argues that for a state to favour any religion or worldview is to impose beliefs on its citizens, which infringes on freedoms that no person should rationally give up, and so the just state should protect religious freedoms but be neutral between religions. Rawls's theory, however, while designed with religious diversity in mind, favours neutrality on all cultural matters, not just religion, and so may not be entirely supportive of Fredrickson's position as quoted. In fact, the dominant multiculturalism in liberal theory departs from Rawls by separating the realm of cultural identities into religion and the rest, and favours explicit recognition in relation to, say, minority languages and customs, but non-recognition in relation to minority religions. For example, Will Kymlicka argues that the strict separation of state and ethnicity, 'the religion model', is incoherent but is content with the separation model as long as it is applied only to religion (1995, 107–108; 2001, 24).

I believe that this secularism is less liberal than it seems and is part of the political culture and policy assumptions that make it difficult for Western societies to be just to Muslims. It is an obstacle to seeing the problems of Muslims and sympathizing with them, to seeing aspects of the oppression of Muslims, to recognizing Muslims and to offering solutions to them similar to those given to other oppressed and disadvantaged groups. I will also add a pragmatic point that I have brought with me from my policy background to my theoretical work. In Britain, there is a political discourse and policy framework around eliminating racial discrimination – laws, policies, agencies, a political movement. Therefore, in addition to the analytical merits of the case, there is an argument for integrating anti-Asian culturalism and Islamophobia within the discourse of racial equality and multiculturalism rather than risk having it marginalized as simply a religious or cultural issue. Racial equality in Britain began with colour, but by the 1980s had gone ethnic (decisively through the judgment of the House of Lords on *Mandala v. Lee* in 1982, which gave legal protection against discrimination to Sikhs; Jews, though white, were already covered). And I extended the analysis to cover Muslims a few years before others had thought about it as an issue. The rest of this book is based on this analysis and the secularist bias that has been an obstacle to the egalitarian inclusion of Muslims and others.

REFERENCES

Anthias, F (1998). 'The Limits of Ethnic "Diversity"'. *Patterns of Prejudice*, *32*(4), 5–19.
Barker, M. (1981). *The New Racism: Conservatives and the Ideology of the Tribe*. London: Junction Books.
Blum, L. (2002). *'I'm Not a Racist But . . . '*. Ithaca, NY: Cornell University Press.
Brah, A. (1996). *Cartographies of Diaspora*. London: Routledge.
CMEB (Commission on Multi-Ethnic Britain). (2000). *The Future of Multi-Ethnic Britain*. London: Profile Books.
Cohen, P. (1996). 'A Message from the Other Shore'. Symposium on Anti-Racism in Britain. *Patterns of Prejudice*, *30*(1), 15–21.
Fredrickson, G. M. (2002). *Racism: A Short History*. Princeton, NJ: Princeton University Press.
Gillborn, D. (1990). *'Race', Ethnicity and Education*. London: Unwin Hyman.
Gillborn, D. (1996). 'Culture, Colour, Power and Racism'. Symposium on Anti-Racism in Britain. *Patterns of Prejudice*, *30*(1), 22–27.
Gilroy, P. (1987). *There Ain't No Black in the Union Jack: The Cultural Politics of Race and Nation*. London: Heinemann.
Hall, S. (2000). 'Conclusion: Multi-Cultural Questions'. In Hesse, B. (ed.) *Un/settled Multiculturalisms: Diasporas, Entanglements, Transruptions*, 209–241. London and New York: Zed Books.

Janmaat, J. G. and Keating, A. (2019). 'Are Today's Youth More Tolerant? Trends in Tolerance among Young People in Britain'. *Ethnicities*, *19*(1), 44–65.

Jansen, Y. (2013). *Secularism, Assimilation and the Crisis of Multiculturalism*. Amsterdam: Amsterdam University Press.

Kymlicka, W. (1995). *Multicultural Citizenship: A Liberal Theory of Minority Rights*. Oxford: Clarendon Press.

Kymlicka, W. (2001). *Politics in the Vernacular: Nationalism, Multiculturalism, and Citizenship*. Oxford: Oxford University Press.

Meer, N. and Modood, T. (2009). 'Refutations of Racism in the "Muslim Question"'. *Patterns of Prejudice*, *43*(3–4), 335–354.

Miles, R. (1982). *Racism and Migrant Labour*. London: Routledge.

Miles, R. (1989). *Racism*. London and New York: Routledge.

Modood, T. (1988). '"Black", Racial Equality and Asian Identity'. *New Community*, *14*(3), 397–404.

Modood, T. (1992). *Not Easy Being British: Colour, Culture and Citizenship*. Stoke-on-Trent, UK: Runnymede Trust and Trentham Books.

Modood, T. (1997). 'Difference, Cultural Racism and Anti-Racism'. In Werbner, P. and Modood, T. (eds.), *Debating Cultural Identity*, 154–172. London: Zed Books.

Rawls, J. (1971). *A Theory of Justice*. Cambridge, MA: Harvard University Press.

Solomos, J. (1991). 'Political Language and Racial Discourse'. *European Journal of Intercultural Studies*, *2*(1), 21–34.

Taylor, C. (1994). 'Multiculturalism and "The Politics of Recognition"'. In Gutmann, A. (ed.) *Multiculturalism and 'The Politics of Recognition'*, 25–74. Princeton, NJ: Princeton University Press.

Wieviorka, M. (1997). 'Is It So Difficult To Be an Anti-Racist?' In Werbner, P. and Modood, T. (eds.), *Debating Cultural Identity*, 139–153. London: Zed Books.

Wittgenstein, L. (1968). *Philosophical Investigations*, trans. G. E. M. Anscombe. Oxford: Blackwell.

Young, I. M. (1992). *Justice and the Politics of Difference*. Princeton, NJ: Princeton University Press.

Chapter Two

Ethno-Religious Assertiveness Out of Racial Equality

The settlement in Britain of new population groups from outside Europe (principally from the Caribbean, South Asia and Africa) made manifest certain kinds of racisms in Britain, and anti-discrimination laws and policies began to be put into place from the 1960s. These laws and policies, initially influenced by contemporary thinking and practice in relation to anti-black racism in the United States, for several decades assumed that the dominant post-immigration issue was 'colour-racism' (Rex and Moore 1967; CCCS 1982; Sivanandan 1985; Gilroy 1987). This perspective was epigrammatically expressed by the writer, Salman Rushdie: 'Britain is now two entirely different worlds and the one you inherit is determined by the colour of your skin' (Rushdie 1982). An alternative view would be that the new populations are best understood as a racialised ethno-religious diversity, though this has only become apparent as the settlements have matured and the minorities have become political actors. The accounting of this perspectival change, and the understanding of ethno-religious minority politics today, requires reviewing the breaking-up of the assumptions of the earlier period.

Until late 2003, it was lawful, except in Northern Ireland, to discriminate against religious minorities unless they were recognised as ethnic groups within the meaning of the law. The latter was the case with Jews and Sikhs, but the courts did not accept that Muslims are an ethnic group and so it was possible, for example, to deny a Muslim a job *qua* Muslim. In such a circumstance, Muslims only had some limited, indirect legal protection *qua* members of ethnic groups such as Pakistanis, Arabs and so on. It was only in 2003, nearly four decades since legislation on 'race', that an offence of religious discrimination was created, though even then confined to employment. Even before issues of international terrorism and foreign affairs intruded into domestic matters, religion in the form of Muslim politics was becoming central to minority-majority relations. No mainstream politician ever desired, let alone anticipated, this. So, how has it happened? While initially unremarked upon, the longstanding exclusive focus on race and ethnicity, and the exclusion of Muslims but not Jews and Sikhs, came to be a source of resentment amongst some Muslims. At the same time, the analyses, campaigns, policies and legislation associated with racial and ethnic equality and diversity were the principal source of precedence and legitimacy as Muslim activists began to make political claims upon British society and the polity. In short, one of the principal ways of seeing the emergence and development of ethno-religious equality is in terms of a grievance of exclusion from the existing equality framework and its utilisation in order to extend it to address the felt exclusion and to develop and seek public recognition for a minority subjectivity ignored by liberal legislators.

THE RISE AND FALL OF POLITICAL BLACKNESS

The minorities' politics, the cutting-edge anti-racism that developed in Britain in the 1970s and early 1980s, first in radical activism and ultra-left corpuscles then, following the Brixton riots of 1981, in some local government, trades unions, radical public sector professional associations and the Labour Party was based on a concept of political blackness. The British population was divided into two groups, black and white. The former consisted of all those people who were potential victims of colour-racism, though in both theory and practice, they were assumed to disproportionately have the characteristics of the African Caribbean population (Modood 1994). Thus a fundamental problem for this conception of political blackness came from an internal ambivalence – namely, whether blackness as a political identity was sufficiently distinct from and could mobilise without blackness as an ethnic pride movement of people of African descent (Andrews 2016). This black identity movement, in a growing climate of opinion favourable to identity politics of various kinds, was successful in shifting the terms of the debate from colour-blind individualistic assimilation to questions about how white British society had to change to accommodate new groups. But its success in imposing or making a singular identity upon or out of a (unlike black America or South Africa) diverse, ethnic, minority population was temporary or illusory. What it did was pave the way to a plural ethnic assertiveness, as South Asian groups, including Muslims, borrowed the logic of ethnic pride and tried to catch up with the success of a newly legitimised black public identity.

A key indicator of racial discrimination and inequality has been numerical under-representation in prestigious jobs, public office and so on. Hence people have had to be (self-)classified and counted, and so group labels, and arguments about which labels are authentic, have become a common feature of certain political discourses. Over the years it has also become apparent that by these inequality measures, it is Asian Muslims, and not African Caribbeans, as policy-makers had originally expected, who have emerged as the most disadvantaged and poorest groups in the country (Modood et al. 1997; Karlsen and Pantazis 2017).[1] To many Muslim activists the misplacing of Muslims into 'race' categories and the belatedness with which the severe disadvantages of the Pakistanis and Bangladeshis came to be recognised by policy-makers meant, at best, that race relations were an inappropriate policy niche for Muslims (UKACIA 1993) and, at worst, it was seen as a conspiracy to prevent the emergence of a specifically Muslim sociopolitical formation (Muslim Parliament 1992).

OUT OF RACE: ETHNICITY AND MUSLIM HONOUR

So, both in relation to identity issues as well as socio-economic disadvantage, a white-black analysis of Britain was becoming unsatisfactory and being challenged by some of those for whom the designation 'black' was meant to be self-illuminating and emancipatory. Indeed, political blackness was unravelling at a grass-roots level at the very time when it was becoming hegemonic as a race relations discourse in British public life (1980s; see Modood 1994). Two important events also show the ways in which practical action in relation to 'colour' was being ethno-religionised.

One was a religion-based political campaign which ran alongside, perhaps even preceded, political blackness and which had a significant effect in shaping the practice of racial equality. This was the campaign by some Sikhs to seek exemption for the Sikh turban from uniform rules (e.g., as bus drivers and conductors) and from the law compelling the wearing of crash helmets on motorbikes, This campaign was successful on several fronts: for example, it achieved an amendment in The Motor-Cycle Crash Helmets (Religious Exemption) Act 1976 and a famous House of Lords decision declared that the Sikhs were not just a religious group but also an 'ethnic group' and therefore a racial group in law (*Mandala v. Lee* 1982). Interestingly, no other religious group has subsequently been recognised as an ethnic group (Muslims and Rastafarians have failed the legal test), and Jews have never had to prove that they are a race, the idea being taken to be self-evident by Parliament, the courts and public opinion. Nevertheless, in this landmark judgement, the legal idea of racial equality was extended into the domain of the rights of ethno-religious groups.

Another notable conflict in which racial equality, ethnicity and religion came to be combined and set an important precedent was 'the Honeyford Affair' (Halstead 1988). Ray Honeyford was a head teacher of a Bradford local authority school in which the majority of pupils were of Pakistani descent and Muslim. In a series of articles in 1983–1984 in a national, right-wing journal, *The Salisbury Review*, he argued that the education of children such as those in his school was being retarded by the cultural and religious practices of their parents, which prevented Pakistani-ethnicity children, especially girls, from gaining rapid proficiency in English, from participating in the full curriculum (for example in sport, dance and drama), from socialising with whites and succeeding fully in British education and society. He was particularly critical of what he said was the widespread practice of Pakistani parents taking or sending their children to Pakistan for weeks or months at a time, disregarding the duty to observe the school calendar. These comments – many of which were and, indeed, continued to be the concerns of educationalists – were presented in an extremely critical, generalising way that portrayed Pakistani, working-class culture and aspects of Islam in a negative way and were augmented by comments about Pakistan as 'obstinately backward', plagued by 'corruption at every level' and the 'heroin capital of the world' (Honeyford 1984, 292). The articles were judged as racist by white anti-racists, locally and nationally, and some secular Asian activists, who initiated a call for Honeyford's resignation, which soon came to be supported by most of the parents and the leading local Muslim organisations, including the Bradford Council of Mosques. The Bradford Pakistani community were stirred up by so much public airing of unflattering comments about themselves, exacerbated by the distribution of Urdu translations of Honeyford's view by his opponents (Samad 1992, 513). This community, largely of peasant Kashmiri background, culturally conservative, and obedient to their clan and religious leaders, began to stand up for itself against what it perceived to be insults to its culture and to its religious restrictions, especially as they applied to gender and sexuality. Left-wing anti-racists therefore came to mobilise conservative Pakistanis on the issue of community honour and in due course the alliance was successful and Honeyford was pressured into early retirement. The wider, and more longer-term effect of the alliance and of other local developments of the time was to develop the Pakistani community, especially the mosque leadership, as a political force in Bradford, at the expense of white anti-racists and others rooted in a secular, multi-ethnic coalition, as the former considerably out-numbered the latter (Samad 1992).

Both the turban campaigns, conducted through self-organisations and outside the frame of 'race' but concluding with significant effect upon the meaning of racial equality, and the defence of Pakistani community honour, initially roused by anti-racists but leading to the empowerment and emboldening of an ethno-religious leadership, were, then, actions which showed that Asian religious communities were emerging as political actors within the race landscape and were capable of winning battles. The single event that most dramatically illustrated the emergence of these new forms of ethno-religious actors – with again Bradford a scene of action and damaged honour a cause of mobilisation – was the battle over the novel, *The Satanic Verses* (*SV*), that broke out in 1988–1989, with Muslims protesting its portrayal of the Prophet Muhammad and other revered figures. This time the secular anti-racists were virtually absent from the conflict, for while many were sensible of the racial stereotyping and divisions it was causing, they were unhappy that it was fuelled by religious anger. Above all they saw it as a case in which freedom of speech should not be compromised, but reluctant to join in the chorus against Muslims, they mainly kept a low profile. On the Muslim side, however, it generated an impassioned activism and mobilisation on a scale greater than any previous national campaign against racism (Modood 1990 and 2005). It is striking that when the public rage against Muslims was at its most intense, Muslims neither sought nor were offered any special solidarity by any non-white minority. It was in fact some white liberal Anglicans that tried to moderate the hostility against the angry Muslims, and it was inter-faith fora rather than political-black organisations that tried to create space where Muslims could state their case without being vilified.[2] Political blackness – seen up to then as the key formation in the politics of post-immigration ethnicity – was seen as irrelevant to an issue which many Muslims insisted was fundamental to defining the kind of 'respect' or 'civility' appropriate to a peaceful multicultural society – that is to say, to the political constitution of 'difference' in Britain (Modood 2005). The *SV* affair, then, divided anti-racists and egalitarians, giving rise to organisations like Women Against Fundamentalists, an off-shoot of Southall Black Sisters, who turned up at Muslim demonstrations to publicly express their support for Rushdie. Other egalitarians tried to assimilate Muslim concerns into the equality movement and to some extent this division has since become a feature within the broad politics of 'multiculturalism' in Britain (for an attempt at reconciliation, see Phillips 2007).

EXPANDING RACIAL EQUALITY TO INCLUDE RELIGIOUS EQUALITY

The campaign to have *The Satanic Verses* banned failed and many people felt more sympathy for the author of the novel than for those who threatened his life. The campaign therefore was not successful in relation to its most basic objectives. Yet, if we consider the broader picture, the campaign marks the entry point of British Muslims into the politics of multicultural equality and one from which they have not ever left; indeed, their concerns became central to multiculturalism. It was also the springboard for organising Muslims politically at a national level. The UKACIA (UK Action Committee on Islamic Action) was created to campaign against the novel, and with support from both the main national political parties, especially New Labour, it proved to be a first step towards the creation of the Muslim Council of Britain (MCB), which sought to represent Muslims on all issues at a national level. It was accepted as such by New Labour from the time it came into power in 1997 until the terrorist attack in London on July, 2005 (7/7). The government was already dissatisfied with the MCB for being a vocal critic of the U.S.-led invasion of Iraq and the U.K. government's involvement in that. Once terrorism in the name of Islam made its appearance in Britain, the government criticised the MCB for not actively and prominently criticising it and began to search for more compliant Muslim organisations as partners. The MCB, however, did manage to achieve much of its founding agenda (Modood 2010). First, it had got Muslim issues and Muslims as a group recognized separately from issues of race and ethnicity; and it had got itself accepted by government, media and civil society as the spokesperson for Muslims, even if after 2005, it did not have a monopoly in this regard. Second, it had achieved the introduction of state funding of Muslim schools on the same basis as Christian and Jewish schools. Third, its aim of getting certain educational and employment policies targeted on the severe disadvantage of the Pakistanis and Bangladeshis (who are nearly all Muslims), as opposed to on minority ethnicity generally, was also achieved to some degree. It also persuaded Tony Blair (against the advice of some civil servants and local authorities and with lukewarm support from the Cabinet) to have a religion question in the 2001 census (Sherif 2011). This last was an important step as it opened the way for a possible later introduction of policies targeting Muslims to match those targeting groups defined by race or ethnicity – or gender (Hussain and Sherif 2014). It took longer in coming and came in increments but the MCB also achieved the legislative protection it sought. Laws against religious discrimination were introduced in 2003, strengthened in 2007 and again in 2010, making them much stronger than anything available in the rest of the European Union. Incitement to religious hatred, the legislation most closely connected to the protests over *The Satanic Verses*, was introduced in 2006, though it was strictly drafted to ensure that its use against literature was most unlikely. Interestingly, the protestors' original demand that the blasphemy law be extended to cover Islam became inoperative when the blasphemy law was abolished in 2008 – with very little protest from Christians or any other religious group. Nevertheless, key aspects of society were learning to exercise restraint even in the absence of law. In relation to the Danish Muhammad Cartoons Affair, which blew up shortly after the abolition of blasphemy, while the cartoons were reprinted in several leading European newspapers, no national newspaper in Britain did so. This suggests that there was a greater understanding in Britain about anti-Muslim racism and about not giving gratuitous offence to Muslims than in some other European countries (for a debate reflecting several sides of the issue and how they have divided liberals, see Modood et al. 2006).

Moreover, even as the MCB fell out of favour with the government,[3] local and national consultations with Muslim groups have continued to grow and probably under New Labour came to exceed consultations with most Christian bodies and certainly any minority group. Inevitably, this has caused occasional friction between Christians and Muslims. On the whole, however, these developments have taken place with the support of the leadership of the Church of England and in a spirit of interfaith respect. (Given how adversarial English intellectual, journalistic, legal and political culture is, religion in England is oddly fraternal and little effort is expended in proving that the other side is in a state of error and should convert, contrary to the popular and intellectuals' view that religion is much more divisive than class or politics.)

ACCOMMODATING MUSLIMS AND SECULARISM IN A COMPARATIVE EUROPEAN CONTEXT

These policy demands no doubt seem odd within the terms of, say, the French or U.S. 'wall of separation'. But it is clear that they virtually mirror existing anti-discrimination policy provisions in the United Kingdom. In any case, it is important to be clear that in the French case, the issue is not simply secularism but a minority-blindness that repudiates 'race' and ethnicity, no less than religion (Scott 2007). The giving up of pre-French identities and assimilation into French culture is thought to go hand in hand with the acceptance of French citizenship. If for some reason assimilation is not fully embraced – perhaps because some people want to retain pride in their Algerian ancestry or want to maintain ethnic solidarity in the face of current stigmatisation and discrimination – then their claim to be French and equal citizens is jeopardised. In any case, the French approach of ignoring racial, ethnic and religious identities does not mean that they, or the related problems of exclusion, alienation and fragmentation, vanish.

For any strong secularist, the single most important issue is to maintain a gap between the state and organised religion. Certainly, this is how secularism is understood in the United States, where churches can be very powerful political actors but the Constitution has a strong 'no establishment clause'. By this measure, it is not at all clear that France is developing a more secularist position than Britain. Britain has two 'national' churches, the Church of Scotland and the Church of England, but it is the latter that most people have in mind when they speak of 'establishment'. In the late 1980s and early 1990s some secular progressives began to argue that the emergence of a multi-faith society meant it was no longer appropriate for the state to privilege one faith and the Church of England ought to be disestablished (the Liberal Democrats passed such a motion at their 1990 conference; see also WAF 1990 and IPPR 1991). Few members of religious minorities initially joined this discussion and so the secular multiculturalists were taken to be speaking for the marginal religious minorities. Yet, when the latter did join this debate, spokespersons of a number of non-Christian religious minorities have actually argued for the importance of maintaining a symbolic and substantive link between religion and the state (Modood 1997). Indeed, somewhat surprisingly, religious minorities, including Muslims, who, as we have seen, have been very assertive across a broad front, have not challenged the Anglican privileges or 'establishment' or even the conception that Britain is/ought to be a Christian country (Modood 1997). When Prime Minister Cameron, who confessed to not being a steadfast believer, made a major speech in 2011 arguing that Britons should not be shy of asserting that Britain is a Christian country (Prime Minister's Office 2011), many secularists protested. The speech was, however, welcomed by the then chair of the Mosque and Community Affairs of the Muslim Council of Britain, Sheikh Ibrahim Mogra (BBC 2011). The minorities seem to prefer an incremental pluralisation of the religion-state linkages, rather than their abolition. This is what is implicit in the demand for including Muslim and Sikh schools within the state sector. It is also echoed in the recommendations of the Royal Commission on the Reform of the House of Lords (2000). It argued that the number of Anglican bishops in the Lords should be reduced from 26 to 16 and that they should be joined by five representatives of other Christian denominations in England, five seats should be allocated to other Christian denominations in the rest of the United Kingdom and a further five should be used to include the presence of non-Christians (for further details see chapter 8). These recommendations have not been accepted but it is interesting that governments have felt the need to create multi-faith consultative bodies. The Conservatives created an Inner Cities Religious Council in 1992, chaired by a junior minister, which was replaced in 2006 with a body with a much broader remit, the Faith

Communities Consultative Council. Indeed in that year, faith communities became a policy area with a Division to itself within the Department of Communities and Local Government, the latter having full representation at Cabinet. It is notable that most of the Muslim goals described in this section have had formal inter-faith support and sometimes would not have been possible without active cross-faith support (for example, the religion question in the Census; see Sherif 2003).

In having an active policy of deepening state-religion linkages Britain is not unusual. Most West European countries are accommodating religious minorities – or at least Muslims. From an E.U. perspective the (belated) British focus on religion/Muslims is normal; it is the focus on American-style race that is peculiar. This is partly because most 'non-whites' in continental Europe are Muslims and mainly from places where the idea of 'blackness' was not prominent. Britain is also unusual in having the degree of minority assertiveness that it has and which has contributed to the character of British Muslim politics and which has been noted by Muslim politicians and activists in other countries (Klausen 2005; for a specific contrast between British Muslim bottom-up policy pressure and its relative absence in Germany, see Lewicki 2014). Continental initiatives have had a much more top-down character. As early as 1974 the Belgian State recognised Islam as one of its national religions, and Muslims in the Netherlands have long had state funded religious schools and television channels as a progressive step in that country's traditional way of institutionally dealing with organized religion – namely, 'pillarization'.[4] Despite a strong anti-multiculturalist, anti-Muslim backlash from the late 1990s (Prins and Saharso 2010) these policies have been maintained (Bader 2011).

Similarly, a 'Muslim community' is slowly and grudgingly becoming recognized by public authorities in parts of Germany by appealing to the historic German idea of a 'religious society' (*Religionsgesellschaft*), though alternative formats are also being tried. Chancellor Merkel assembled a group of Muslims in 2006 for an *Islamkonfrenz* at the highest level of government, an exploratory body, yet with an extensive political agenda, and this has been continued on a periodic basis, despite neither side being happy with the (lack of) outcomes so far. Again, a series of French Interior Ministers have taken a number of steps to 'normalise' Islam in France by creating an official French Islam under the authority of the state in ways that make it identical to other faiths. Those who think that French *laïcité* consists of a wall of separation between the state and church are badly mistaken. The French state has formal institutional and financial connexions with the Catholic and Protestant churches, the Jewish Consistory and now a Council of the Muslim Faith (Bowen 2007; for more on various European cases see Modood and Kastoryano 2006, Stepan 2011, and Koenig 2009).

The British approach has in some ways been less statist and corporatist in its accommodation of Islam and the other newly present faiths than its continental neighbours. It has also been more liberal. This can be illustrated by reference to one of the most illiberal cases, the French ban on the wearing of the Muslim headscarf, the hijab (and other 'ostentatious' religious symbols) in French state schools in February 2005. In contrast, the hijab hardly attracts any controversy in Britain. The niqab (face veil) has been an object of a fierce and intense debate, launched by the senior governmental figure, Jack Straw MP, but he was careful to insist that he was not advocating the use of the law but was voluntarily requesting that Muslim women remove the niqab when speaking to him at his surgery (Straw 2006). France, however, in 2010 banned the covering of the face in public places – a move clearly targeting the niqab or what in France is called the 'bourka' – leading to a number of Muslim women being arrested and convicted. In July 2014, the European Court of Human Rights rejected an appeal against this law and meanwhile related bans have been enacted in Belgium, Germany and Denmark, and other European states are considering doing the same (Ferrari and Pastorelli 2016).

In certain ways the minority politics described in this chapter has been joined – perhaps even dominated – by foreign policy and security concerns from around the time of the terrorist attacks of 9/11, and especially after the invasion of Iraq in 2003 and the London bombings of 7/7.[5] Moreover, especially following the change in government in 2010, government and politicians, both in relation to security and cultural integration, have become more top-down and coercive, with a corresponding increase in media and public hostility to Muslims.

CONCLUSION

The purpose of this chapter has been to put the politics of Muslim accommodation in some historical context, to show that it was based upon bottom-up campaigns and facilitated by using and developing a prior racial equality activism, laws and policies. That the Muslim equality agenda has got as far as it has is because of the liberal and pragmatic British political culture on matters of religion, as opposed to a more thoroughgoing secularism that requires the state to control religion. Yet, a more fundamental ideological reason is that Muslims utilised and extended previously existing arguments and policies in relation to racial and multicultural equality. By emphasising discrimination in educational and economic opportunities, political representation and the media, critiquing 'Muslim-blindness' in the provision of healthcare and social services; and arguing for remedies which mirror existing legislation and policies in relation to sexual and racial equality, most politically active Muslims in respect of domestic issues have adjusted to and become part of British political culture in general and British multiculturalist politics in particular. Indeed, it could be said that they achieved a significant measure of political integration. Most of this progress has taken place under a New Labour administration. Cynics have argued that the success of the Muslim agenda is because New Labour has had to placate Muslim anti-Iraq War anger. A more long term analysis, as offered here, shows that Labour's attentiveness to that agenda precedes the war or even 9/11. As part of its effort to advance racial and religious equality, the New Labour government consciously, albeit not always enthusiastically, pursued policies that did not exist before 1997 – such as the funding of Muslim schools, the creation of Muslim peers and legislation to prevent religious discrimination and hatred, currently the strongest in the European Union. In general, while the data would be partial and complex to assemble, my impression is that not just in relation to ethnic or ethnoreligious minorities in general, but specifically in relation to Muslims, there is greater political and public presence in Britain than in any other E.U. country, and while in every country, post 9/11, dominant discourses and politics manifest relentless hostility to Muslims and Muslim activities, real or imagined, Muslims in Britain continue to be not just the objects of debates and policies but participants (O'Toole et al. 2013).

NOTES

1. As Somalis became a settled group in Britain, at the turn of the century, they joined the Pakistanis and the Bangladeshis as the three most disadvantaged ethnic groups in Britain, each being almost entirely Muslim.
2. A few years later the large Fourth Survey found that nominal Christians and those without a religion were more likely to say they were prejudiced against Muslims than those Christians who said their religion was of importance to them (Modood et al. 1997, 134).
3. The government played an active role in encouraging the formation and the promotion of alternative, national Muslim organisations on the grounds that they were more moderate and representative, especially the Sufi Muslim Council and the British Muslim Forum. With the realisation that no single Muslim organisation was fully reflective of non-jihadi Muslims, the New Labour government readmitted the MCB back into the fold – but now as only part of a plurality, and this policy continued under the Coalition, whilst the subsequent Conservative governments have been reluctant to give the MCB any prominence.
4. This principle that recognized that Protestants and Catholics had a right to state resources and some publicly funded autonomous institutions officially ended in 1960. It is, however, still considered as a 'relevant framework for the development of a model that grants certain collective rights to religious groups' (Sunier and von Luijeren 2002) in such matters as state funding of Islamic schools. So, the accommodation of Muslims is being achieved through a combination of mild pillarization and Dutch minority policies (Bader 2011).
5. Though this has not led to the 'death' of multiculturalism that so many have discerned in the events following 9/11 and 7/7 (Modood 2007/2013; and Meer and Modood 2009).

REFERENCES

Andrews, K. (2016). 'The Problem of Political Blackness: Lessons from the Black Supplementary School Movement'. *Ethnic and Racial Studies*, *39*(11), 2060–2078.
Bader, V. (2011). 'Associational Governance of Ethno-Religious Diversity in Europe: The Dutch Case'. In Smith, R. (ed.), *Citizenship, Borders, and Human Needs*, 273–297. Philadelphia: University of Pennsylvania Press.
BBC. (2011). 'David Cameron on Christianity – Views'. BBC News, 18 December: http://www.bbc.co.uk/news/uk-16231223 [last accessed 23/9/2018].
Bowen, J. (2007). *Why the French Don't Like Headscarves: Islam, the State, and Public Space*. Princeton, NJ: Princeton University Press.
Centre for Contemporary Cultural Studies (CCCS). (1982). *The Empire Strikes Back: Race and Racism in 70s Britain*. London: Hutchinson.
Ferrari, A. and Pastorelli, S. (eds.). (2016). *The Burqa Affair across Europe: Between Public and Private Space*. London: Routledge.
Gilroy, P. (1987). *There Ain't No Black in the Union Jack: The Cultural Politics of Race and Nation*. London: Heinemann.
Halstead, J. (1988). *Education, Justice and Cultural Diversity: An Examination of the Honeyford Affair, 1984–85*. London: Falmer Press.
Honeyford, R. (1984). 'Education and Race: An Alternative View'. *Salisbury Review*, Winter, *9*, 292.
Hussain, S. and Sherif, J. (2014). 'Minority Religions in the Census: The Case of British Muslims'. *Religion*, *44*(3), 414–433.
Institute of Public Policy Research (IPPR). (1991). *The Constitution of the United Kingdom*. London: IPPR.
Karlsen, S. and Pantazis, C. (2017). 'Better Understandings of Ethnic Variations: Ethnicity, Poverty and Social Exclusion'. In Dermott, E. and Main, G. (eds.), *Poverty and Social Exclusion in the UK: Volume 1—The Nature and Extent of the Problem*, 115–133. Bristol, UK: Policy Press.
Klausen, J. (2005). *The Islamic Challenge: Politics and Religion in Western Europe*. Oxford: Oxford University Press.
Koenig, M. (2009). 'How Nation-States Respond to Religious Diversity'. In Bramadat, P. and Koenig, M. (eds.), *International Migration and the Governance of Religious Diversity*, 293–322. Kingston, ON: School of Policy Studies, Queen's University.
Lewicki, A. (2014). *Social Justice through Citizenship? The Politics of Muslim Integration in Germany and Great Britain*. Basingstoke, UK: Palgrave.
Meer, N. (2007). 'Muslim Schools in Britain: Challenging Mobilisations or Logical Developments?'. *Asia-Pacific Journal of Education*, *27*(1), 55–71.
Meer, N. and Modood, T. (2009). 'The Multicultural State We Are In: Muslims, "Multiculture" and the "Civic Re-balancing" of British Multiculturalism'. *Political Studies*, *57*(3), 473–497.
Mirza, M., Senthilkumaran, A. and Ja'far, Z. (2007). *Living Apart Together: British Muslims and the Paradox of Multiculturalism*. London: Policy Exchange.
Modood, T. (1990). 'British Asian Muslims and the Rushdie Affair'. *The Political Quarterly*, *61*(2), 43–160; also in Donald, J. and Rattansi, A. (eds.), *'Race', Culture and Difference*, 260–277. London: Sage.
Modood, T. (1994). 'Political Blackness and British Asians'. *Sociology*, *28*(4), 859–876.
Modood, T. (ed.). (1997). *Church, State and Religious Minorities*. London: Policy Studies Institute.
Modood, T. (2005). *Multicultural Politics: Racism, Ethnicity, and Muslims in Britain*. Minneapolis and Edinburgh: University of Minnesota Press and University of Edinburgh Press.
Modood, T. (2007/2013). *Multiculturalism: A Civic Idea* (2nd ed., 2013). Cambridge: Polity Press.
Modood, T. (2010). *Still Not Easy Being British*. Stoke-on-Trent, UK: Trentham Books.
Modood, T., Berthoud, R., Lakey, J., Nazroo, J., Smith, P., Virdee, S. and Beishon, S. (1997). *Ethnic Minorities in Britain: Diversity and Disadvantage*. London: Policy Studies Institute.

Modood, T., Hansen, R., Bleich, E., O'Leary, B. and Carens, J. (2006). 'The Danish Cartoon Affair: Free Speech, Racism, Islamism, and Integration'. *International Migration*, *44*(5), 3–57.
Modood, T. and Kastoryano, R. (2006). 'Secularism and the Accommodation of Muslims in Europe'. In Modood, T., Triandafyllidou, A. and Zapata-Barrero, R. (eds.), *Multiculturalism, Muslims and Citizenship: A European Approach*, 162–178. London: Routledge.
Modood, T., Triandafyllidou, A. and Zapata-Barrero, R. (eds.). (2006). *Multiculturalism, Muslims and Citizenship: A European Approach*. London: Routledge.
Muslim Parliament of Great Britain. (1992). *Race Relations and Muslims in Great Britain: A Discussion Paper*. London: The Muslim Parliament.
O'Toole, T., DeHanas, D. N., Modood, T., Meer, N. and Jones, S. (2013). *Taking Part: Muslim Participation in Contemporary Governance*. Bristol, UK: Centre for the Study of Ethnicity and Citizenship, University of Bristol: http://www.bristol.ac.uk/media-library/sites/ethnicity/migrated/documents/mpcgreport.pdf [accessed 23/09/2018].
Phillips, A. (2007). *Multiculturalism without Culture*. Princeton, NJ: Princeton University Press.
Prime Minister's Office. (2011). 'Prime Minister's King James Bible Speech'. gov.uk, 16 December: http://www.number10.gov.uk/news/king-james-bible [accessed 21/04/2015].
Prins, B. and Saharso, S. (2010). 'From Toleration to Repression: The Dutch Backlash against Multiculturalism'. In Vertovec, S. and Wessendorf, S. (eds.), *Backlash: European Discourses, Policies and Practices*, 72–91. London: Routledge.
Rex, J. and Moore, R. (1967). *Race, Community and Conflict*. Oxford: Oxford University Press.
Runnymede Trust Commission on British Muslims and Islamophobia. (1997). *Islamophobia: A Challenge for Us All*. London: The Runnymede Trust.
Runnymede Trust Commission on British Muslims and Islamophobia. (2004). *Islamophobia: Issues, Challenges and Action*. Stoke-on-Trent, UK: Trentham Books.
Rushdie, S. (1982). 'The New Empire within Britain'. *New Society*, 9 December.
Samad, Y. (1992). 'Book Burning and Race Relations: Political Mobilisation of Bradford Muslims'. *New Community*, *18*(4), 507–519.
Scott, J. W. (2007). *Politics of the Veil*. Princeton, NJ: Princeton University Press.
Sherif, J. (2003). *Campaigning for a Religion Question in the 2001 Census*. http://www.mcb.org.uk/downloads/census2001.pdf [accessed 31/01/2008].
Sherif, J. (2011). 'A Census Chronicle – Reflections on the Campaign for a Religion Question in the 2001 Census for England and Wales'. *Journal of Beliefs & Values*, *32*(1), 1–18.
Singh, G. (2005). 'British Multiculturalism and Sikhs'. *Sikh Formations*, *1*(2), 157–173.
Sivanandan, A. (1985). 'RAT and the Degradation of Black Struggle'. *Race & Class*, *26*(4), 1–33.
Straw, J. (2006). 'I Felt Uneasy Talking to Someone I Could Not See'. *Guardian*, 5 October: https://www.theguardian.com/commentisfree/2006/oct/06/politics.uk [accessed 23/09/2018].
Sunier, T. and von Luijeren, M. (2002). 'Islam in the Netherlands'. In Haddad, Y. (ed.), *Muslims in the West: From Sojourners to Citizens*, 144–158. New York: Oxford University Press.
Swann, Lord. (1985). *Education for All: Final Report of the Committee of Inquiry into the Education of Children from Ethnic Minority Groups, Cmnd 9453*. London: HMSO.
Stepan, A. (2011). 'The Multiple Secularisms of Modern Democratic and Non-Democratic Regimes'. In Calhoun, C., Juergensmeyer, M. and Van Antwerpen, J. (eds.), *Rethinking Secularism*, 114–144. Oxford: Oxford University Press.
UK Action Committee on Islamic Affairs (UKACIA). (1993). *Muslims and the Law in Multi-Faith Britain: Need for Reform*. London: UKACIA.
Women Against Fundamentalism (WAF). (1992). 'Founding Statement'. *Women Against Fundamentalism Journal*, *1*(1).

Chapter Three

Maintaining Civility and the Feelings of the Hated

In discussion of free speech and incitement to religious hatred, there is a tendency to draw an analogy with blasphemy. This becomes the point of departure or more than the point of departure. But I want to suggest that a better analogy, as a starting point, is incitement to *racial* hatred or (in a slightly different but related challenge) the legal and other issues around Holocaust denial.

Clearly there is sometimes a public order concern about the forms of dangerous speech that incite hatred. We recognize occasions on which the law has to intervene to stop people saying certain things or things in a certain way or saying those things in a certain time and place. For a classic illustration used by political theorists and others, take a situation in which there is a threat of immediate violence. Such a case is sketched by John Stuart Mill in *On Liberty* (1956 [1859]). He is championing freedom of speech but he says,

> [E]ven opinions lose their immunity, when the circumstances in which they are expressed are such as to constitute their expression a positive instigation to some mischievous act. An opinion that corn-dealers are starvers of the poor, or that private property is robbery, ought to be unmolested when simply circulated through the press, but may justly incur punishment when delivered orally to an excited mob assembled before the house of a corn-dealer, or when handed about among the same mob in the form of a placard. (Mill 1956 [1859], 67–68)

The crowd are outside the house of the corn merchant, cannot afford to buy food for themselves and their families and are protesting about their hunger. The orator or demagogue says, 'There, that is the man who is responsible. The corn merchant lives in this house. He is in here'. The orator does not have to add, 'Go and get him' for us to know from the context that he is provoking the mob to violence. The demagogue here is threatening violence; and anyone framing legislation must clearly have such cases in mind. I want to suggest, however, that when we think about legislation we go well beyond such threats of immediate violence. Let us tease out the rationale behind the current law (for more details, see Modood 1993).

Where feelings run deep in a society, a climate of opinion can be exacerbated – or a climate of opinion can be created – in which victimization or racial attacks may take place, or where some forms of speech or literature may create emotive perceptions of a group as an enemy within. Such speech or literature is likely to lead to acts of discrimination against this putatively undesirable group of people, although perhaps not to immediate violence. That is my point: perhaps not to *immediate* violence. The speech or literature is nevertheless likely to create fear in the vulnerable group; and in mentioning this fear we introduce a new feature which complicates the initial picture of incitement which we drew from Mill's example of the corn merchant. We start considering the effects not just on the emotions of the incited rabble but of its *targets*. What are the corn merchant and his family feeling, trapped inside with this baying mob outside? Fear, obviously; but the victims of such incitement are likely to undergo other and longer-term forms of distress.

For example – and now we are talking about real social-political cases – to taunt people of some backgrounds with images of slavery and of lynching is to remind those people of subjugation: 'This is how you were treated or your parents or ancestors were treated, and this is perhaps what you deserve. Do not feel cocky here; this is the treatment appropriate for you'. Similarly with racist materials that portray black people as simian, as of less than human intelligence and sensibility – and again with images, held aloft or put on a wall or banner in Northern Ireland, of Protestant victories over Catholics. And so on.

Only if we focus on the emotions of *victims*, of targeted groups and targeted people, can we understand the fact that most countries in the European Union have legislation against Holocaust denial, with the offences typically punished by prison sentences of some years.[1] No one has ever suggested that the literature of Holocaust denial would lead to immediate violence. But it would, we all recognize, have a very distressing effect on some people – in particular, on people whose family histories are tied up with the Holocaust; almost certainly on Jewish people more generally; and probably on others. Such literature poses as well the danger of legitimizing the particularly gross dictatorship of the Nazis as having been just another political regime. My point is this: when we specify what is wrong with incitement, we think about its effect on the victims and not just on those who are incited.

Among the effects that we might anticipate and which we might attempt in our legislation to prevent are the emotional reactions in the victims that may lead *them* into violent responses. So we are working to prevent both the violence of the victimizer and violent responses from the victim. This, too, is of course a public order concern, but is again not apparent in the image of incitement with which I began.

Incitement to hatred, then, involves not just the danger of immediate violence, but the production as well of a climate of opinion or emotions, or the exploitation of that climate – not just the arousal of certain hatreds in the dominant group but also a fear and humiliation in the victim group that can lead in turn to conflict and violence. These dangers all inform any agenda for the prevention of incitement to hatred.

An objection might be raised here, that everything we have said so far is about protecting people, not their religious beliefs. Yes, that is exactly my concern: protecting people, not religious beliefs. But the people in question may be people marked by religious identity: Roman Catholics in Northern Ireland, for instance; Jewish people, as I have already mentioned; and in relation to this chapter, Muslims in Britain.

Now what if a group of religious people, let us say some Muslims (and this is close to a real example), are connected to aspects of their faith with such deep emotion that disrespectful attacks upon it will cause them the kind of distress that is caused to other groups by reference to (say) images of black bestiality or by Holocaust denial? Add to this a set of domestic and geopolitical circumstances in which these Muslims – and here we might include as well Muslims who are less intense in their religion – feel that they are being targeted and harassed as culturally backward, as disloyal and as terrorists – in short, as not belonging here, as unwanted and under threat. And is not that, if somewhat briefly and over-simply stated, the Britain and other parts of Europe in which we are living? And will that not explain the explosions of protest, anger and violence sparked by *The Satanic Verses*, for example, or to the cartoons of the prophet Muhammad published in the Danish newspaper, *Jyllands-Posten* (Modood et al. 2006; Levey and Modood 2009)?

I am not justifying everything that was done in the name of those protests. I am pointing to certain chain reactions and to the need for us to understand how they may be prevented. Of course certain Muslims (let us call them 'extremists'), in their responses to *The Satanic Verses* and the cartoons, exploited the situations, feelings and ignorance of other Muslims. That is true; but there would have been nothing to exploit without the deep significance of these feelings to those other Muslims. Some people undoubtedly worsened the situation; but they could do so only because some Muslims think as they do about the prophet Muhammad's centrality to their sense of the sacred, of their faith and of the dignity of that faith.

At this point we can appreciate that not only should there be some legislation to curb incitement to religious hatred, but that in some cases and contexts the legislation may touch directly on religious feelings and beliefs and so may indeed appear to be protecting those feelings and beliefs, such as the intense devotion for the prophet Muhammad found among some Muslims. Such legislation then may seem to *privilege* those feelings and beliefs. But this would not be accurate. The legislation may come to have such a secondary consequence but that would not be its *purpose*; its purpose would be protection against incitement to religious hatred in the wider meaning of incitement that I have been elaborating.

This may seem to be putting Islam, alone of all religions, above all censure or criticism; but I do not want any religion to enjoy such a privileged position. We just need to acknowledge that what hurts different people – often reopening the historical wounds that they already bear – varies over place and time: it may be racial slurs, or bigotry in Northern Ireland, or anti-Semitism. And now Muslims are very much in the frame. What hurts them is historically contingent; and we need to respond to such hurt, as it arises. If certain actions are likely to provoke Muslims in ways that are harmful to their status as fellow and equal citizens and that are likely to lead to conflict, then there is a problem we need to address. Islam is not being privileged here; it is just a contingent fact (if it is accepted as a fact) that some actions hurt some Muslims just as other actions – which we acknowledge for this reason to be reprehensible – hurt other groups.

No religion should be protected from criticism. But how is that criticism to be stated? There are ways of criticising the actions of some Jewish people or of the Jewish state that might be considered racist; and there are ways of making the same criticisms that are not racist (for how to distinguish between racism and reasonable criticism in relation to Muslims, see chapter 4). Here it is not a matter of protecting Islam or Muslims from criticism but of the *kind* of criticism that will be permitted. Should others enjoy the right of mocking and ridiculing and hurting religious people to the point where some such people lose their self-control? Should that right take priority over the endeavour – of higher priority to me – to create a society in which mutual respect and civic equality prevail over people's right to castigate, ridicule and offend?

This of course raises the question, Who shall be the arbiter of what is offensive? Shall it be the religious community that is the subject matter of the material in question? In answer I would emphasise again that we are not dealing primarily with a theological decision over blasphemy to be made by Islamic scholars, but with equality of respect and dignity. We see people feeling hurt and humiliated and reacting in aggrieved and angry ways. It is only civil to ask what has affected them in this way, and to seek to reduce the hurt. The pain of the victim, therefore, will indeed be one criterion of what should or should not be admissible. It will not be the only criterion; we will want to investigate the circumstances, to clarify what is really at issue and whether those who are hurt are running together in their grievance a number of concerns. And there may also be questions of other people's rights, to be balanced against the hurt. But my argument runs with the grain of the understanding reached by the criminal justice system of racial and (in the workplace) sexual harassment: the lead is often given by what the victim thinks. If the victim thinks he or she is harassed, there is a presumption of harassment; such presumption does not decide the matter, but the matter must then be investigated and aired. It is for such a principle that I am arguing.[2]

CENSOR OR CENSURE?

Let me, however, make two qualifications that address the issue of limits. The first concerns a distinction between freedom of enquiry and freedom of expression. John Stuart Mill and many libertarians who followed his lead have wanted to argue for freedom of expression in every social and intellectual sphere. Even if an opinion is wrong, Mill argued, present and future generations lose by its suppression

> the clearer perception and livelier impression of truth, produced by its collision with error. . . . The beliefs which we have most warrant for have no safeguard to rest on but a standing invitation to the whole world to prove them unfounded. . . . Since the general or prevailing opinion on any subject is rarely or never the whole truth, it is only by the collision of adverse opinions that the remainder of the truth has any chance of being supplied. (Mill 1956 [1859], 21)

These arguments place a value upon truth; they are arguments for the freedom of *enquiry*. Yet non-propositional expression is not – or at least may not be – a contribution to enquiry or to truth. So we may want to reaffirm the freedom of enquiry in relation to people's religions and faith – including of course Islam – without thereby entitling people to express their views about Islam in any offensive or insulting way that they like. As we know from our experience, almost every day of our life, there are gracious ways and there are aggressive ways of making a point. I want then to place freedom of enquiry on a higher level than freedom of expression. We may sometimes need to curb freedom of *expression* for the reasons I gave earlier about incitement, whereas freedom of *enquiry* should be curbed, if at all, only under very severe circumstances.

My second point about limits is this: in thinking about incitement to hatred and how to limit and prevent it, it may be more important to censure than to censor. The law is a very blunt instrument, and its capacity to deal with opinions and expressions is extremely limited. We cannot expect the law to do a lot of work where the issue is respect for people as people, including religious people as religious people. That does not imply that everything should be perfectly acceptable on which the law is silent. There need to be limits to avoid disrespect, offence and provocation, and to prevent fear and humiliation. These limits are exercised through personal and institutional self-restraint. (By 'institutional self-restraint' I mean such restraint as editors of newspapers have to exercise in their professional, editorial capacity.) Most of the ways in which we show courtesy, civility and respect for each other as fellow citizens are through ordinary behaviour where the law is silent, where the law leaves the space for us to be either offensive or civil.

Let us go back to the two examples we have mentioned: *The Satanic Verses* and the cartoons. A certain kind of education took place between those two affairs, an *education of sensibility* in what is offensive – gratuitously insulting – to Muslims. When some Muslims first protested about *The Satanic Verses* (published in 1988), the reaction of many people in the United Kingdom – and most noticeably of people contributing to the serious media – was almost supercilious: what, they asked, was all the fuss about; the book was just a novel; Muslims should get over it and live with it. Most Muslims of course had not read the novel; they knew of it from garbled hearsay or photocopied extracts. But on all sides they heard prestigious and influential and literary people praise the novel and ask whether Muslims knew how to read a book. Now that was really insulting and for some caused more hurt than the novel itself. Muslims heard both that novelists should be able to portray the prophet however they liked and that any Muslims who could not see this novel's merits were culturally low and backward and lacking in sensibility.

The British reaction to the cartoons (published in 2005) was quite different. Those cartoons, originally published in a Danish newspaper, were reproduced in newspapers in several other countries – Germany and France, for instance – as a kind of political declaration: the papers were taking a stand; they were insisting on their right to publish cartoons that offended Muslims. But not a single British newspaper – right-wing, left-wing or in the centre – published the cartoons. All the papers in Britain thought the cartoons were unworthy of reprinting; that they would do harm; and in particular, that they would, without satisfying any particular principle, damage the good relations that should exist between Muslims and non-Muslims. In this there is a more general lesson to be learnt: that editors should exercise responsible judgement which may include a decision not to publish certain things. When the leaders of society and of institutions, alive to what is hurtful, exercise self-restraint, then the law can be minimally and rarely exercised. So an important principle is coming centre stage: to censure rather than censor.

I would suggest that of *The Satanic Verses* and the cartoons, *The Satanic Verses* was by far the more serious affair. Of the twelve cartoons that were published, some were only mildly offensive, some were innocuous and one was even poking fun at the very exercise. We assumed (perhaps because we did not see them) that they were all offensive when they were not. There was one that I would say was racist: the cartoon that became famous, of a bearded man wearing a large turban with an Islamic declaration and from which is protruding a lit fuse. Nothing in that cartoon showed that it was of Muhammad, but it was clearly of a Muslim. Its point was, I think, that Muslims are terrorists or that, at least, there is something about Muslims and terrorism that goes together. It was not, then, a remark about the prophet Muhammad as such but a remark about Muslims; and on this basis it was racist. This is similar to how a cartoon of Moses with a large nose and holding the Ten Commandments under one arm and moneybags under the other, or something similar, might be used to make a comment about Jews in general and not just about one religious figure. I am thinking of some of the cartoons from *Der Stürmer* from the 1920s and 1930s in Germany.[3] The cartoonist would be making a statement not about Moses but about Jews; and on that basis it would be offensive and racist. That was the character of the cartoon with the turban-bomb.

Should such a cartoon therefore have been banned? Not necessarily. There are some forms of racism that it is better to legally live with. But they should be censured. And that brings me back to *The Satanic Verses*, and the grounds for seeing the novel as a far more serious hurt for Muslims: there was no censure. At the time of the Danish cartoons a strong current of opinion in the media ran against their publication: the cartoons were offensive and improper and should not be circulated. Nobody had said that about *The Satanic Verses*. This is not to set aside the novel's content. Of course Muslims do not like being thought of, in the terms encouraged by the cartoons, as terrorists. But *The Satanic Verses* introduced various forms of what most people (not just Muslims) regard as vulgarity. The eroticization of the sacred in *The Satanic Verses* was far more hurtful then anything in the cartoons.

In the face of *The Satanic Verses* it was that sense of humiliation, of being (as it were) culturally naked, that was so hurtful to Muslims. At first there was nobody of any authority, nobody who might be a respectable voice of Britain, who acknowledged why Muslims were hurt or who questioned the novel's propriety. When at last important figures in the Church of England and the Roman Catholic Church began to moderate the debate, they did not call for the novel to be banned, but they did at least publicly recognise why Muslims were hurt. Those opening months were so serious because nobody could see – as they *could* see seventeen years later when the cartoons were published – why Muslims were hurt.

I am not so naïve as to believe that all the editors who chose to not reprint the cartoons did so only out of respect for Muslims. At the very least some may have had mixed motives. Some may have been more concerned about the safety of their staff and premises, for example. I am unhappy that some Muslim protestors have created fear of reprisals, even murder, in relation to issues of respect and disrespect. Without seeking to justify intimidation, threats and violence of that sort, we should bear in mind that force and violence often, even if only by a minority of activists, accompanies passionate protests against perceived injustice. This is true of demonstrations by students, trade unionists, animal rights activists, CND (Campaign for Nuclear Disarmament) and so on. One consequence is that public discussion often focuses on the behaviour of the protestors rather than an evaluation of their grievance. Another is that if people in power accede to the demands of the protestors it can be unclear whether they were persuaded by the force of argument or merely to avoid further violence. Nevertheless, it is the case that moral learning, political reform and violent protests can be part of a related dynamic and play a part in effecting justifiable social change.

Justice Sachs makes an important point about *The Satanic Verses* and the importance of its publication: the novel is a move towards Muslim self-reflection (Sachs 2013). Of course I support such self-reflection (as I support freedom of enquiry), and I value any contribution to it; I value, too, the enquiry into Islam that is shared with non-Muslims. But here I want to exercise my distinction between freedom of enquiry and of expression. Would a less offensive portrayal, even within fiction, undermine the enquiry? Why can the enquiry not be conducted in less hurtful ways?

I do believe that there should be legislation against incitement to religious hatred, as we now have in Great Britain and which we have had in Northern Ireland for some time[4]; but I would put the weight upon censure. In relation both to *The Satanic Verses* and to the Danish cartoons, it is more appropriate to censure than to censor. We do not necessarily want to prohibit actions by law, but we should be censuring people who, we think, are being gratuitously offensive. We may well be condemning at the same time some behaviour of protestors against the offence. To decide whether something shall count as offensive or not, we do not ask whether those protesting against it are even more offensive. They may well be; they may be threatening to kill those who have offended them. But what caused the original offence is not thereby rendered inoffensive. Indeed our failure to censure now may create social divisions that will be more difficult to heal in the future and may require *more* – not *less* – legislation, legislation that may mean *less* – not *more* – freedom in the future.

THE FEELINGS AND BELIEFS OF THE HATED

Jeremy Waldron has argued that certain 'reputational attacks amount to assaults upon the dignity of the persons affected – 'dignity' in the sense of their recognition as social equals and as bearers of human rights and constitutional entitlements' (2012, 58–59). He believes that this justifies legislation against hate speech. I think this is broadly right, but that dignity or recognition as social equals requires paying more attention to group subjectivities than Waldron consistently holds, and this has implications for understanding hate and laws protecting the dignity of members of vulnerable groups.

Waldron seems to have two positions in relation to laws and the hurt that some groups may experience. On the one hand he says that 'I accept the point, which many critics make, that offense is not something the law should seek to protect people against' (Waldron 2012, 15) and that '[p]rotecting people's feelings against offense is not an appropriate objective for the law' (Waldron 2012, 106). On the other hand, he also writes, 'The idea, then, that it might be unlawful to wound people's feelings is not an incoherent one, and we know how to recognise legal principles whose aim is to protect people from this sort of harm' (Waldron 2012, 111). Even if unsure on this point, Waldron is sure that protecting people's feelings against offense has nothing to do with his dignitarian rationale. Feelings of hurt, distress, anger, fear and so on are not definitive and may only sometimes be symptoms of indignity: 'That someone's feelings are hurt is more or less definitive of offense, but it is not definitive of indignity. Shock, distress, or wounded feelings may or may not be symptomatic of indignity' (Waldron 2012, 108).

I would like to push Waldron away from the above ambivalence and to draw the line between offence and hate in a different place. I think we do need to sometimes prevent the giving of offense; or, to put it another way, that our defining of hate cannot be independent of the feelings and beliefs of the hated. The feelings referred to in the last quote are not merely symptoms, they are part of the experience of being hated, and so they are or should be part of what hate speech laws are trying to prevent. This has not always been recognised in law but has gradually come to be so in some countries, especially in liberal democracies; for Western Europe, protecting Jews from Holocaust deniers was the catalyst. The distress caused to the hated may not always be decisive or a sufficient condition for protective legislation, but they are a necessary condition and not merely a symptom of an undermining of equal civic standing.

Up to about the 1980s, incitement to hatred was understood as focused on stopping the 'stirring up of hatred' and on public order, but since then laws have increasingly focused not just on acts or agents of hate but also on the feelings of the victims. Britain's way of dealing with incitement to racial and religious hatred has its own distinctive history, yet is an example of what I mean. Before the existence of any race relations legislation in Britain, hateful speech could be dealt with only under common law powers relating to breach of the peace or under the Public Order Act 1936: in effect this meant that public disorder had to be imminent. Section 6 of the Race Relations Act 1965 broadened this offence by not restricting the criteria to those of outcome but including the intentions of the speaker or writer in question: intending to stir up racial hatred, regardless of the measure of success, became an offence. This in effect meant (and this is how the courts interpreted the few cases that came before them) that stirring up racial hatred could not be construed as an action with an immediate outcome but as something that, if not challenged, undermined the official commitment to racial equality and led to racial conflict. This is very much along the lines of an understanding of hate speech protection that Waldron offers. The British offence, however, was further amended by the Race Relations Act 1976 and later incorporated in Section 5, Public Order Act 1986 and Sections 28 and 31, Crime and Disorder Act 1998/2001: '[A]ny writing, sign or other visible representation which is threatening, *abusive or insulting*, within the hearing or sight of a person likely to be caused harassment, *alarm or distress* thereby' (my italics).

Moreover, it is considered racially or religiously aggravated if it is 'motivated (wholly or partly) by hostility towards members of a racial or religious group based on their membership of that group'.[5] The offence having been earlier disconnected from any strict likelihood of the breach of the peace, it no longer depends on the speaker's/author's intentions or interpretation of his speech/text but on what a person may reasonably conclude is the likely effect on one or more racial groups, especially the group(s) referred to in the speech/text. If the group is likely to feel that as a group it is being rubbished – that old wounds are being reopened, enmities rekindled, images of domination invoked – then it can legitimately argue that the level of hate is being increased even if that is not the intention of the author and even if no specific act of violence is imminent. The Commission for Racial Equality, almost from its inception in the late 1970s, was of the view that such legislation is necessary to avoid the feelings of humiliation, indignity and insecurity that minority groups would experience if subject to the unchecked use of inflammatory language.

Waldron, then, conceives of hate and allied offences too narrowly, relative to contemporary U.K. law, with the result that the feelings of the victim are made secondary and contingent, whereas they are part of what hate is about. Hate speech is not only about feelings but also includes what Waldron refers to as 'indignity'; but feelings are part of what the law is and should rightly be trying to prevent. The feelings are not incidental, they are crucial. The feelings of the hated may not be sufficient to justify a law but the law would be unnecessary if there were no such feelings, and so the law needs to show understanding of such feelings and address them where it is thought that law, rather than censure, is the best remedy.

I share Waldron's view that the law should protect people, not beliefs. Michael Ignatieff (1989; 1990) gave a version of this argument at the time of *The Satanic Verses* affair when he said that he supported legislation against people shouting 'You filthy Muslim' to Muslims, but people should be free to say what they like about Islam in any manner of their choosing – presumably including in a 'threatening, abusive or insulting' manner. My view is that people can be hated because they are perceived to be members of a group, but sometimes a group can be hated through attacks upon its beliefs, and this combination is especially relevant to our times. I would like to spell out what I mean through three images concerning Muslims and Islam.

In *Norwood v. Director of Public Prosecutions (DPP)* 2003, the Divisional Court upheld the conviction against Norwood, arguing that displaying a British National Party poster bearing the words 'Islam out of Britain' and 'Protect the British People' accompanied by a picture of the 9/11 attack on the Twin Towers amounted to an offence of causing alarm or distress. The High Court argued that evidence of actual alarm or distress was not necessary if it was determined that 'any right thinking member of society' is likely to be caused harassment, alarm or distress (*Norwood v. Director of Public Prosecutions [DPP]* 2003). It concluded, therefore, that the poster was racially insulting and additionally, religiously aggravated. I expect this judgement sits well with Waldron's argument. It should be clear that this poster is not very religious. The word 'Islam' is there, as well as the general knowledge that the perpetrators of the attack on the Twin Towers in New York were religiously motivated, acted in the name of Islam and saw their action as on behalf of and for the sake of the liberation of Muslims from U.S. imperial and financial power. Yet religion is backgrounded.

Contrast this with a case I have already referred to – namely, the Danish cartoon that is often referred to 'the turban bomb', with its suggestion that the cartoon is of the Prophet Muhammed and he blows himself and other people up. As far as I know this image has not been banned anywhere, but some people argue that it should be (e.g., the U.S. political scientist, Erik Bleich [2012]). As I argued above, I believe the picture is offensive because it racialises Muslims: it is not really a comment on Muhammad, rather he is drawn to stand for Muslims in general (see the debate on the Danish cartoons in Modood et al. 2006; and Levey and Modood 2009). The racist cartoon, however, centred as it is on the Prophet, has a religious dimension missing in the Norwood poster. The religious dimension is not incidental to its being hatred: it hurts or humiliates by referring to something Islamic – expressing hatred by evoking and negatively characterising the religion of the hated. And it is has the effect it does because of what the Prophet means to so many Muslims. For many Muslims what is most hurtful is not the racializing as such but using the Prophet to attack Muslims. The racializing is offensive and does effect the civic standing and reputation of Muslims. But the pain of many Muslims is much greater if the image is meant to be that of the Prophet. The key point is that anti-Muslim images (or discourses) can be and typically are simultaneously racialising and trying to hurt through attacking Muslim feelings and beliefs – through attacking what we might call 'the Muslim spot'.

My third image is also connected with the Danish cartoons affair. It was not part of the *Jyllands-Posten* set but was included in the portfolio that some radical Danish Muslims took with them to Arab capitals to rouse anger against the Danish government (Modood et al. 2006, 25). In fact the cartoon has a French provenance and portrays a pig in an Arab male headdress with 'Mohamed' (in French and Arabic) written on its side, writing in a book on which is written 'Koran' (in French and Arabic). There is some anecdotal evidence to suggest that this is the picture that triggered the violent response in the Arab world and led Arab governments to initiate boycotts of Danish goods, thereby both making the controversy violent and making the Danish government respond more sympathetically to the feelings of Danish Muslim protestors. While the meaning of the Norwood poster and the turban-bomb cartoon was fairly clear, what is the meaning of this picture, which not only is not about terrorism but does not seem to be evidently about any specific event or action? It is perhaps not that unusual for a 'racial' group or a minority to be portrayed in bestial terms. Black people for example have often been depicted as apes. The idea of such a depiction is that black people are less intelligent, less civilised, indeed, less human and more ape-like. In the cartoon I am discussing the idea is not that there is something piggy-like about Muslims' appearance (certainly not their colour) or behaviour. So, why a pig? There can only be one answer. Because of the status of a pig in Islam – namely, that it is considered a pollutant and thus to be avoided and not to be consumed. Why is the pig signified to be the Prophet? Because the artist knows that this will hurt Muslims. While the choice of the image foregrounds religion more clearly than the Twin Towers poster or the turban-bomb, it has no message or purpose other than hate. While the other two images could be said to have something like a political message or argument – something to do with the undesirability of terrorism or (some) Muslims being a security threat that needed to be acted against – the third image seems to be devoid of such content and seems to be pure hate. It seems to have no purpose other than to hurt Muslims. And it succeeds. I have asked a number of Muslims which image do they think is more hurtful to Muslims, the turban-bomb or the pig-prophet, and each has instantly and without hesitation chosen the latter. When after a symposium on his book, I posed the same question to Jeremy Waldron, he conceded that the pig-prophet was probably more hurtful to more Muslims but noted that the turban-bomb came closer to his concept of 'hate speech'. I take this to be evidence of a flaw in a concept of hate speech, which cannot properly capture the more hurtful and less ambiguous case of a hate-motivated cartoon.

The flaw, I think, is based on two things that I have been trying to show. First, certain feelings in members of the target group are standardly relevant to hate speech and are part of what speech laws and other hate speech measures are trying to prevent. If the victim group feels attacked then we have a prima facie case of hate. Second, hate speech can be directed at or at least utilise the beliefs of the victim groups, so that the liberal claim that the law should protect people, not belief, is right; but sometimes when people are hatefully attacked or racialised through their beliefs or as people who hold certain beliefs, then the matter is not so simple. In protecting people in such cases, one will be stopping others from attacking them through their beliefs. In such cases if one ignores their beliefs then one cannot identify the hate and so a fortiori one cannot protect the hated.

NOTES

1. Holocaust denial is punishable in 16 European countries (Austria, Belgium, Czech Republic, France, Germany, Hungary, Liechtenstein, Lithuania, Luxembourg, Netherlands, Poland, Portugal, Romania, Russia, Slovakia and Switzerland) and Israel. 'Laws against Holocaust Denial', Wikipedia, https://en.wikipedia.org/wiki/Laws_against_Holocaust_denial.
2. A principle that has been made prominent recently in the #MeToo movement.
3. An anti-Semitic illustrated magazine produced by the Nazis, '[t]he semi-pornographic *Stürmer* was effectively the private vehicle of the Franconian Gauleiter Julius Streicher. . . . A sort of news of the sewers, it specialised in anything of a salacious nature. . . . Streicher claimed it was the only paper Hitler read from cover to cover' (Burleigh 2000, 210).
4. The offence of stirring up religious hatred, created by the Racial and Religious Hatred Act (2006), requires threatening words or behaviour (abusive or insulting words or behaviour would not be sufficient), and there must be an actual intention to stir up religious hatred; a likelihood of its being stirred up is not enough to constitute the offence. The Northern Irish legislation dates back to Prevention of Incitement to Hatred Act 1970.
5. Following '9/11' an Anti-terrorism, Crime and Security Act was quickly passed and extended the phrase 'racially aggravated' to 'racially or religiously aggravated'.

REFERENCES

Bleich, E. (2012). 'Free Speech or Hate Speech? The Danish Cartoon Controversy in the European Legal Context'. In Khory, K. R. (ed.), *Global Migration*, 113–128. Basingstoke, UK: Palgrave.
Burleigh, M. (2000). *The Third Reich: A New History*. Basingstoke, UK: Macmillan.
Ignatieff, M. (1989). 'Defenders of Rushdie Tied Up in Knots'. *Observer*, 2 April.
Ignatieff, M. (1990). 'Protect People, Not What They Believe'. *Observer*, 11 February.
Levey, G. B. and Modood, T. (2009). 'Liberal Democracy, Multicultural Citizenship, and the Danish Cartoon Affair'. In Levey, G. B. and Modood, T. (eds.), *Secularism, Religion and Multicultural Citizenship*. Cambridge: Cambridge University Press. http://www.cambridge.org/gb/knowledge/isbn/item1174366/?site_locale=en_GB.

Mill, J. S. (1956). (1859). *On Liberty and Other Essays*. Indianapolis: Bobbs-Merrill.
Modood, T. (1993). 'Muslims, Incitement to Hatred and the Law'. In Horton, J. (ed.) *Liberalism, Multiculturalism and Toleration*. Basingstoke, UK: Macmillan; also in Modood, T. (2005). *Multicultural Politics: Racism, Ethnicity, and Muslims in Britain*. Edinburgh: University of Edinburgh Press.
Modood, T., Hansen, R., Bleich, E., O'Leary, B. and Carens, J. (2006). 'The Danish Cartoon Affair: Free Speech, Racism, Islamism, and Integration'. *International Migration*, 44(5), 3–62.
Sachs, A. (2013). 'In Praise of "Fuzzy Law"'. In Griffith-Jones, R. (ed.), *Islam and English Law Migration*, 225–235. Cambridge: Cambridge University Press.
Waldron, J. (2012). *The Harm in Hate Speech*. Cambridge, MA: Harvard University Press.

Chapter Four

Islamophobia and the Struggle for Recognition

It was not very long ago that anglophone scholars of racism understood it in terms of biology, and specifically in terms of the black-white binary. At the same time, other scholars, especially in continental Europe, understood racism in terms of anti-Semitism, especially in the recent biologized forms that Europe has manifested. When it began to be clear that these two paradigms were failing to capture some contemporary experiences, such as anti-Asian cultural racism in Britain or anti-Arab cultural racism in France, some scholars began to move away from these paradigms (see chapter 1). Yet, following the assertive Muslim agency triggered off by *The Satanic Verses* affair and other Muslim controversies, as Muslims responded to such hostilities and articulated their misrecognition, they were constantly told, especially in Britain, that there is no such thing as anti-Muslim racism because Muslims are a religious group and not a race. Hence Muslims could legitimately ask for toleration and religious pluralism but not for inclusion in anti-racist egalitarian analyses and initiatives. While this view continues to be expressed even today, and some deny that there is a racism that could be labelled 'Islamophobia', it no longer has the hegemony it once was.

The origins of the term Islamophobia have been variously traced to an essay by two French Orientalists (Dinet and Ben Ibrahim 1918), to 'a neologism of the 1970s' (Rana 2007, 148), to an early 1990s American periodical (Sheridan 2006), and, indeed, in Britain, even to an article of mine (see Modood 1991, quoted in Moo 2006). What is less disputed is that the term received its public policy prominence with the Runneymede Trust's Commission on British Muslims and Islamophobia (CBMI 1997), *Islamophobia: A Challenge for Us All*. It is defined as 'an unfounded hostility towards Islam, and therefore fear or dislike of all or most Muslims' (CBMI 1997, 4).

While a number of anglophone authors, including myself, started using the concept of Islamophobia in the late 1980s and early 1990s, it was the Runnymede Trust's 1997 report which launched the career of the term as a concept of public discourse in Britain and much beyond it. While the report was groundbreaking and played a crucial role in getting people to think about anti-Muslim prejudice, I felt it did not sufficiently locate Islamophobia as a racism as, say, anti-Semitism.[1] I continued to write about Islamophobia as a form of cultural racism, which may be built on racism based on physical appearance (e.g., colour-racism) but was a form of racism in its own right – again, as anti-Semitism is. This also became the approach of UNESCO and I am pleased to see that it has been explicitly embraced by the new 2017 Runnymede Trust report, *Islamophobia: Still a Challenge for Us All* and by the All Party Group on British Muslims' 2018 Report, *Islamophobia Defined*.

In this chapter, I want to bring together five propositions:

1. Islamophobia is a form of othering or cultural racism (among other things).
2. A racialised group cannot be reduced to a race.
3. Critique of othering/Islamophobia presupposes non-othered knowledge of the other.
4. Critique of Islamophobia presupposes a normative framework which needs to be justified.
5. Islamophobia can be distinguished from reasonable criticism of Islam and Muslims.

1. ISLAMOPHOBIA IS A FORM OF OTHERING OR CULTURAL RACISM

Islamophobia is a form of cultural racism because while the perception and treatment of Muslims clearly has a religious *and* cultural dimension, it, equally clearly, bears a physical appearance or ancestral component. For while it is true that 'Muslim' is not a (putative) biological category in the way that 'black' or 'south Asian' (aka 'Paki'), or Chinese is, neither was 'Jew'. In that instance it took a long, non-linear history of racialisation to turn an ethno-religious group into a race. More precisely, the latter did not so much replace the former but superimposed itself because even though no one denied that Jews were a religious community, with a distinctive language(s), culture(s) and religion, Jews still came to be seen as a race, and with horrific consequences. Similarly, Bosnian Muslims were 'ethnically cleansed' because they came to be identified as a 'racial' group – that is to say, as having a perceived line of descent by people who actually were phenotypically, linguistically and culturally the same as themselves. The ethnic cleanser, unlike an Inquisitor, wasted no time in finding out what people believed, if and how often they went to a mosque and so on: their victims were *racially* identified as Muslims in terms of membership based on a perceived line of descent (as argued in chapter 1).

Race, then, as I understand it, is not just about biology or even 'colour', for while racialization has to pick on some features of a people related to physical appearance and ancestry (otherwise racism cannot be distinguished from other forms of groupism), physical appearance need only be a marker, and not necessarily denote a form of determinism. This is illustrated in the conceptualisation of cultural racism as a two-step process (see chapter 1). While biological racism is the antipathy, exclusion and unequal treatment of people on the basis of their physical appearance or other imputed physical differences – saliently, in Britain their non-'whiteness', cultural racism builds on biological racism a further discourse which evokes cultural differences from an alleged British, 'civilised' norm to vilify, marginalise or demand cultural assimilation from groups who may also suffer from biological racism. Post-war racism in Britain has been simultaneously culturalist and biological, and while the latter is essential to the racism in question, it is, in fact, the less explanatory aspect of a complex phenomenon. Biological interpretations have not governed what white British people, including racists, have thought or done – how they have stereotyped, treated and related to non-whites – and biological ideas have had increasingly less force both in the context of personal relationships and in the conceptualisation of groups. As white people's interactions with non-white individuals increased, they did not become necessarily less conscious of group differences but they were far more likely to ascribe group differences to upbringing, customs, forms of socialisation and self-identity than to biological heredity. The interesting question, as posed in chapter 1, arises as to whether it could be a one-step racism: could colour racism decline and fade away and yet cultural racism – seeing a descent-based people as culturally 'other' – remain and perhaps even grow?

Cultures and cultural practices are usually internally diverse, containing and omitting various 'authentic' elements, and adaptations and mixes. To racially group all Jews or Muslims together as one cultural 'race' or as one ethno-religious entity is to catch most, if not all, cultural minorities in that targeted group. For example, a non-religious Muslim might still be targeted as a cultural Muslim or Muslim by community; which of course means Muslim by background; which means birth and ancestry. Hence my point that Muslims, no less than Jews, are identified 'racially' and not simply in terms of religious beliefs or behaviour. Moreover, if we accept that racism does not necessarily involve attributing qualities which inhere in a deterministic, law-like way in all members of a group, then we do not have to rule out cultural racism as an example of racism. As such we should guard against the characterisation of racism as a form of 'inherentism' or 'biological determinism' which leaves little space to conceive the ways in which *cultural racism* draws upon physical appearance as one marker among others (chapter 1).

2. A RACIALISED GROUP CANNOT BE REDUCED TO A RACE

While understanding some contemporary treatment of Muslims and aspects of their societal status in terms of 'racialisation' clearly is an advance, we should beware that the conceptualisation of Muslims in the West is not reduced to racialisation or any other 'ing' theoretical frame such as Orientalism. By definition, 'othering' sees a minority in terms of how a dominant group negatively and stereotypically imagines that minority as something 'other', as inferior or threatening, and to be excluded. Indeed, the dominant group typically projects its own fears and anxieties onto the minority. Minorities, however, are never merely 'projections' of dominant groups but have their own subjectivity and agency through which they challenge how they are (mis)perceived and seek to not be defined by others but to supplant negative and exclusionary stereotypes with positive and prideful identities. Oppressive misrecognitions, thus, sociologically imply and politically demand recognition. Our analyses therefore should be framed in terms of a struggle for recognition (Modood 2007/2013).

The danger of reducing Muslims to racialised identities is particularly high at the moment because the Islamophobic 'othering' of Muslims is acute, and if anything, rising. This can be seen in how aggressive negative portrayals of Muslims is standard in so much right-wing nationalism, whether in President Trump's Muslim bans, Marine Le Pen's Front National, Alternative fur Deutschland in Germany or in various parties in central and Eastern Europe, including the Freedom Party in Austria, which has now entered government. Discourses about Muslims have recently been central to the internal debates in UKIP (United Kingdom Independence Party) about whether to become a working class party of welfarism or one defending 'our way of life' against the alleged threats of Islamisation. Western media routinely present Muslims as un-British, un-French, un-German and so on and with a degree of hostility that no other group in Europe suffers (except perhaps the Roma in parts of central Europe). It is therefore right that scholarly and public attention should be focussed on this racialisation of Muslims that is creating a deep, long-term division in our societies which may be very difficult to reverse. Yet, as all ethnic or religious groups, Muslims are not merely created by their oppressors but have their own sense of identity too. Multicultural inclusivity means recognising and respecting these identities.

Recognition of course does not mean thinking of Muslims as a group with uniform attributes or a single mindset, all having the same view on religion, personal morality, politics, the international world order and so on. In this respect Muslims are just like any other group – they cannot be understood in terms of a single essence. No one in the social sciences thinks that identities are based on cognitive or behavioural properties that are shared by all who may be members of a relevant group such as women, black people, gay and lesbians and so on. If group members do not share a common essence then they cannot be simply demarcated from non-group members because there will be many cases where individuals are not simply on one side of the boundary or the other. So, groups cannot have discrete, nor indeed, fixed boundaries as these boundaries may vary across time and place, across social contexts, and will be the subject of social construction and social change. This 'anti-essentialism' is rightly deployed in the study of Islamophobia and Muslims. It is a powerful way of handling ascriptive discourses, of showing that various popular or dominant ideas about Muslims, just as in the case of women, gays and so on, are not true as such but are aspects of socially constructed images that have been made to stick to those groups of people because the ascribers are more powerful than the ascribed. Anti-essentialism is an intellectually compelling idea and a powerful resource in the cause of equality.

It is also common, though, for authors to accuse each other of essentialism. This is because there are different versions of anti-essentialism. To pave the way for my third and fourth propositions I want to briefly rehearse two interpretations which I discussed in my book, *Multiculturalism* (Modood 2007/2013). The first is the sceptical interpretation that the critique kills the groups as real entities and they only live on as ascriptions or reactions to ascriptions or political make-believe. Rogers Brubaker, for example, argues that 'ethnicity, race and nation are not things in the world but perspectives on the world; ways of seeing, interpreting and representing the social world' (Brubaker 2005, 17, 79 and 219; cf. 11, 65). One way to interpret this claim might be to conclude that there is something false, fictitious and illegitimate about appeals to culture, ethnicity and so on in understanding oneself, let alone others or society. Stuart Hall's words sometimes lend themselves to this radical conclusion: 'If we feel we have a unified identity . . . it is only because we construct a comforting story or 'narrative of the self' about ourselves. . . . The fully unified, completed, secure and coherent identity is a fantasy (Hall 1992a, 277).

Sceptics do not necessarily want to kill off worthwhile political projects around, say, a black identity or feminism and so some allow for something called 'strategic essentialism' (Spivak 1990; cf. Kristeva 1981), where pretending that there is a black or national identity is permitted because of the politics, but analysts know that these identities are only 'necessary fictions' (Hall 1992b, 254). I think, however, groups are not just strategically but also conceptually necessary to both social science and to anti-racism or egalitarian politics and so I offered an alternative interpretation of anti-essentialism. I suggested that Wittgenstein's concept of family resemblance offers a way of recognising that just as it does not make sense to say that games or languages do not exist because they do not share a common, definitional essence, so the lack of group essences and discrete, bounded populations with unchanging characteristics was not a good reason to assert in an *a priori* way that groups did not exist. Rather, we had to have a more flexible, looser and variable notion of a group and of group membership that allowed for open-textured and overlapping boundaries and overlapping memberships. If it seems difficult to reconcile this with our *a priori* concept of group, let us call the entities, 'groupings'. The key point was that once we stopped demanding that groups measure up to our impossible definitions we would lose the temptation to conclude that groups suffered from an ontological deficiency, that they were merely 'perspectives upon the world', ontologically no superior to the products of othering. Another way of putting it is that just as the complete self-made individual of some liberal theories does not exist, it does not follow that individuals do not exist, that we have to give up 'individual' from social science vocabularies; so similarly with groups.

3. CRITIQUE OF OTHERING PRESUPPOSES NON-OTHERED KNOWLEDGE OF THE OTHER

The value of othering as a way of studying minorities is that it can be used to challenge blanket generalisations about a minority. Othering sometimes takes the form of attributing certain features to a group, which are alleged to be found in all members of the group. 'All blacks are muggers', 'All Muslims are fanatics' and so on. Theorists of racialization typically add that even when no explicit biological ideology is in play, these generalisations are being asserted by the racists in a quasi-naturalistic way – that is to say that like the laws of nature, they brook no exceptions (Modood 1997; and chapter 1 above).

The problem with this is that it is an implausible analysis of racialised thinking. Racists often do admit of counter-examples. 'My best friend is black and no mugger and if only all blacks could be like that but alas they are not'. Moreover, these racialised statements, which identify groups on the basis of their physical appearance, are not necessarily seeking biological or natural bases for the racialised generalisations. The racialiser is unlikely to believe that black mugging and Muslim fanaticism is genetic and much more likely to think that it is something to do with upbringing, family structure, community norms and so on – in short, what we might call 'culture' in the manner of cultural racism that I have already described. Yes, the concept of othering has the power to point out to racists that their generalisations do not hold of every member of the putative 'race', that their thinking suffers from quasi-naturalism or essentialises a group. However, all the racist has to do to escape the critique is to say that they are not talking about all members but some members or many members or most members, or more precisely, of more members than is true for other groups or society as a whole.

So, to make effective the anti-racist critique, one needs to engage with probabilistic statements and that means relating it to what is known or can be researched empirically about the population in question. More fundamentally, the question that my discussion here raises is, When a dominant group attributes certain characteristics to a subordinate group, how do we work out which of those characteristics that are meant to constitute the otherness of the minority is an imagined and malign projection onto the minority and which is a genuine feature of cultural difference? Another way of putting this is that the analysis of othering is not a self-sufficient intellectual perspective or disciplinary inquiry – for example, as Orientalism or anti-racism studies. It is dependent on an inquiry *into the group as such* and *not just its othering*. If we knew nothing about Muslims, we would have no way of knowing when they were being othered.

We must, however, allow for and investigate the interaction between the construction of the other and the group that is being othered; they are likely to influence each other in an ongoing dialectic. This is a significant point because it draws attention to the fact that the character of a minority is not 'pure'. Indeed, one could make this point stronger: the minority may be subtly altered by the coexistence with or the pressures of the dominant society, including the pervasive presence of certain kinds of othering, such that the minority in question even while unaware of these alterations, may have its subjectivity and its groupness reshaped.

The interaction, then, between othering and Muslim or any other ethno-religious groupness has two aspects:

1. Products of othering or a stereotype must have some basis in fact if it is to be at all effective, otherwise it will not be a *prima facie* plausible stereotype of group X;
2. Othering shapes the group subjectivity to some extent: it can have sociological weight, creating situations which one has to constantly negotiate and some of it will be internalised, becoming part of one's biography, even a focus of group identity assertions, solidarities and

mobilisations, which by an energetic engagement with othering can subtly influence group identity.

This emphasis on interaction is of course not original to me. Indeed, one could say that it is standard in most social scientific explanations (e.g., Weberian, Barthian, 'racialisation' etc.). My point is that these standard explanations are often accompanied by bad philosophy or meta-theory – namely, the claim that there is no such thing as ethnicity or groups. Granted that most researchers are in favour of a model of interaction, my doubt is whether their theories or meta-theories are consistent with the practice of an interactionist perspective. My argument is that interaction between X and Y presupposes the conceptualisation of X and Y separately because interaction presupposes a relation between two items and the approaches I have just mentioned, like the othering approach, allows for no independent way of identifying the ethnic or minority group dimension. Against me, it may be said that the reason such independent identification is not in the model is that minority ethnicity does not ever exist in a 'pure' form; it is always already shaped by othering or other externalities. I think this 'never' is too big a generalisation. It should also be noted that even if it were true, the objection does not hold. I am not so much concerned to create analytical space for 'pure' ethnicity (and so by implication for ethno-religious groups such as Muslim minorities) as to ensure that there is some space for ethnicity – that it is not reduced to other social, economic or political factors. Works of art have an economic value, a market price, for instance; in that sense they do not exist in a 'pure' space called 'art'. But that does not mean that we cannot identify a work of art independently of its economic value. So, similarly, I am saying that the fact that ethnicity and othering, or ethnicity and labour markets interact, creating impurities, does not mean that we cannot identify ethno-religious factors independently of othering or labour markets and so on. If it indeed were the case that a group could not be identified independent of its othering, then how could there be a critique of othering which was not at the same time a critique of the group itself?

So, while an emphasis on interaction is standard, my account of the interaction is meant to underline that a group may be – usually is – more than just an other – for example, that the othered Muslim does not exhaust the possibilities of being a Muslim because it interacts with non-othered Muslimness. Moreover, while such alterations and cross-influences will be happening all the time, we must not assume that they are all bad, all exercises of malign power. Which means that we need a normative framework or at least a reference point to judge the benign from the malign exercises of power or social effects. This takes me to my next proposition.

4. CRITIQUE OF OTHERING PRESUPPOSES A NORMATIVE FRAMEWORK WHICH NEEDS TO BE JUSTIFIED

Othering nearly always identifies the group in question in terms of negative features. These can take many different forms. Some of the most common are to do with having lower intelligence, less capable of disciplined, responsible behaviour, and with a propensity for criminal or violent behaviour. In relation to Muslims, these are some of the negative traits: an obsession with religion over other aspects of life; moral conservatism, especially in relation to sexuality; patriarchy; tendency to act on religion or politics in extreme and violent ways.

Analysis of othering is clearly an important tool when it can be deployed to show the operation of these negative perceptions in the media, in news reports, in political discourses and the way public concerns are raised and expressed (e.g., in relation to 'radicalisation' or women's dress), in television programme content, in the activities of the security services and so on. There is, however, a limitation to such analyses of othering or racialisation – namely, that sometimes there is a lack of agreement between those doing the othering and those being othered about whether certain features are necessarily negative. Most people will agree that to describe a group as less intelligent is to have said something negative about it. But is this the case with religious strictness and moral conservatism? Here it is possible that the dominant group may take one view of the matter – namely, that such attitudes and behaviours are negative and backward, but the minority – that is to say, substantial numbers within the minority, may refuse that such characterisations are negative. In recent years, we have seen this most starkly in Europe, in the dominant society's view that wearing the hijab – the headscarf – or the burqa by Muslim women is a sign of oppression (Göle and Billaud 2012). Despite the dominant society delivering this judgement through the popular and intellectual media, the numbers of women engaged in such practices has increased and the increase has been accompanied by the women in question saying that they are choosing to don such clothes out of choice and not as compliance with the demands of Muslim men. To accept, to qualify or to resist such Muslim women's perspective is not just a matter of empirical inquiry but invokes a normative framework. In recent years, aspects of feminism and liberalism (e.g., 'Western feminism' and 'muscular liberalism') have been cynically and insincerely used to critique and undermine various Muslim practices and claims for accommodation, including issues of women's dress (Göle and Billaud 2012). However, not all such appeals have to be cynical or insincere. They can be principled and reasonable. Without trying to spell out in any detail the sincere and insincere versions of these highly complex and varied '-isms', I am simply making the point that some such normative framework is necessary. An analysis of othering – for example, of how the fact of living within a hegemonic secularism subtly influences Muslim subjectivity – is incomplete without an appeal to a normative framework, for without that, we cannot know to what extent the influence is a result of an exercise of self-interested power, of domination, and to what extent it is an aspect of benign social change on the part of Muslims themselves, who on a reasoned basis come to adapt their practices and modify their sense of what it means to be a Muslim. To stick with my earlier example, to argue that the hijab, or niqab or burqa are or are not a form of oppressive othering is not just a matter of empirical inquiry or discourse analysis but implicitly or explicitly appeal to how to distinguish between what is negative and what is positive in the characterisation of Muslims. If it is implicit, it needs to be made explicit. Either way the normative presuppositions need to be questioned – that is to say, they cannot be taken for granted but stand in need of argument and justification. Without such justification not only may an analysis of othering be incomplete or distorted, but also it may itself be an exercise in othering – namely, in seeing groups in question as prejudicially othered – as, for example, religious conservatives – when that is exactly how the group may wish to think of itself and to be respected for being as such. This will of course be an empirical matter: hence my earlier point that critique of othering presupposes empirical knowledge of the other. But, depending on the facts, it may also be a refusal to accept the group on its own terms. That may not be wrong as such.

My point is that to accept or not to accept will require a normative argument and so a perspective such as Orientalism or anti-Islamophobia are incomplete without normative argument. So, the kind of normative disavowal that one finds in the influential work of say, Talal Asad (2003; 2009) is misplaced. He has been a powerful force for getting us to rethink secularism but his conceptual framework does not explicitly help us to determine whether secularism is a good thing, or which version of secularism is better than another. Or, to put it another way. Everyone will agree that Islamophobia must be distinguished from reasonable criticism of Muslims and aspects of Islam, but not only is this a difficult distinction to make, but it also begs the question what are reasonable criticisms that Muslims and non-Muslims may make or discuss in relation to some Muslim views about, say, gender or education or secularism. Not only must the study of Islamophobia not squeeze out the possibility of such discussion, but by showing us where it becomes Islamophobic, it should help to guide us on to the terrain of reasonable dialogue. Merely identifying the unreasonable and the populist is not enough; our frames of analysis should lead us to the reasonable: to what criticisms may be made of Muslims and/or Islam and what criticisms that Muslims want to make of contemporary Western societies, too, are worthy of hearing. The minority in question must be able to negotiate, modify, accept criticism and change in its own way; a dialogue must be distinguished from a one-sided imposition.

Islamophobia should therefore be studied within a normative framework and not just one that exposes the normative presuppositions of others while evading the challenge of justifying one's own normative presuppositions. My own framework, multiculturalism or a struggle for recognition and institutional accommodation, prioritises groups fighting negative outsider perceptions by giving normative and political weight to insider identifications in all their plurality.

5. ISLAMOPHOBIA CAN BE DISTINGUISHED FROM REASONABLE CRITICISM OF ISLAM AND MUSLIMS

Yet, how, it may be asked, are we to distinguish reasonable criticism from Islamophobia? Take the proposition:

'Muslim views about women are oppressive and not appropriate for modern Britain'.

Is this Islamophobia or reasonable criticism?

My suggestion is that we should apply the following five tests:

1. Does it *stereotype* Muslims by assuming they all think the same?

    - Does the criticism(s) seem to suggest that all or most Muslims have this blameworthy characteristic and that this feature defines Muslims – indeed, drowns out any worthy characteristics and ignores contextual factors?

2. Is it *about* Muslims rather than a dialogue *with* Muslims, which they would wish to join in?

    - Does the mode of criticism consist of generalising about a group in a way that tends to exclude them rather than treat them as conversational partners who share common concerns?

3. Is mutual learning possible?

    - For example, one may criticise some Muslims for sexual conservatism or puritanism but is one willing to listen to those Muslims who think that contemporary societies like Britain are over-sexualised and encourage sexually predatory and undignified behaviour?[2]

4. Is the language civil and contextually appropriate?

- Is the behaviour or practice being criticised in an offensive way and seems to make Muslims the target rather than stick to the issue? (A good analogy here is how reasonable, contextual criticism of Zionism can become a diatribe against Jewish people as such.)

5. Is it insincere criticism for ulterior motives?

- Does the person making the criticism really care about the issue or is using it to attack Muslims (in the way that some have come to use feminism and homosexuality)?

If the answer to questions 1, 2 and 5 is a 'Yes' or a 'No' to 3 and 4, then we may be dealing with Islamophobia or anti-Muslim racism. Any discourse can of course have a mixed character but the more the answers align with the pattern mentioned, the more that discourse needs to be examined closely as to its potentially Islamophobic character. This of course is not a litmus test with as single decisive colour result. I hope, however, it indicates what we should be looking for and why and so can be the basis for a discussion about whether a particular discourse is Islamophobic or reasonable criticism.

NOTES

1. I am grateful for Robin Richardson reminding me that the Runnymede Trust did emphasise that its work on Islamophobia was a direct follow-up to its work on antisemitism, and within months of the report's publication its reconstituted commission on Islamophobia under Richard Stone was lobbying for amendments regarding Islamophobia to draft legislation on racist hate crimes and on racial discrimination. Moreover, in 2001 it made much use of the concept of anti-Muslim racism as a result of the advocacy, including by Stuart Hall and myself.

2. In the post–Harvey Weinstein and #MeToo climate it might be easier to understand the point here than it might have been a few years ago.

REFERENCES

Asad, T. (2003). *Formations of the Secular: Christianity, Islam, Modernity*. Stanford, CA: Stanford University Press.
Asad, T. (2009). *Genealogies of Religion: Discipline and Reasons of Power in Christianity and Islam*. Baltimore, MD: Johns Hopkins University Press.
Brubaker, R. (2005). *Ethnicity without Groups*. Cambridge, MA: Harvard University Press.
Commission on British Muslims and Islamophobia (CBMI). (1997). *Islamophobia: A Challenge for Us All*. London: Runnymede Trust.

Dinet, E. and Ben Ibrahim, Sliman. (1918). *The Life of Mohammed, The Prophet of Allah*. Paris: Paris Book Club.
Göle, N. and Billaud, J. (2011). 'Islamic Difference and the Return of Feminist Universalism'. In Triandafyllidou, A., Modood, T. and Meer, N. (eds.), *European Multiculturalisms: Cultural, Religious and Ethnic Challenges*, 116–141. Edinburgh: Edinburgh University Press.
Goodwin, M. J., Cutts, D. and Janta-Lipinski, L. (2014). 'Economic Losers, Protestors, Islamophobes or Xenophobes? Predicting Public Support for a Counter-Jihad Movement.' *Political Studies*, Early View online, 19 August 2014, doi:10.1111/1467-9248.12159.
Hall, S. (1992a). 'The Question of Cultural Identity'. In Hall, S. and McGrew, T. (eds.), *Modernity and Its Futures*, 274–316. Cambridge: Polity.
Hall, S. (1992b). 'New Ethnicities'. In Donald, J. and Rattansi, A. (eds.), *'Race', Culture and Difference*, 252–259. London: Sage.
Kristeva, J. (1981). 'Woman Can Never Be Defined', trans. M. A. August. In Marks, E. and de Courtivron, I. (eds.), *New French Feminisms*, 137–141. New York: Schocken.
Modood, T. (1997). '"Difference", Cultural Racism and Anti-Racism'. In Werbner, P. and Modood, T. (eds.), *Debating Cultural Hybridity: Multicultural Identities and the Politics of Anti-Racism*, 154–172. London: Zed Books.
Modood, T. (2005). *Multicultural Politics: Racism, Ethnicity, and Muslims in Britain*. Minneapolis: University of Minnesota Press and Edinburgh: University of Edinburgh Press.
Modood, T. (2007/2013). *Multiculturalism: A Civic Idea* (2nd ed., 2013). Cambridge: Polity Press.
Moo, Mr. (2006). 'Notes on Islamophobia'. Yahya Birt, December 31: https://yahya-birt1.wordpress.com/2006/12/31/notes-on-islamophobia/ [accessed 02/10/2018].
Rana, J. (2007). 'The Story of Islamophobia'. *Souls*, *9*(2), 148–161.
Sheridan, L. P. (2006). 'Islamophobia Pre– and Post–September 11th, 2001'. *Journal of Interpersonal Violence*, *21*(3), 317–336.
Spivak, G. C. (1990). *The Post-Colonial Critic: Interviews, Strategies, Dialogues*. New York: Routledge.

Chapter Five

Pointing to a Multicultural Future

Rethinking Race, Ethnicity, Religion and Britishness

INTRODUCTION

The purpose of this chapter is to consider the place of religion in relation to post-immigration diversity in Britain and British national identity as reflected in three national commission reports stretching over thirty years.[1] This means that the immigration I am concerned with is mainly the primary, non-white immigration from the Commonwealth of the 1950s–1970s, and the secondary or family reunification migration it led to in the 1970s–1980s, and of course the children and grandchildren of these settlements. The 1990s saw the beginning of a new wave of migration into the United Kingdom, mainly of refugees and asylum seekers from non-Commonwealth countries such as Bosnia, Somalia, Afghanistan, Kurds from Turkey and so on. From 2004 onwards large inflows of migration from the newly acceded E.U. states of Eastern Europe has also taken place. The latter two waves have certainly deepened the diversity, perhaps creating a 'superdiversity' (Vertovec 2007) but the diversity I am interested in relates to not being white and/or not Christian and the core of that as a settled British population relates to the two earlier waves of migration indicated above.

The three Commission reports, stretching over 30 years, are *Education for All: Report of the Committee of Inquiry into the Education of Children from Ethnic Minority Groups* (Swann 1985), *The Future of Multi-Ethnic Britain* (CMEB 2000) as its successor, and the Commission on Religion and Belief in British Public Life – namely, *Living With Diversity: Community, Diversity and the Common Good* (CORAB 2015) as one which picks up on an aspect of its work.[2] I chose them as they each presented a positive view of

British post-immigration ethnic and/or religious diversity. My interest is not on the specific policy recommendations of these Commissions but on the general approach or understanding of the context exhibited in relation to the place of religion in a changing Britain.

While Swann was a government inquiry, CMEB and CORAB were run by an independent organisation (a campaigning organisation, The Runnymede Trust, and an educational institution, The Woolf Institute, Cambridge respectively). All three public inquiries were led by members of the House of Lords[3]: the scientist and former vice chancellor, Michael Swann, the political philosopher and former vice chancellor, Bhikhu Parekh and the former senior judge, Elisabeth Butler-Sloss.[4] Each commission focused on the changing nature of minorities and their place in British society and how they were changing British society and how British society should be further changed to accommodate the minorities. Having said this, it should, however, be noted that Swann was specifically confined to the disadvantages and the (lack of) progress of primarily black and Asian children in English schools,[5] and CORAB did not have a direct or exclusive minority-oriented focus.

Of course the choice of the commissions involves some selection. I could have chosen otherwise. For example, in relation to issues of ethnic diversity and equality, are not the Scarman Report (1982, the first major inquiry commissioned by the government) (Scarman 1981) and the Macpherson Report (Macpherson 1999) of much greater policy significance? Yet, the above three Commissions were of a reflective kind and not directly a response to an immediate crisis, while Lord Justice Scarman's brief was 'to inquire urgently into the serious disorder in Brixton on 10–12 April 1981'. The same point, namely, an urgent focus on a specific set of events also applies to Macpherson's report, another judge-led inquiry commissioned by the British government, this time on the murder of Stephen Lawrence and its investigation by the London Metropolitan Police.

Our Shared Future (2007), the report of the government appointed Commission on Integration and Cohesion (COIE), did indeed have a much wider brief (COIE 2007). It however is not on a par with the three I have chosen. It is a rare national report on race and ethnicity that is published without considerable debate and engagement, even controversy, but that was the case with this report, which was perceived as having been overly guided by the government minister which appointed it (Hunter and Boswell 2015). The Scarman Report was thought by many in the government, probably including the Prime Minister, Mrs. Thatcher, and its right-wing supporters as excusing criminality and riotous behaviour by focusing on 'racial disadvantage' and blaming the riots on the police through its use of the concept of 'institutional discrimination'.[6] The CMEB/Parekh Report was vociferously attacked for being anti-British, anti-patriotic and for portraying Britain as inherently racist (Richardson 2000; McLaughlin and Neal 2007; Modood 2014). CORAB got attacked for suggesting that Christianity was no longer adhered to by the majority of Britons and so Britain was no longer 'a Christian country'.[7] Moreover, the COIE is much less referred to either generally or in terms of an intellectual impact than the reports mentioned above.[8]

In having chosen the commissions I have there is a further advantage of an even spread across time, as each is separated by the next nearest in time to it by exactly 15 years, making a symmetrical triad.[9]

THE SWANN REPORT (1985)

Swann marks the early wave of British multiculturalism and includes some of the key ideas of racial disadvantage, discrimination and racism but explicitly tends towards a conceptualisation of the non-white minorities in terms of ethnic pluralism rather than racial dualism, despite the latter being the dominant perspective of the 1980s (Modood 1988; 1994). It reframes the concern with race into a conception of an ethnically plural Britain, which has been one of the dominant themes of British multiculturalism. Swann is, then, not just a pioneering expression of multiculturalism in general but in particular of this central feature of multiculturalism. Its deliberations on education were cast within a vision of accommodating cultural diversity within a framework of shared values and a pluralised and expanded sense of what it is to be British. While this vision was expressed in a brief introductory chapter, it has become the idea of multiculturalism in Britain or of multicultural Britishness. It argued,

> [W]e are not looking for the assimilation of the minority communities within an unchanged dominant way of life, we are perhaps looking for the 'assimilation' of all groups within a redefined concept of what it means to live in British society today. We are not seeking to fit ethnic minorities into a mould which was originally cast for a society, relatively homogeneous in language, religion and culture, nor to break this mould completely and replace it with one which is in all senses 'foreign' to our established way of life. We are instead looking to recast the mould into a form which retains the fundamental principles of the original but within a broader pluralist conspectus – diversity within unity.
> (Swann 1985, 8)

It is a sentiment which perhaps harks back to Roy Jenkins's unelaborated but famous definition of integration in 1966 during his period as Home Secretary: 'not as a flattening process of assimilation but as equal opportunity, accompanied by cultural diversity, in an atmosphere of mutual tolerance' (Lester 2004). It can be seen more clearly in an essay by Bhikhu Parekh, when in the early 1970s he had argued that 'pluralistic integration within the framework of a generally accepted conception of the good life should be the ideal governing Britain's relations with her immigrant population' (Parekh 1974, 230). While Parekh saw racism in its various manifestations as a significant obstacle to this integration, the aspect in which he was ahead of his time is his going on to say,

> In the ultimate analysis pluralistic integration entails that the Briton's perception of his identity should be revised. . . . Only when it is acknowledged as a matter of course that a Briton is not by definition white but could be black, brown or yellow, that he might speak Swahili, Mandarin or Hindustani as his first and English as his second language, and that his 'kith and kin' might be found in Bombay, Barbados and Ibadan as well as in Salisbury and Wellington, can the non-white minority feel as authentically British as the native, and can be so accepted by the latter. (Parekh 1974, 230–231)

Hence, it is perhaps not very surprising that a commission in which Parekh had been a member in its early period expressed a very similar idea. We shall see this theme was to become central to CMEB 15 years later, under Parekh's chairmanship.

Swann included a discussion of religion (devoting to it one of its 16 chapters[10]), but in a not altogether positive way. For example, despite considerable submissions to the contrary and open dissent from six ethnic minority members (Swann 1985, 515), it explicitly argued against extending state funding from Christian and Jewish (voluntary-aided) state-funded faith schools to Islam, Hinduism and Sikhism.

THE COMMISSION ON MULTI-ETHNIC BRITAIN (2000)

According to its chair, Bhikhu Parekh, 'The Commission's remit was to analyse the current state of multi-ethnic Britain and to propose ways of countering racial discrimination and disadvantage and making Britain a confident and vibrant multicultural society at ease with its rich diversity' (CMEB/Parekh Report 2000, iix). The report was summarised as this: 'Building and sustaining a community of citizens and communities will involve:

- rethinking the national story and national identity;
- understanding that all identities are in a process of transition;
- developing a balance between cohesion, equality and difference;
- addressing and eliminating all forms of racism;
- reducing material inequalities;
- building a pluralistic human rights culture' (CMEB/Parekh Report 2000, xii).

The Commission on Multi-Ethnic Britain had a number of unusual features for a national commission. It was created by an independent race-relations think tank, The Runnymede Trust, and while it was launched by the Home Secretary, Jack Straw, it was wholly independent of the government and included no members of the judiciary or representatives of the government. Of its 25 members (not all of whom served the full term) more than a third were non-white and nearly a third were academics.[11] Besides its distinguished chair, it included prominent public intellectuals and race equality professionals such as the late Professor Stuart Hall; the late Professor (later, Sir) Bob Hepple, who went on to become the Master of Clare College, Cambridge; the journalist and writer, Yasmin Alibhai-Brown; the Chair of the Greater London Assembly (and later of the Commission for Racial Equality, and after that, the Equality and Human Rights Commission), and broadcaster, Trevor Phillips; Sir (later Lord) Herman Ouseley, the Chair of the Commission for Racial Equality at the time; and Andrew Marr, Chief Political Editor at BBC Television at the time. As a result of this mix, some of the report had an academic character, such as Part I, 'A Vision for Britain', which began with 'Rethinking the National Story', included several sociological chapters and a political theory chapter entitled 'Cohesion, Equality and Difference'. These chapters attempted, as the report did as a whole, to be accessible to the general as well as the public policy reader, and wore their academic apparel lightly; nevertheless they offered an intellectual framework for thinking about minority-majority relations in Britain and, so, for the more concrete analyses of the rest of the report. It may be the case however that the Commission did not have the personnel composition and balance that people are accustomed to and that it had a more theoretical and academic orientation than journalists and politicians would expect. A consequence of this was the wilful misunderstanding of the report so that it could be accused by the right-wing press of being an overly minority perspective and unpatriotic and dismissed as an expression of an out-of-touch liberal intelligentsia (Parekh 2000b; Modood 2014).

The CMEB broke new ground in a number of ways in relation to discourses and understanding of post-immigration minorities and how they should be accommodated in Britain. One of these was the inclusion of religious community identification and needs within the conceptualisation of the 'multi-ethnic'; though this marks a continuity with Swann, there is much development beyond it too. For example, in the 1990s it was clear that historic colour-racism was now also accompanied by new contemporary forms of 'cultural-racism' (Modood 1997; and chapter 1 above) and forms of anti-Muslim hostility or Islamophobia (Runnymede Trust 1998) and both of these were features of CMEB's conceptualisation of 'racism' (CMEB 2000, chapter 5; see also chapter 1 above). In this respect, the CMEB marks a transitional point, where, subsequent to the Rushdie Affair of 1988–1989, the effects of Muslim and other minority religious political assertiveness is seen to be changing the nature of multi-ethnicity, yet without becoming prominent in the report (the report being prior to the emergence of domestic terrorism in the name of Islam and the international 'war on terror'). 'The future of multi-ethnic Britain' that the report desires consists of promotion of (in the key phrases of the report) 'race equality and cultural diversity' and 're-thinking the national story' in relation to 'black and Asian people'. The CMEB clearly – and up to that point unprecedently for a public report on race and ethnicity – acknowledges that religion has been neglected within the frame of racial equality. Its (self-) critical remarks include these:

> Most race equality organisations are broadly secular, not religious. It is perhaps for this reason that they frequently appear insensitive to forms of racism that target aspects of religious identity. For example, they are widely perceived by British Muslims to be insensitive to distinctive Muslim concerns, by Jewish people to be uninterested in antisemitism, and by Irish people to be indifferent to sectarianism and anti-Catholicism. People with Indian cultural backgrounds and ties to Sikhism or Hinduism similarly feel that anti-racist organisations have little or nothing to say about their religious affiliations and identities. (CMEB/Parekh Report 2000, 237)

Yet the CMEB does not fully integrate the dimension of religion into its vision of equality and diversity. In the building of a 'community of communities', it is primarily ethno-racial and ethno-cultural individuals and communities that are in mind, rather than the ethno-religious. 'Religion and belief' is largely confined to one chapter and five recommendations in a report of 20 chapters and 135 recommendations. None of those five are cross-referenced or mentioned in the recommendations under the headings of Education, Employment, Policing and so on. They are supplementary rather than integrated. The five specific recommendations are:

1. In all faith communities there should be closer connections between anti-racism and work to improve interfaith relations.
2. Legislation should be introduced prohibiting direct and indirect discrimination on grounds of religion or belief.
3. A statement of general principles should be drawn up on reasonable accommodation in relation to religious and cultural diversity in the workplace and in schools, and case-study examples of good practice should be provided.
4. A study should be made of police responses to hate crimes containing a religious component.
5. A commission on the role of religion in the public life of a multifaith society should be set up to make recommendations on legal and constitutional matters.

In relation to national identity, the Commission had an overarching message, which was then qualified in certain ways. The overarching message was that the rethinking and political action to make Britain more inclusive, which had begun, had to continue and had to focus on British identity itself if the country was to continue to progress towards an inclusive, non-racial, multicultural Britishness. The argument was that the inequalities and exclusions associated with racism, including material inequalities and disadvantages, could not be countered by merely materialist strategies but required 'rethinking the national story', our collective identity, in a plural way. A qualifying message was that there could be no complacency about the importance of anti-racism, which needed more political will, if Britishness was to be made inclusive in fact and not just rhetoric. Another qualifying message was that old-fashioned, monistic, assimilationist, majoritarian nationalism was past its usefulness and had to be replaced by a new, plural kind of national identity (sometimes referred to as 'post-national' in the report). It is argued that this was happening as ethnic minorities were assuming a British identity and qualifying it with a minority ethnicity, and thus not just passively accepting Britishness but making it their own – which, together with affirmation of their minority identity, is a mark of a new confidence (CMEB/Parekh Report 2000, para 3.29). The report notes however that there is one major and so far insuperable barrier to this development. Britishness, as much as Englishness, has systematic, largely unspoken, racial connotations. Whiteness nowhere features as an explicit condition of being British, but it is widely understood that Englishness, and therefore by extension, Britishness is racially coded (CMEB/Parekh Report 2000, para 3.30). Unfortunately, these few qualifying remarks about racism and how the perception that Britishness means whiteness unleashed a hysterical reaction in the right-wing press which influenced more generally the reception of the report. The overall message was ignored and the Commission was condemned by many for being unpatriotic and even denying that Britain was or could be a unified country (Richardson 2000).

The right-wing media was so successfully able to caricature the Commission thus, that even the Home Secretary of the time, Jack Straw, who had given the Commission its blessings at its launch, was now reported as saying, under the headline '"Proud to be British" Straw Raps Race Report':

> [H]e was appalled when he read part of the document suggesting that the term British had racial connotations and was no longer appropriate in a multicultural society. He ripped up a speech prepared for the launch of the document yesterday and instead delivered a strong attack on the part which he believed lacked intellectual rigour.
>
> 'Unlike the Runnymede Trust I firmly believe that there is a future for Britain and a future for Britishness', Mr Straw declared. 'I am proud to be British and of what I believe to be the best of British values'. (Ford 2000)

That these remarks were based on a false reading of the report is evidenced by an article that had been published in the *Guardian* on the previous day by Parekh as the chair of the CMEB, in which he argued,

> The report recognises that, while cherishing cultural diversity, Britain must remain a cohesive society with a shared national culture. That culture is based on shared values, including such procedural values as tolerance, mutual respect, dialogue and peaceful resolution of differences, as well as such basic ethical norms as respect for human dignity, equal worth of all and equal life chances.
>
> The common national culture includes shared symbols and a shared view of national identity, and these are best evolved through a democratic dialogue between our various communities. The report sees Britain both as a national community with a clear sense of collective purpose and direction and also made up of different communities interacting with each other within a shared moral framework.[12]

Despite such statements, the reception of the CMEB report was a catastrophe for the multiculturalist cause which it espoused. However, what is interesting is that on this specific point of controversy, if we look only a few years forward we see that what was deemed by the press and politicians to be unacceptable has come to be thought of as necessary, even relatively uncontroversial, among senior politicians.[13] Soon afterwards, Cabinet members started expressing exactly the view that had been lambasted – or to put it more precisely, which was not sufficiently identified because of the lambasting. In 2001, John Denham argued that Britishness, as it existed, was insufficient, hence 'positive action must be taken to *build* a shared vision and identity' (Denham 2001, 19, italics added), and in 2007, Jack Straw himself said that it was necessary 'to *develop* an *inclusive* British story which reflects the past, takes a hard look at where we are now and *creates* a potent vision . . . to make sense of our shared future' (Straw 2007, italics added). Note the active verbs: 'build', 'develop', 'creates' – exactly the view that had motivated the CMEB. Nor were such views confined to New Labour. A project within a Leverhulme Trust Bristol-UCL Programme that took interviews from New Labour Cabinet Ministers and Conservative Shadow Cabinet Ministers during 2007–2008 did not find a uniformity of views on this matter but found considerable cross-party agreement that British national identity had to be opened up to include minorities and that politicians and the state had a role to play in this process.[14] It is a point of view that is not always lived up to but the opening ceremony of the Olympic Games in London in July 2012 was an excellent expression of a multicultural Britishness that New Labour tried to articulate without ever quite succeeding and its positive reception in the British media – including the same papers that had lambasted the CMEB – shows what is possible (Katwala 2012). An Australian political theorist opined that the Britain displayed at the Olympics meant that '[m]any countries are [now] looking to Britain as an example of a dynamic multicultural society united by a generous patriotism' (Soutphommasane 2012). Yasmin Alibhai-Brown, the left-wing journalist and a member of the CMEB, who returned her MBE as a protest against the Iraq War, wrote,

> [T]hese two weeks have been a watershed of true significance. There has been a visceral reaction among black and Asian Britons to what we have seen. For some, it has been perhaps the first time they have really felt a part of this country. For others, the promise of tolerance and integration has come true. (Alibhai-Brown 2012)[15]

So, while the initial media reception misunderstood the Parekh Report on British national identity – partly it should be added because of some ambivalent phrases in the report (Modood 2014) – it underlined, even in the period before 9/11 and the 'multiculturalism has failed' discourse, how multiculturalists and race egalitarians approached the question of British national identity was one of the most charged topics that they could address. On the other hand, the report brings out how central the question of national identity, especially the idea of remaking or multiculturalizing national identity, is to multiculturalism.

COMMISSION ON RELIGION AND BELIEF IN BRITISH PUBLIC LIFE (2015)[16]

In one way or another nearly all the CMEB recommendations in relation to religion (quoted in full above) have been pursued, with the last having now been realized in the existence of the Commission on Religion and Belief in British Public Life (CORAB).[17] Convened by the Woolf Institute, Cambridge, and chaired by Baroness Butler-Sloss. The terms of reference of this commission which ran from 2013 to 2015 were to

a. consider the place and role of religion and belief in contemporary Britain, and the significance of emerging trends and identities;
b. examine how ideas of Britishness and national identity may be inclusive of a range of religions and beliefs, and may in turn influence people's self-understanding;
c. explore how shared understandings of the common good may contribute to greater levels of mutual trust and collective action, and to a more harmonious society;

d. make recommendations for public life and policy. (https://www.corab.org.uk/background-information/, last accessed 26/02/2019)

CORAB is dual aspected. On the one hand, it is not concerned directly with the position of minorities but the place of religion in public life generally. On the other hand, it has – I believe – come into being because of the fact of expanding and deepening religious diversity which is the principal cause of the new public salience of religion in Britain. Specifically, while the terms of reference do not refer to race, ethnicity or even minorities, some of the mechanics of the origins of CORAB display a direct continuity with the Parekh Report. This was achieved through Mohammed A. Aziz, who had been a commissioner in the Commission for Racial Equality and a consultant senior advisor on race and religion to ministers and cabinet secretaries. Subsequent to leaving Government in 2011, he formulated the idea of the Commission and proposed it to the Woolf Institute, Cambridge, whose director, and later also the vice-chair of CORAB, Dr Ed Kessler, warmly received the suggestion that the Woolf Institute host CORAB and Mohammed went on to raise the necessary funds, seek out suitable commissioners and head the Secretariat. The link with the CMEB was directly present through the chair of the CMEB, Lord Parekh becoming not just one of four patrons of the CORAB but the only one who participated actively in its deliberations throughout the life of the Commission; Robin Richardson had drafted the CMEB report and was given the same responsibility in relation to the CORAB report; and I, having been an active part of the CMEB, was appointed a commissioner and member of the Steering Group of CORAB. More substantively, it should be clear that religion has primarily re-entered public life, political debates, mobilisation and policy making because of – in Britain as in the rest of Western Europe and beyond – the presence, assertiveness and terrorism of Muslims – even though the terrorism in question is supported, let alone engaged in, by a very small proportion of Muslims. While the reference '9/11' is the most relevant here in terms of public consciousness, its specificity in relation to terrorism means that it is less relevant in relation to the themes of this chapter – namely, those of equality, diversity and national identity. In relation to the latter, the pivotal events could be said to be those captured by the terms, 'the Rushdie Affair' and 'l'affaire du foulard', both occurring independently yet simultaneously in 1988–1989 (see chapters 2 and 9).

A good way to approach the CORAB is through the argument that Britain consists of a Christian legacy, new faiths and the non-religious (Weller 2005, 117). More specifically, that current debates about multiculturalism in relation to religion can I think be seen in terms of three contending forces, which may be expressed in the contentions that Britain's public institutions and national identity should reflect that it is

1. still predominantly a Christian country,
2. now a multifaith country,
3. mainly a secular country.

In relation to the last we need to distinguish between several meanings of 'secular'. First, 'secular' may refer to philosophical and ethical perspectives; non-religion not as an absence but a presence; not as the opposite of religion but in terms of its status as a conversational partner of religion or even as one of many 'spiritual families' that constitute belief in modernity (Taylor 2009, xii). One of the most fundamental conceptual features of the CORAB report is the importance it gives to such secular worldviews, what it refers, using the vocabulary of French legislation in relation to freedom of belief, as 'les convictions' (CORAB 2015, 14). While the CORAB report notes that such ideas developed during the Enlightenment and are at the core of ideas of equality and liberal democracy, and at times have been in an antagonistic relationship to religion, actually '[t]he two sets of values have also at times intermingled and converged, and have deeply influenced each other' (CORAB 2015, para 2.11). Yet the decision to place religion and secular convictions on the same plane was arrived at not by a philosophical or a theological discussion but by a resolution at the first meetings to fully embrace the legal non-discrimination concept of 'religion or belief' and to express this in the title and terms of reference. The U.K. Equality Act, 2010, itself following the European Convention on Human Rights in relation to freedom of religion, expresses the legal offence of religious discrimination by reference to 'religion or belief' – that is to say, religion and secular beliefs are treated on a par. CORAB took the legal category 'religion or belief', up to now only applied in relation to non-discrimination and freedom of religion and applied it to all aspects of the report – for example, to education and the media and not just the law. Humanistic beliefs, principles and conscience are treated on a par with religion, one might say, though CORAB does not use this vocabulary – an almost quasi-religion or alternative to religion.[18] It did not mean that everyone who in a census or attitude survey said they had no religion had a humanist philosophy or participated in humanist meetings or rituals, but that was no disability as this simply paralleled the situation of those who identified as Christian or Muslim. It is possible however that CORAB did not fully appreciate the implications of generalising the equality between religious and non-religious beliefs. An example of this egalitarian inclusion, what I have elsewhere called 'equalising upwards' (see chapter 6), is the recommendation that '[f]unding for chaplaincies in hospitals, prisons and higher education should be protected, but with equitable representation for those from non-Christian religious traditions and for those from humanist traditions' (CORAB 2015, para 3.27).

A second meaning of 'secular' can be understood in relation to political secularism. As a concept, 'secular' might be said to have several alternative contemporary understandings:

a. Religion is a private matter and the state may act to confine it thus.
b. Some British people often think that political secularism has the first of these meanings until they reflect on Anglican participation in the national rituals such as the remembrance of the dead in wars or a royal wedding or state-funded faith schools, which most British people have long supported and in the main continue to support. This then tends to lead British people to express this alternative view:
c. Religion has something to contribute to the public good but should do so within liberal democratic constitutionalist norms and framework. What most British people approve of in political secularism is not an absolute separation between religion and the state but that religion as a feature of the public life of the country works within – indeed freely and actively supports – the liberal democratic constitutional character of the British state and politics (see chapter 8).

It is perhaps not surprising that the first of these is not represented in a commission investigating the place of religion in public life, but it should also be noted that judging by the composition of CORAB, secularist philosophies are not significantly represented.[19] Indeed, there is only one commissioner whose affiliation is indicated by reference to a secularist philosophy – namely, Andrew Copson, the chief executive of the British Humanist Association (now called Humanists UK). Given, though, the fact of multiple identities, it would be appropriate to recognise that at least some members with a religious community, if not a religious organisation identification, are likely to overlap with secularist as well as religious perspectives.[20] So even though the CORAB could be said to limit the scope of the secular vis-a-vis public religion relative to the concept of privatisation and radical secularism (as per (a) above), of more significance is how, by embracing an extensive concept of 'religion and belief', the Commission adjusted the balance within the triangular relationship in favour of secularism – not because of any animus to Christianity but in an inclusive spirit in the context of socio-demographic trends, to which I now turn.

According to the census, the number of people who identified themselves as Christian in England and Wales declined from 71 per cent to 58 per cent between 2001 and 2011 (p. 86).[21] While the censuses are of the full population, they are a relatively superficial measure of identification. In this regard it is best to supplement the census with the British Social Attitudes (BSA) survey findings, which is what CORAB does. The BSA, which includes Scotland, only has a sample of 3,000 but it is a systematic, purposive attitudes survey and has been measuring religious attitudes annually since 1984. It shows that Christian identification has gone down from 68 per cent in 1984 to 43 per cent in 2014 (p. 16). This shows a steeper drop than the census and so we might suppose that Christian identification has different meanings in different contexts and/or the true picture is somewhere between the two figures. The BSA offers data by Christian denominations and shows that during 1984–2014 the numbers identifying as Anglicans declined from 40 per cent to 17 per cent; and Catholics, from 10 per cent to 8 per cent. Other Christians remain steady at about 18 per cent of the British population. While there has been a decline in older Protestant churches such as Methodists and Baptists, there has been a growth in newer churches such as Pentecostals and Seventh Day Adventists, many of which are black majority led. The findings are, then, that Christians are barely or not at all a majority in England and Wales, and Anglicans are no longer a majority among Christians; though of course 'Anglican' is an elastic identity, as indeed is 'Christian' itself, as comparing the census and the BSA shows. Yet Anglicanism does seem to have suffered a particularly steep decline.

On the other hand, those who say they have no religion have gone up from 15 per cent to 25 per cent between the 2001 census and 2011 census (p. 86); and in the BSA from just under a third in 1984 to almost half in 2014 (p. 16) – the two datasets being more discrepant on this point than on Christians. The key point is that both datasets show the same trend and strongly suggest that it is not short-term.

As for religions other than Christianity, the BSA sample sizes are too small to be useful but the 2001 and 2011 censuses show that significant number of non-Christian religious minorities are to be found in all the major cities and towns and doubled in size over that decade, comprising nearly 10 per cent of England and Wales in 2011.[22] Being younger and having larger families, they will continue to grow. For example, while Muslims are about 5 per cent of the population, they are 8 per cent of those under 25. While Hindus, Sikhs, Jews and Muslims are about 12 per cent of 9–13-year-olds (three quarters being Muslims), they are double this proportion in London.

THE NEW RELIGIOUS DIVERSITY AND SIGNIFICANCE OF RELIGION

While for some right-wing newspaper commentators and editorials the big story of the Commission allegedly was one of Christian marginalisation and secular majoritarianism, my interest here is in the third point of the triangular relationship – namely, the minority faiths.[23]

While each new generation across the last century seems to be less Christian than its predecessor and so few young people today deem Christianity to be important to their life, this generational indifference is not found among post-immigrant groups. Indeed, among ethnic minorities expressions of commitment among the young can be exceptionally high: more than a third of Indians, and two-thirds of Pakistani and Bangladeshi 16–34-year-olds said in a national survey at the end of the twentieth century that religion was very important to how they led their lives, compared to a fifth of Caribbeans and 5 per cent of whites (Modood et al. 1997, 301). In the case of young Muslims, the importance of religion has been rising and overtaking their elders (GfK, NOP 2006; see also Mirza, Senthilkumaran and Ja'far 2007).

Beyond that, religion has a social importance for minorities. In South Asia, from where the majority of British Hindus, Sikhs and Muslims originate, religious identity has a salience much higher than in Britain, so it is not surprising that during the last few decades, religion – rather than, say, colour or linguistic heritage or national origins – has risen in the individual and community self-identities of these minorities together with their sense of Britishness.[24] Of course groups are partly defined by not what they say they are, but what others – usually a dominant group – says they are. British society, as it happens, has been very receptive to ethnic minority self-definitions and redefinitions. For example, when West Indians said they were African Caribbean; when non-whites said they were not 'coloured' but blacks; when Asians said they were not 'black'; ethnic minority collective self-projections quickly altered public discourses and prevailed over older nomenclature. So, similarly, when ethnic minority groups such as Pakistanis started dismissing 'Pakistani' and 'Asian' for themselves in preference for 'Muslim', the wider British public, especially the media and public organisations, fell in line. Since the 1980s–1990s onwards there seems to have been a constant rise in religious community identification among South Asians to supplement or demote race/ethnic identifications, and in a very few years they moved from 'black' to 'Asian' to Indian/Pakistani/Bangladeshi to Sikh/Muslim/Hindu.[25] This was then picked up and reinforced by the media, politicians and public discourse in relation to those groups or more widely. For example, the spring-summer 2001 riots in northern cities like Bradford and Oldham were originally reported by the national press as 'Asian' (though South Asians themselves were referring to the rioters as Muslim), but as the months passed that term shifted to 'Muslim', a transition completed by the events of '9/11' in September and discussions thereof.[26] This does not necessarily refer to religiosity but is a recent manifestation of the well-known phenomenon that Jews generally and Catholics in locations like Northern Ireland can call themselves and can be called by others as Jews and Catholics respectively even if they are not religious and may even be anti-religious. We are here clearly talking about group identity or ethno-religious community membership, not belief.[27]

Of course, as indicated above, what minorities are usually unable to do is to control the meaning of terms. This again is most evident in the recent period, especially after 9/11 and in Britain especially after the July 2005 bombings in London ('7/7'), in relation to Muslims and Muslim identity or public discourses of Islam. Muslims may have demanded recognition qua Muslims and may have propelled that identity into public discourse and popular consciousness but very few Muslims have sought to have 'Muslim' mean fanatic, fundamentalist, misogynist, separatist or terrorist, but anyone familiar with current affairs and how it is reported in the British media knows that this is what 'Muslim' currently connotes to many in Britain (Morey and Yaqin 2011). This stereotyping of Muslims, part of the phenomenon generally called Islamophobia, can be understood as 'racialisation'. Not simply because that is what happens to groups designated as 'races', nor even because non-whiteness is closely associated with being a Muslim,[28] but because it is to treat Muslims as if they were a single, racial or quasi-racial group as argued in the introduction and chapters 1 and 4. The dissonance that one might experience here in accepting the idea that a religious group is a 'race' can be eased by considering the general case of how the Jews have been racialized (indeed in continental Europe, the Jews are the quintessential race), as well as the specific case of Catholics in Northern Ireland or Muslims in the 'ethnic cleansing' rampages in the former Yugoslavia (chapter 1; Modood 2005; Meer and Modood 2009).[29] In this regard it is worth noting that the CMEB recommendation that discrimination on the grounds of religion or belief should be outlawed (quoted above) began to be fulfilled from 2003 onwards; initially only in relation to employment, following an E.U. directive, later also covering services and was fully implemented in the Equality Act, 2010. In that Act, religion or belief as a ground for discrimination was put on a par with all other grounds for discrimination in the strongest anti-discrimination legislation in Europe. The CORAB was very mindful of the phenomenon of religious discrimination and of how it was often based on a racialized view of religion and intertwined with racial discrimination, suggesting that the term 'ethno-religious' – a legal concept in Australia – captures an aspect of this (CORAB 2015, para 2.5). It did make a recommendation for the law to better understand this intertwining (CORAB 2015, paras 8.18–8.21) but in the light of the 2010 Equality Act there was much less scope for it to make recommendations in relation to discrimination than might be the case in many other countries.

It should be clear from the above that the meaning of religion can vary between religions, in particular between Christians and non-Christians, or between being a member of a majority or a minority religion: for Jews,

Muslims, Hindus and Sikhs religion is not just about belief but also sometimes primarily about community and cultural heritage or identity, including resisting stereotypes about one's own community or discriminatory treatment. Yet another way in which religion is not just about belief is that it often requires a public performance or a behaviour – for example, in relation to codes of dress or food – and so is much more publicly visible and sometimes requires institutional adaptation in order to be accommodated.[30] While this is barely a feature of modern, especially Protestant, Christianity, where 'inner belief' can be considered sufficient and it is often deemed unnecessary, perhaps even inappropriate, to display markers – even a cross – of one's faith, this is quite exceptional in global, and now British, terms. Most religions require the observance of rules of piety and Britain is experiencing such practice-based religions re-entering the public space – Muslim dress being the most visible and contentious – after quite a long period in which such religion has been eroded away or transformed into private belief. Institutions and areas of public life which have given up the need to accommodate Christians are now having to adjust to the needs of minority faiths, and sometimes stimulating Christian reappraisal of its retreat from public piety (e.g., the display of a wearer's cross, as in the Eweida case at the European Court of Human Rights). Dietary requirements, space for worship and gender relations, besides dress, are also prominent as elements of religious praxis that institutions such as schools, hospitals and prisons, and even workplaces are being asked to adjust to. Adaptations of codes of dress or uniforms; or provision of vegan, vegetarian, kosher and halal meals; places for worship and time off to use them are the kinds of requests being made upon state institutions, universities, employers even when no parallel provision exists for Christians and is not being requested for by Christians. This praxis-based accommodation is a significant multiculturalist challenge because it is not simply a matter of granting minorities provisions already enjoyed by the majority but a matter of respecting minority religions in ways that Christians may be indifferent, too, in relation to their own faith. And of course it is not just a symbolic recognition that is being requested as substantive provisions or institutional changes are sometimes necessary.

Partly because minority faiths are behaving in ways that most British people are not familiar with and, at least prima facie, sometimes may not approve of, and whose accommodation require some funding or others to change their behaviour – especially at the level of institutional rules and the shared public space – there is some majoritarian unease. Even when minority claims of public recognition and respect can be met with modest policy and resource commitments, some people, perhaps a growing number at the moment, are uncomfortable with and believe there is an over-religionising – specifically over-Islamising – of the public sphere. Some of this cultural anxiety and antipathy to (too much public) religion merges with aspects of cultural hostility which may be forms of racism and Islamophobia. It may even be that in the standard case it overlaps with anti-minorities, especially anti-Muslim, sentiment. Nevertheless, the cultural anxiety I am referring to is not the same as cultural racism and needs to be identified and engaged with in its own right. CORAB partly acknowledged this in one of its grandest recommendations:

> A national conversation should be launched across the UK by leaders of faith communities and ethical traditions to create a shared understanding of the fundamental values underlying public life. It would take place at all levels and in all regions. The outcome might well be – in the tradition of Magna Carta and other such declarations of rights over the centuries – a statement of the principles and values which foster the common good, and should underpin and guide public life. (CORAB 2015, para 3.30)

Of course the anxieties – no less than the hostility and collective blaming – is considerably heightened when we are not simply talking about cultural difference, public religion or institutional accommodation but of terrorism and security. Some Muslims are involved in international terror campaigns and so, for this reason, too, are a source of public anxiety and suspicion, and the object of state surveillance, which in turn leads Muslims to be alienated and distrustful. Here CORAB recommends a governmental approach that works with and not against the Muslim community and with academic research (CORAB 2015, paras 8.22–8.25).

The net result of what I have been describing in this section is that minority religions have come to have a significant – even if contested – public presence (Modood 2005; Dinham and Lowndes 2009). Public campaigns for inclusion and equality, conflicts over faith schools, women's dress and gender more generally, not to mention all the issues to do with the 'war on terrorism' and Islamist radicalism, has made religion much more politically prominent and in public affairs generally. Public dialogue, representation and leadership is often sought and realised by those who define themselves in terms of religious community organisations.

While these are some of the reasons in which religion has become more publicly salient and in which the meaning of religion has changed, so some appropriate public learning is required. It has also to be acknowledged that most people are losing touch with their own religious heritage, let alone understanding the new significance and variety of religion. At this juncture of simultaneous growth in ignorance about religions and their rising public, political, international and geo-strategic importance, CORAB makes one of its central recommendations – namely, that there is a substantial need for raising the level of religion and belief literacy among the public, journalists, policymakers and various kinds of professionals (CORAB 2015, 9). The suggestion that the low level of public understanding of religion is a problem and needs to be remedied is not new to CORAB (Dinham and Lowndes 2009). What I believe is distinctive about CORAB is the understanding of religion that it is said greater literacy is needed of – namely, religion which is extended to include secular belief systems; yet which is not reducible to belief for it includes pious practice, as for example, in relation to dress; which is a community or ethnic identity, especially for minorities; and which is intertwined with racism such as in the case of anti-Semitism or Islamophobic racializing of Muslims as an 'other'. This complex, multidimensional understanding of religion, the lack of literacy in which is a serious problem of public life, is a thread across the report and is fundamental in the report's discussions of law, the media, education, social action and dialogue. Just as CORAB's generalisation of the legal concept of 'religion or belief' has extended religion in one direction, so the ideas of praxis, racialisation and identity in the concept of 'ethno-religious' has extended it in another. Moreover, religious literacy is required across society and especially by opinion formers and policy shapers and implementers because religion in this extended sense has something to contribute to the common good. But this is not a crudely pro-religion view. Nor just because secular beliefs and ethno-religious communities are folded into it. CORAB recognises religion as 'a public good', but also as 'a public bad', and so for both these reasons governments have a legitimate and indeed a necessary interest in it (CORAB 2015, para 2.6; see chapter 8 below).[31]

If religion and belief literacy is primarily intended to remedy the educational deficits of adults, it is of course important to bring up the next generation with fewer of these deficits. In some of its educational recommendations, if taken together, the 'living with difference' (as the report was entitled) approach of CORAB comes out nicely. For example, it recommended the ending of the current statutory requirement of Christian worship in state schools – in reality more observed in the breach – and suggested the development of inclusive but non-compulsory school assemblies. This angered some Christian observers but it should not do so when it is taken together with the recommendation that 'publicly funded schools to be open for the provision of religion- or belief-specific teaching and worship on the school premises outside of the timetable for those who request it and wish to participate' (CORAB 2015, para 4.28). Moreover, it pressed for all schools to teach a subject dealing with religious and non-religious worldviews, which should have the same status as other humanities subjects (CORAB 2015, 83). It also affirmed state-funded faith schools, and while recognising that they can increase segregation and have a divisive effect that needs to be actively addressed by seeking a mix of pupils, it resisted the imposition of any form of quota of non-faith pupils upon some schools, as it was urged to do. In this way I think it avoided being either pro or anti any one part of the Christian-secular-diversity triangle that I said characterises contemporary Britain but sought to achieve a reasonable balance and interdependence between the points of the triangle. With a judicious mix of the compulsory and the encouraging it avoided a one-size-fits-all solution and ensured space for difference while making sure that there be a commonality, a learning together of all religions and belief systems in mixed-class settings (Modood 2015). This set of recommendations is clearly trying to strike a balance between inclusivity and allowing some space for difference; recognising that the latter can be divisive but at least in state schools it would be in a context of everyone taught together to acknowledge and respect difference as well as commonality. Beyond that, all faith traditions may continue to run independent schools and state-supported schools but encouraged to include diversity too. I therefore do not accept, as one-sided commentators have claimed, that in its educational recommendations CORAB erased the idea of Britain as a Christian nation. It was not a turning back on the meaning that Christianity has in the formation of an evolving national identity but a weaving together of all three points of the national triangle in a way that is inclusive of each and balances the cultivation of a common life with the nourishing of difference for whom that is important.

CONCLUSION

It has been remarked that the CMEB had some ambivalence about Britishness. While it was wrongly perceived as suggesting that to be British or wanting to be British was racist, and it firmly put 'rethinking the national story' on the race-equality agenda, it was ambivalent about whether Britain was a nation and could achieve the goal of an anti-racist, multicultural belonging, or whether it was a 'post-nation' (Modood 2014; Uberoi 2015). CORAB's terms of reference, cited above, indicate a much more affirmative view of Britain by making 'ideas of Britishness and national identity' central to its purpose. A dialogical or multilogical Britishness seems to suggest itself as a goal, the solution to the problems discussed by CORAB. It is interesting that at a time when academic attention has been on globalisation, the postnational and transnationalism, British diversity has been centred on the national. In many ways, this is a more general European trend in which, when politicians talk of 'integration', they are not usually talking about European integration but about how to make the new minorities truly French, more German and so on. In so far as Britain differs, it is that the national identity is seen as something which itself should be understood in terms of diversity. This is present in the central message of the two latter Commissions discussed, though perhaps it is carried further in CORAB. While the CMEB top bullet-pointed summary item above emphasised 'rethinking the national story and national identity', CORAB explicitly foregrounded in its terms of reference the dialogical relationship between commonality and difference: '[E]xamine how ideas of Britishness and national identity may be inclusive of a range of religions and beliefs, and may in turn influence people's self-understanding'. The difference is perhaps slight, but while CMEB emphasised – too one-sidedly in the view of its critics – the interrogation of dominant ideas of British national identity, CORAB emphasised the dialogical remaking of inherited national identities which are both productive of minority inclusion and reflective of difference. Perhaps CORAB was merely trying to state the message of the CMEB more clearly and avoid the brickbats received by the latter. If CMEB was interpreted as over-emphasising the deconstructive attitude towards received notions of national identity, CORAB was careful to project a more constructive tone.

The 30 years trajectory from Swann via CMEB to CORAB shows not just an effort to think through equality and diversity in a period in which the minorities were growing in size and becoming more significant in relation to British national identity. It is also a thinking about the nature of multiculturalism in a context which changes in ways that few if any would have predicted. This is certainly to do with how religion and not just colour becomes the marker of minority status and of otherness. Most importantly it is about the interaction of race/ethnicity and religion in the 'ethno-religious', which when combined with an extensive concept of 'religion and belief', displays in the British context a reworked concept of religion. At the same time there is – despite some ambivalence in the CMEB – a line of affirmation in an evolving, plural, British national identity – one which cannot be taken for granted but must be revisited as a work in progress. This happens at a time, 1985–2015, when many have been anticipating a fading away of the national in favour of the global and the local (Antonsich and Matejskova 2015).

NOTES

1. I would like to thank Geoff Levey, Bhikhu Parekh, Robin Richardson and Varun Uberoi for their comments on this chapter and for numerous conversations over the years on some of the topics of the chapter. They, of course, are not responsible for the views expressed here.

2. Declaration of interest: I was the academic adviser and contributor to CMEB and an active part of the collective authorship of its report (aka as 'The Parekh Report') and a commissioner and steering group member of CORAB. Of course all views expressed in this chapter are my own and no doubt others from CMEB and CORAB might express some points differently or perhaps disagree in some instances.

3. Though Parekh became a peer only towards the end of the life of his commission.

4. Actually, Bhikhu Parekh served on all three Commissions – as a member (resigned November 1981 to become Vice Chancellor, University of Baroda), as a chair, and as an active patron, respectively.

5. The final report also contained chapters on the educational needs of Italian, Cypriot, Traveller and Ukrainian children as well.

6. '1981 Brixton Riot', Wikipedia: https://en.wikipedia.org/wiki/1981_Brixton_riot, accessed on 26/02/2019.

7. John Bingham and Steven Swinford, 'Britain Is No Longer a Christian Country and Should Stop Acting As If It Is, Says Judge', *Daily Telegraph*, 7 December 2015: http://www.telegraph.co.uk/education/12036287/Britain-is-no-longer-a-Christian-country-and-should-stop-acting-as-if-it-is-says-judge.html, accessed 10/01/2016. See also Gledhill 2015.

8. Ralph Grillo also identifies these three reports as having a special significance and shares the point just made about COIE (Grillo 2018). In relation to the latter, see Hunter and Boswell 2015. For more general discussions about how research on immigrant integration is used in public or policy discourses across Europe, see Scholten et al. 2015; and Husband 2015.

9. It is worth mentioning a certain continuity of personnel: Bhikhu Parekh was present in all three (see note 3), I was present in the two most recent (as per note 2) and Robin Richardson was the editor of those two commission reports.

10. Chapter 8: Religion and the Role of the School: Religious Education and the 'Separate' Schools Debate.

11. CMEB/Parekh Report 2000, 366–371. I include the report's editor, Robin Richardson, who is not listed on pp. 366–371 but who played a key role in the shaping and drafting of the report.

12. Parekh 2000a. For a fully philosophically elaborated statement, see Parekh 2000c. For a discussion of Parekh's understanding of multiculturalism and national identity and how it is present in the CMEB report, see Uberoi 2015 and 2018.

13. Actually most of the report's more than 140 recommendations were acted upon quite soon after its publication (Runnymede 2004).

14. Uberoi and Modood 2013, 23–41. For more on the Leverhulme programme see 'Leverhulme', University of Bristol: Centre for the Study of Ethnicity and Citizenship: http://www.bristol.ac.uk/ethnicity/projects/leverhulme/, last accessed on 26/02/2019; and Modood and Salt 2011.

15. As CORAB (2015) later commented, 'What the ceremony portrayed, essentially, was a multinational nation that was rooted in but not stuck in the past, proud yet also self-deprecating, open to the future, open to the wider world, and concerned with the common good' (para 3.8).

16. CORAB is also discussed in Malik 2018 and set in the context of a useful discussion of the role of Commissions in Britain and of non-legal regulation.

17. 'Reasonable accommodation' in the workplace has not been made into law as in the United States and Canada. CORAB argued that where a legal offence of indirect discrimination is in place, the additional right to reasonable accommodation achieves no material benefit (para 8.10).

18. Interestingly, in 2013 two Britons, Sanderson Jones and Pippa Evans, started The Sunday Assembly because they 'wanted to do something that was like church but totally secular and inclusive of all – no matter what they believed'. There are now more than 70 Sunday Assembly chapters in eight different countries where people sing songs, hear inspiring talks, and create community together. 'Our Story', Sunday Assembly, https://www.sundayassembly.com/story. Meanwhile, there is a 'growing network of over 300 celebrants trained and accredited by the British Humanist Association' to conduct non-religious weddings, funerals, and other ceremonies. 'Humanist Ceremonies', Humanism, https://humanism.org.uk/ceremonies/. In July 2016, following the likes of Harvard, Westminster University created the first British paid post of secular advisor to join its multifaith chaplaincy. Aftab Ali, 'Westminster University Achieves First by Hiring First-Ever Secular Advisor for Staff and Students', *Independent*, 14 July 2016, http://www.independent.co.uk/student/news/westminster-university-secular-humanist-adviser-isabel-millar-jane-flint-a7137196.html.

19. Members of the Commission can be seen at http://www.corab.org.uk/background-information.

20. A point not taken into account by some who commented on the membership of the Commission (e.g., David Voas, 'Can the Commission Justify Religious Privilege?', *Public Spirit*, 14 October, 2014: http://www.publicspirit.org.uk/can-the-commission-justify-religious-privilege/; and Morris 2016). The steering group commissioner, Lord Harries, the former Bishop of Oxford and the most senior Christian on the commission, was happy to describe

himself as a Christian humanist. The final report was clear that while religious and humanistic values may sometimes conflict, and certainly have done so historically, they may also overlap and indeed be intertwined and influence each other (CORAB 2015, paras 2.11–2.12). I would suggest that most, perhaps all, the commissioners shared this orientation of a religion-friendly humanism and a humanist-friendly religionism.

21. A religion question was only introduced in 2001 and so there is no earlier census data on this. There is less diversity in Scotland, though a higher proportion are non-religious. In Northern Ireland, Christian affiliation is much higher (with Protestants and Catholics about 40 per cent each).

22. Or 7.4 per cent of the U.K. population, consisting of Muslims (4.8 per cent), Hindus (1.5 per cent), Sikhs (0.8 per cent), Jews (0.5 per cent) and others (0.8 per cent), and double these proportions in many urban areas.

23. The reception of the report included some anger in certain Christian quarters, where it was interpreted it as anti-Christian and a secularist hollowing out of a Christian legacy and especially objected to as a proposal to end compulsory Christian worship in all schools. This point of view was reflected in the *Daily Telegraph*, *Daily Express*, *Daily Mail*, and *Spectator*. More favourable were the centrist/mainstream responses, as in *The Times*, *Independent*, and *Guardian* and the BBC, who saw it as appropriately recognising the growth of non-religion as well as diversity.

24. It is doubtful for example that most South Asians in Britain ever thought of themselves in terms of colour identities such as black or brown as much as some observers thought to be the case (Modood 1994; Modood et al. 1997, 291–297). In relation to Britishness, see Modood et al. 1997, 338–331; and Heath and Demireva 2014.

25. The first South Asian group to assert a religious rather than an ethnic (Indian) identity were the Sikhs in relation to workplace bans on the wearing of turbans in the 1960s–1980s and in favour of a Sikh separatist movement in the Punjab or in response to how it was combatted by the Indian state in the 1980s (see chapter 2).

26. I rely here on memory as interestingly this does not seem to have been documented in detail, though see Lewis, 2002, 210–211.

27. Modood 1998. Of course historically speaking, it could be said that the Jews were a people who had a religion (which came to be called Judaism) rather than a religious group; the same could perhaps be said of Hindus and Hinduism. The term 'ethno-religious' here is therefore most apt.

28. That is, 'Muslim' is racially coded (as colour, cultural alienness, and not being European) in the way the CMEB argued 'Britishness' is racially coded as whiteness.

29. Note, however, the point made in footnote 33. Jews may be considered as a racialized religious group or as a religionised ethnic group or 'nation'.

30. Modood 2015; cf. DeHanas 2016. It is often said of some religions – for example, Judaism and Hinduism – that they do not really have (many) core beliefs but are lived out and transmitted through core practices. This relates to the limitations of the word 'religion' as alluded to in footnote 32.

31. As applied to the role of universities, see Modood and Calhoun 2015.

REFERENCES

Alibhai-Brown, Y. (2012). 'Mo's Joyful Embrace of Britishness and Why These Games Mark a Truly Historic Watershed'. *The Independent*, 12 August. https://www.dailymail.co.uk/debate/article-2187469/Mo-Farahs-joyful-embrace-Britishness-Games-mark-truly-historic-watershed.html, last accessed 26/02/2019.

Antonsich, Marco and Matejskova, Tatiana. (2015). 'Immigration Societies and the Question of "the National"'. *Ethnicities*, *15*(4), 495–508.

Commission on Integration and Cohesion (COIE). (2007). 'Our Shared Future'. http://image.guardian.co.uk/sys-files/Education/documents/2007/06/14/oursharedfuture.pdf, last accessed on 26/02/2019.

Commission on Multi-Ethnic Britain (CMEB/Parekh Report). (2000). *The Future of Multi-Ethnic Britain*. London: Profile Books.
Commission on Religion and Belief in British Public Life (CORAB). (2015). *Living with Difference: Community, Diversity and the Common Good*. Cambridge: The Woolf Institute.
DeHanas, Daniel Nilsson. (2016). *London Youth, Religion, and Politics: Engagement and Activism from Brixton to Brick Lane*. Oxford: Oxford University Press.
Denham, John. (2001). *Building Cohesive Communities: A Report of the Ministerial Group on Public Order and Community Cohesion*. London: Home Office.
Dinham, Adam and Lowndes, Vivien. (2009). 'Faith in the Public Realm'. *Faith in the Public Realm: Controversies, Policies and Practices*, 1–20. Bristol, UK: Policy Press.
Dinham, Adam and Francis, Matthew (eds.). (2015). *Religious Literacy in Policy and Practice*. Bristol, UK: Policy Press.
Ford, Richard. (2000). '"Proud to be British" Straw Raps Race Report'. *The Times*, 12 October.
GfK, N. O. P. Social Research. (2006). 'Attitudes to Living in Britain – A Survey of Muslim Opinion'.
Gledhill, Ruth. (2015). 'New Butler-Sloss Religion Report "Destroys Our Nation's Defence against Evil"'. *Christian Today*, 7 December.
Grillo, R. (2018). 'Religion, Belief and Diversity in Transition: The Commission on Religion and Belief in British Public Life'. In Alidadi, K. and Foblets, M. C. (eds.), *Public Commissions on Cultural and Religious Diversity: National Narratives, Multiple Identities and Minorities*. Abingdon, UK: Routledge.
Heath, Anthony and Demireva, Neli. (2014). 'Has Multiculturalism Failed in Britain?'. *Ethnic and Racial Studies*, 37(1), 161–180.
Hunter, Alistair and Boswell, Christine. (2015). 'Research-Policy Dialogues in the United Kingdom'. In Scholten, P., Entzinger, H., Penninx, R. and Verbeek, S. (eds.), *Integrating Immigrants in Europe: Research-Policy Dialogues*, 233–251. Cham, Switzerland: Springer Open.
Husband, Charles, ed. (2015). *Research and Policy in Ethnic Relations: Compromised Dynamics in a Neoliberal Era*. Bristol, UK: Policy Press.
Katwala, S. (2012). 'An Island Story: Boyle's Olympic Opening Was Irresistibly British', *OpenDemocracy*, 31 July: http://www.opendemocracy.net/ourkingdom/sunder-katwala/island-story-boyles-olympic-opening-was-irresistibly-british.
Lester, A. (2004). 'The Home Office Again'. In Adonis, A. and Thomas, K. (eds.), *Roy Jenkins: A Retrospective*. New York: Oxford University Press.
Lewis, Phillip. (2002). *Islamic Britain, Religion, Politics and Identity among British Muslims*. 2nd ed. London: I. B. Tauris.
Macpherson, Sir William. (1999). 'The Stephen Lawrence Inquiry, Report of an Inquiry,' Presented to Parliament by the Secretary of State for the Home Department by Command of Her Majesty. February. Cm 4262-I.
Malik, M. (2018). 'Religion, Belief and Diversity in Transition: The Commission on Religion and Belief in British Public Life'. In Alidadi, K. and Foblets, M.-C. (eds.), *Public Commissions on Cultural and Religious Diversity*, 91–109. London: Routledge.
McLaughlin, Eugene and Neal, Sarah. (2007). 'Who Can Speak to Race and Nation? Intellectuals, Public Policy Formation and the Future of Multi-ethnic Britain Commission'. *Cultural Studies*, 21(6), 910–930.
Meer, Nasar and Modood, Tariq. (2009). 'Refutations of Racism in the "Muslim Question"'. *Patterns of Prejudice*, 43(3–4), 335–354.
Mirza, Munira, Senthilkumaran, Abi and Ja'far, Zein. (2007). 'Living Apart Together'. *Policy Exchange*, January 27.
Modood, Tariq. (1988). '"Black", Racial Equality and Asian Identity'. *Journal of Ethnic and Migration Studies*, 14(3), 397–404.
Modood, Tariq. (1994). 'Political Blackness and British Asians'. *Sociology*, 28(4), 859–876.
Modood, Tariq. (1997). '"Difference", Cultural-Racism and Anti-Racism'. In Werbner, Pnina and Modood, Tariq (eds.), *Debating Cultural Hybridities: Identities and the Politics of Anti-Racism*, 154–172. London: Zed Books.

Modood, Tariq. (1998). 'Anti-Essentialism, Multiculturalism and the "Recognition" of Religious Groups'. *Journal of Political Philosophy*, 6, 378–399.
Modood, Tariq. (2003). *Multiculturalism, Muslims and the British State*. Leeds, UK: British Association for the Study of Religions.
Modood, Tariq. (2005). *Multicultural Politics: Racism, Ethnicity and Muslims in Britain*, Minneapolis: University of Minnesota Press and Edinburgh: University of Edinburgh Press, 11–18.
Modood, Tariq. (2013). *Multiculturalism: A Civic Idea*. 2nd ed. Cambridge, UK: Polity Press.
Modood, Tariq. (2014). 'Multiculturalism and Britishness: Provocations, Hostilities and Advances'. In *The Politics of Ethnic Diversity in the British Isles*, 21–37. Basingstoke, UK: Palgrave Macmillan UK.
Modood, Tariq. (2015). 'Religion in Britain Today and Tomorrow', Public Spirit, 26 January: http://www.theosthinktank.co.uk/comment/2015/01/29/religion-in-britain-today-and-tomorrow.
Modood, Tariq. (2015). 'Schools Need to Do More to Improve Children's Religious Literacy', *The Conversation*, December 7: https://theconversation.com/schools-need-to-do-more-to-improve-childrens-religious-literacy-51926.
Modood, Tariq, Berthoud, Richard, Lakey, Jane, Nazroo, James, Smith, Patten, Virdee, Satnam and Beishon, Sharon. (1997). *Ethnic Minorities in Britain: Diversity and Disadvantage*, no. 843. London: Policy Studies Institute.
Modood, Tariq and Calhoun, Craig. (2015). *Religion in Britain: Challenges for Higher Education*, Stimulus Paper, London: Leadership Foundation in Higher Education.
Modood, Tariq, and Salt, John. (2011). 'Global Migration, Ethnicity and Britishness'. In *Global Migration, Ethnicity and Britishness*, 248–268. Basingstoke, UK: Palgrave Macmillan UK.
Morey, Peter and Yaqin, Amina. (2011). *Framing Muslims*. Cambridge, MA: Harvard University Press.
Morris, Bob. (2016). '"Living with Difference": The Butler-Sloss Commission's Report Reflects the Interests of Its Members Rather Than the Public Interest'. UCL Constitution Unit, January 5: https://constitution-unit.com/2016/01/05/living-with-difference-the-butler-sloss-commissions-report-reflects-the-interests-of-its-members-rather-than-the-public-interest/.
Parekh, B. (1974). *Colour, Culture and Consciousness: Immigrant Intellectuals in Britain*. London: Allen & Unwin.
Parekh, B. (2000a). 'A Britain We Can All Belong To'. *Guardian*, 11 October.
Parekh, Bhikhu. (2000b). 'Reporting on a Report'. *The Runnymede Bulletin*, (June), 1–8;
Parekh, B. (2000c). *Rethinking Multiculturalism: Cultural Diversity and Political Theory*. Cambridge, MA: Harvard University Press.
Richardson, Robin. (2000). 'Children Will Be Told Lies: Distortions, Untruths and Abuse in the Media Coverage'. *Runnymede Trust Bulletin*, 324, 12–13.
Runnymede Trust. (1998). *Islamophobia: A Challenge for Us All*. London: Runnymede Trust.
Runnymede Trust. (2004). *Realising the Vision: Progress and Further Challenges*. London: Runnymede Trust.
Scarman, Leslie. (1981). *The Scarman Report: The Brixton Disorders 10–12 April 1981: Report of an Inquiry'*. London: Penguin.
Scholten, P., Entzinger, H., Penninx, R. and Verbeek, S. (2015). *Integrating Immigrants in Europe: Research-Policy Dialogues*. Springer Open.
Soutphommasane, Tim. (2012). 'Labour Can Make the Most of a Britain Alive with Olympic Spirit'. *The Observer*, 19 August. https://www.theguardian.com/commentisfree/2012/aug/19/tim-southphommasane-labour-olympic-spirit-new-britain, last accessed 26/02/2019.
Straw, Jack. (2007). Cyril Foster Lecture, 25 January.
Swann, Lord. (1985). *Education for All: Report of the Committee of Inquiry into the Education of Children from Ethnic Minority Groups*. London: HMSO.
Taylor, Charles. (2009). 'Foreword: What Is Secularism?'. In Levey, Geoffrey Brahm and Modood, Tariq (eds.), *Secularism, Religion and Multicultural Citizenship*. Cambridge: Cambridge University Press.

Uberoi, Varun. (1966). 'National Identities and Moving Beyond Conservative and Liberal Nationalism'. In Uberoi, Varun and Modood, Tariq (eds.), *Multiculturalism Rethought*, 75–94. Edinburgh University Press.

Uberoi, Varun. (2015). 'The "Parekh Report" – National Identities without Nations and Nationalism'. *Ethnicities*, *15*(4), 509–526.

Uberoi, Varun. (2018). 'National Identity – A Multiculturalist's Approach'. *Critical Review of International Social and Political Philosophy*, *21*(1), 46–64.

Uberoi, Varun and Modood, Tariq. (2013). 'Inclusive Britishness: A Multiculturalist Advance'. *Political Studies*, *61*(1), 23–41.

Vertovec, Steven. (2007). 'Super-Diversity and Its Implications'. *Ethnic and Racial Studies*, *30*(6), 1024–1054.

Weller, Paul. (2005). *Time for a Change: Reconfiguring Religion, State and Society*. London: Bloomsbury Publishing.

II

Multiculturalism and Secularism

Chapter Six

Muslims, Religious Equality and Secularism

The initial development of anti-racism in Britain, as explained in the Introduction, followed the American pattern, and indeed was directly influenced by American personalities and events. Just as in the United States the colour-blind humanism of Martin Luther King Jr. came to be mixed with an emphasis on black pride, black autonomy and black nationalism as typified by Malcolm X, so too the same process occurred in the United Kingdom (both these inspirational leaders visited Britain). Indeed, it is best to see this development of racial explicitness and positive blackness as part of a wider socio-political climate which is not confined to race and culture or non-white minorities. Feminism, gay pride, Québécois nationalism and the revival of a Scottish identity are some prominent examples of these new identity movements which have become an important feature in many countries, especially those in which class politics has declined in salience; the emphasis on non-territorial identities such as black, gay and women is particularly marked among anglophones. Moreover, it would be fair to say that what is often claimed today in the name of racial equality, again especially in the English-speaking world, goes beyond the claims that were made in the 1960s. Iris Young (1990, 157) expresses well the new political climate when she describes the emergence of an ideal of equality based not just on allowing excluded groups to assimilate and live by the norms of dominant groups, but on the view that 'a positive self-definition of group difference is in fact more liberatory'.

This significant shift takes us from an understanding of 'equality' in terms of individualism and cultural assimilation to a politics of recognition; to 'equality' as encompassing public ethnicity. This perception of equality means not having to hide or apologise for one's origins, family or community, and requires others to show respect for them. Public attitudes and arrangements must adapt so that this heritage is encouraged, not contemptuously expected to wither away.

These two conceptions of equality may be stated as follows:

- the right to assimilate to the majority/dominant culture in the public sphere, with toleration of 'difference' in the private sphere;
- the right to have one's 'difference' (minority ethnicity, etc.) recognised and supported in both the public and the private spheres.

While the former represents a classical liberal response to 'difference', the latter is the 'take' of the new identity politics. The two are not, however, alternative conceptions of equality in the sense that to hold one, the other must be rejected. Multiculturalism, properly construed, requires support for both conceptions. For the assumption behind the first is that participation in the public or national culture is necessary for the effective exercise of citizenship, the only obstacle to which are the exclusionary processes preventing gradual assimilation. The second conception, too, assumes that groups excluded from the national culture have their citizenship diminished as a result, and sees the remedy not in rejecting the right to assimilate, but in adding the right to widen and adapt the national culture, and the public and media symbols of national membership, to include the relevant minority ethnicities.

It can be seen, then, that the public-private distinction is crucial to the contemporary discussion of equal citizenship, and particularly to the challenge to an earlier liberal position. It is in this political and intellectual climate – namely, a climate in which what would earlier have been called 'private' matters had become sources of equality struggles – that Muslim assertiveness emerged as a domestic political phenomenon. In this respect, the advances achieved by anti-racism and feminism (with its slogan 'the personal is the political') acted as benchmarks for later political-group entrants, such as Muslims. As I will show, while Muslims raise distinctive concerns, the logic of their demands often mirrors those of other equality-seeking groups.

RELIGIOUS EQUALITY

So, one of the current conceptions of equality is a difference-affirming equality, with related notions of respect, recognition and identity – in short, what I understand by political multiculturalism (Modood 2007/2013, chapter 3). What kinds of specific policy demands, then, are being made by or on behalf of religious groups and Muslim identity politics in particular, when these terms are deployed?

I suggest that these demands have three dimensions, which get progressively 'thicker' – and are progressively less acceptable to radical secularists.

No Religious Discrimination

The very basic demand is that religious people, no less than people defined by 'race' or gender, should not suffer discrimination in job and other opportunities. So, for example, a person who is trying to dress in accordance with their religion or who projects a religious identity (such as a Muslim woman wearing a headscarf, a *hijab*), should not be discriminated against in employment. This however was not unlawful in Britain until 2003. Initially it was only a partial 'catching-up' with the existing anti-discrimination provisions in relation to race and gender. It did not extend to discrimination in provision of goods and services or create a duty upon employers to take steps to promote equality of opportunity. These latter and full parity for religion with all other grounds of discrimination were not achieved until the Equality Act of 2010.

Even-Handedness[1] Relative to Historically Established Religions

Many minority faith advocates interpret equality to mean that minority religions should get at least some of the support from the state that longer-established religions do. Muslims have led the way on this argument, and have made two particular issues politically contentious: the state funding of faith schools and the law of blasphemy. The New Labour government of 1997–2010 initiated the funding of non-Christian and non-Jewish schools. By 2017, there were 48 Jewish, 27 Muslim, 11 Sikh and 5 Hindu out of a total of 6,814 state-funded schools in England (Long and Bolton 2018). These schools, mainly Anglican and Catholic, represent 37 per cent of all mainstream primaries and 19 per cent of all mainstream secondary schools in England. They must teach mainly the national curriculum monitored by local authorities or central government.

Some secularists are unhappy about the proliferation of faith schools. They accept the argument for parity but believe this should be achieved by the state's withdrawing its funding from all religious schools. Most Muslims reject this form of equality in which the privileged lose something but the underprivileged gain nothing. More specifically, the issue between 'equalising upwards' and 'equalising downwards' here is about the legitimacy of religion as a public institutional presence.

Muslims have failed to get the courts to interpret the existing statute on blasphemy to cover offences beyond what Christians hold sacred; indeed the blasphemy law was abolished in 2008 without much fuss or debate. Muslim organisations such as the Muslim Council of Britain had put their effort in getting an incitement to religious hatred offence, as has existed in Northern Ireland for many years, mirroring the existing one of incitement to racial hatred. (The latter extends protection to cover certain forms of anti-Jewish literature, but not anti-Muslim literature.) Such a proposal was in the Queen's Speech in October, 2004, but was part of the raft of legislation that was abandoned to make way for the General Election of May, 2005, yet was reintroduced in the Queen's Speech in May 2005 and placed before Parliament in June. Despite the controversy that this has created, few people noticed how the law on race was already being stretched to cover religion so that anti-Muslim literature was becoming covered in the way that anti-Jewish literature has been covered from decades.[2]

Nevertheless, the government continued to have difficulties getting support for such legislation, not least from its own supporters, both inside and outside Parliament, where it especially provoked resistance from comedians, intellectuals and secularists, who feared that satire and criticism of religion was at risk (Chittenden 2004). Finally, Parliament passed a bill in early 2006 to protect against incitement to religious hatred. Yet it was only passed after members of both houses of Parliament – supported by much of the liberal intelligentsia – forced the government to accept amendments that weakened its initial proposals. Unlike the incitement to religious hatred offence in Northern Ireland, and the incitement to racial hatred offence in the United Kingdom, mere offensiveness was not an offence, and moreover the incitement must require the intention to stir up hatred. Nevertheless, a controversy shortly after this bill was passed showed that the media were coming to voluntarily restrain themselves. This was the case with the Danish Muhammad cartoons affair, the cartoons being reprinted in several leading European newspapers but not by any major organ in Britain, suggesting there was a greater understanding in Britain about anti-Muslim racism and about not giving gratuitous offence to Muslims than in some other European countries (see chapter 3).

Positive Inclusion of Religious Groups

The demand here is that religion in general, or at least the category of 'Muslim' in particular, should be a category by which the inclusiveness of social institutions may be judged, as they increasingly are in relation to race and gender. For example, employers should have to demonstrate that they do not discriminate against Muslims by explicit monitoring of Muslims' position within the workforce, backed up by appropriate policies, targets, managerial responsibilities, work environments, staff training, advertisements, outreach and so on (FAIR 2002; CBMI 2002; MCB 2003). Similarly, public bodies should provide appropriately sensitive policies and staff in relation to the services they provide, especially in relation to (non-Muslim) schools, social and health services; Muslim community centres or Muslim youth workers should be funded in addition to existing Asian and Caribbean community centres and Asian and black youth workers.

To take another case: the BBC currently believes it is of political importance to review and improve its personnel practices and its output of programmes, including its on-screen 'representation' of the British population, by making provision for and winning the confidence of women, ethnic groups and young people. Why should it not also use religious groups as a criterion of inclusivity and have to demonstrate that it is doing the same for viewers and staff defined by religious community membership?

In short, Muslims should be treated as a legitimate group in their own right (not because they are, say, Asians), whose presence in British society has to be explicitly reflected in all walks of life and in all institutions; and whether they are so included should become one of the criteria for judging Britain as an egalitarian, inclusive, multicultural society. A significant victory was made when the government agreed to include a religion question in the 2001 census. The question was voluntary but only 7 per cent did not answer it, yet to date its full potential to introduce 'religious monitoring' in the way that the inclusion of an ethnic question in 1991 had led to the more routine use of 'ethnic monitoring' has not been realised.

These policy debates may seem odd within the terms of, say, the U.S. 'wall of separation' between the state and religion or French *laïcité*, and can be uncomfortable for secularists in Britain too. Yet they more or less mirror existing U.K. anti-discrimination policy provisions. Moreover, Muslim assertiveness, though triggered and intensified by what are seen as attacks on Muslims, is primarily derived not from Islam or Islamism but from contemporary Western ideas about equality and multiculturalism. While simultaneously reacting to the latter in its failure to distinguish Muslims from the rest of the 'black' population and its uncritical secular bias, Muslims positively use, adapt and extend these contemporary Western ideas in order to join other equality-seeking movements. Some political Muslims do, therefore, have an ambivalence in relation to multicultural discourses (Modood and Ahmad 2007). On the one hand, as a result of previous misrecognition of their identity, and existing biases, there is distrust of 'the race relations industry' and of 'liberals'; on the other hand, the assertiveness is clearly a product of the positive climate created by liberals and egalitarians (Modood 2005). This ambivalence can tend towards antagonism when it is joined by Islamist discourses. There is a sense among many Muslims that Muslim populations across the world are repeatedly suffering at the hands of their neighbours, aided and abetted by the United States and its allies, and that Muslims must come together to defend themselves. There is a useful analogy with the black power movement here – not just in its internationalism, but one can also say that as black nationalism and Afrocentrism developed as one ideological expression of black power, so, similarly, we can see political Islamism as one confrontational version of a search for Muslim dignity and power.

A PANICKY RETREAT TO A LIBERAL PUBLIC-PRIVATE DISTINCTION

If the emergence of a politics of difference out of and alongside a liberal assimilationist equality created a dissonance, as indeed it did, the emergence of a British Muslim identity out of and alongside ethno-racial identities has created an even greater dissonance. Philosophically speaking, it should create a lesser dissonance, for a move from the idea of equality as sameness to equality as difference is a more profound conceptual movement than the creation of a new identity in a field already crowded with minority identities. But to infer this is to naively ignore the hegemonic power of secularism in British political culture, especially on the centre-left. While black and related ethno-racial identities were welcomed by, indeed were intrinsic to the rainbow coalition of identity politics, this coalition has been deeply unhappy with Muslim consciousness. While for some this rejection is specific to Islam, for many the ostensible reason is that it is a politicized religious identity. What is most interesting is that in this latter objection, if it is taken at its face value, the difference theorists, activists and paid professionals revert to a public-private distinction that they have spent two or three decades demolishing.

We thus have a mixed-up situation where secular multiculturalists may argue that the sex lives of individuals – traditionally, a core area of liberal privacy – is a legitimate feature of political identities and public discourse, and seem to generally welcome the sexualisation of culture, while on the other hand, religion – a key source of communal identity in traditional, non-liberal societies – is to be regarded as a private matter, perhaps as a uniquely private matter. Most specifically, Muslim identity is seen as the illegitimate child of British multiculturalism. Indeed, the Rushdie Affair made evident that the group in British society initially most politically opposed to (politicised) Muslims weren't Christians, or even right-wing nationalists, but the secular, liberal intelligentsia.[3]

Just as the hostility against Jews, in various times and places, has been a varying blend of anti-Judaism (hostility to a religion) and anti-Semitism (hostility to a racialised group), so it is difficult to gauge to what extent contemporary British Islamophobia is 'religious' and to what extent 'racial'. Even before September 11 and its aftermath, it was generally becoming acknowledged that of all groups, Asians face the greatest hostility today, and Asians themselves feel this is because of hostility directed to Muslims (Modood 2005). It has taken time but British anti-racists have come to acknowledge that Islamophobia is a form of cultural racism (as discussed in chapters 1 and 4). One has also to acknowledge that there must be analytical space for forthright criticism of aspects of Muslim doctrines, ideologies and practice without its being dismissed as racism – this being a parallel problem to, say, distinguishing anti-Zionism and anti-Semitism (see chapter 4).

IS RELIGIOUS EQUALITY A LESSER EQUALITY?

The multiculturalism or politics of difference that I am advocating has four major implications for liberal citizenship. First, it is clearly a collective project and concerns collectivities and not just individuals. Second, it is not colour/gender/sexual orientation 'blind' and so breaches the liberal public-private identity distinction which prohibits the recognition of particular group identities so that no citizens are treated in a more privileged or less privileged way or divided from each other.

Third, it takes race, sex and sexuality beyond being merely ascriptive sources of identity, merely categories. Race is of interest to liberal citizenship only because no one can choose their race and so should not be discriminated against on something over which they have no control. But if equality is about celebrating previously demeaned identities (e.g., in taking pride in one's blackness rather than in accepting it merely as a 'private' matter), then what is being addressed in anti-discrimination, or promoted as a public identity, is a chosen response to one's ascription. Exactly, the same applies to sex and sexuality. We may not choose our sex or sexual orientation but we choose how to politically live with it. Do we keep it private or do we make it the basis of a social movement and seek public resources and representation for it?

Muslims and other religious groups utilise this kind of argument, claiming that religious identity, just like gay identity and just like certain forms of racial identity, should not just be privatised or tolerated, but should be part of the public space. In their case, however, they come into conflict with an additional fourth dimension of liberal citizenship that we can refer to as 'secularism': the view that religion is a feature, perhaps uniquely, of private and not public identity.

The response that woman, black and gay are ascribed, unchosen identities while being a Muslim is about chosen beliefs, and that Muslims therefore need or ought to have less legal protection than the other kinds of identities is sociologically naïve and a political con. The position of Muslims in Britain today is similar to the other identities of 'difference' in relation to the contemporary concept of equality. No one chooses to be or not to be born into a Muslim family. Similarly, no one chooses to be born into a society where to look like a Muslim or to be a Muslim creates suspicion, hostility, or failure to get the job you applied for. Though how Muslims respond to these circumstances will vary. Some will organise resistance, while others will try to stop looking like Muslims (the equivalent of 'passing' for white); some will build an ideology out of their subordination, others will not, just as a woman can choose to be a feminist or not. Again, some Muslims may define their Islam in terms of piety rather than politics; just as some women may see no politics in their gender, while for others their gender will be at the centre of their politics.

Those who see the current Muslim assertiveness as an unwanted and illegitimate child of multiculturalism have only two choices if they wish to be consistent. They can repudiate the idea of equality as identity recognition and return to the 1960s liberal idea of equality as colour/sex/religion, and so forth, blindness. Or they can argue that equality as recognition does not apply to oppressed religious communities, perhaps uniquely not to religious communities. To deny Muslims positive equality without one of these two arguments is to be open to the charge of double standards.

Hence a programme of racial and multicultural equality is not possible today without a discussion of the merits and limits of secularism.[4] Secularism can no longer be treated as 'off-limits', or, as President Jacques Chirac said in a major speech in 2004, 'non-negotiable' (Cesari 2004, 166). Not that it's really a matter of being for or against secularism, but rather a careful, institution-by-institution analysis of how to draw the public-private boundary and further the cause of multicultural equality and inclusivity.

SECULARISM: DIFFERENT PUBLIC-PRIVATE BOUNDARIES IN DIFFERENT COUNTRIES

At the heart of secularism is a distinction between the public realm of citizens and policies, and the private realm of belief and worship. While all Western countries are clearly secular in many ways, interpretations and the institutional arrangements diverge according to the dominant national religious culture and the differing projects of nation-state building and thus makes secularism a 'particular' experience.

For example, the United States has as its First Amendment to the Constitution that there shall be no established church and there is wide support for this and in the last few decades there has been a tendency among academics and jurists to interpret the church-state separation in continually more radical ways (Sandel 1994; Hamburger 2002). Yet, as is well known, not only is the United States a deeply religious society, with much higher levels of church attendance than in Western Europe (Greely 1995), but there is also a strong Protestant, evangelical fundamentalism that is rare in Europe. This fundamentalism disputes some of the new radical interpretations of the 'no establishment clause', though not necessarily the clause itself, and is one of the primary mobilising forces in American politics. It is widely claimed that it decided the presidential elections of 2004 and 2016. The churches in question – mainly white, mainly in the South and Midwest – campaign openly for candidates and parties, indeed raise large sums of money for politicians and introduce religion-based issues into politics, such as positions on abortion, HIV/AIDS, homosexuality, stem-cell research, prayer at school and so on, as well as support a right-wing nationalism. It has been said that no openly avowed atheist has ever been a candidate for the White House and that it would be impossible for such a candidate to be elected. It is not at all unusual for politicians to publicly talk about their faith, to appeal to religion and to hold prayer meetings in government buildings. On the other hand, in establishment Britain, bishops sit in the upper chamber of the legislature by right and only the senior Archbishop can crown a new head of state, the monarch, but politicians rarely talk about their religion. It was noticeable, for example, that when Prime Minister Blair went to a summit meeting with President Bush to discuss aspects of the Iraq War in 2003, the U.S. media widely reported that the two leaders had prayed together. Yet, Prime Minister Blair, one of the most openly professed and active Christians ever to hold that office, refused to answer questions on this issue from the British media on his return, saying it was a private matter. The British state may have an established church but the beliefs of the Queen's first Minister are his own concern.

France draws the distinction between state and religion differently again. Like the United States, there is no state church but unlike the United States, the state actively promotes the privatisation of religion. While in the United States, organized religion in civil society is powerful and seeks to exert influence on the political process, French civil society does not carry signs or expressions of religion. Yet, the French state, contrary to the United States, confers institutional legal status on the Catholic and Protestant Churches and on the Jewish Consistory, albeit carefully designating organized religions as 'cults' and not communities. Almost as many French schoolchildren (about a fifth) are taught in state-subsidised religious schools (nearly all Catholic) as in England. In Germany, a secular constitution goes hand in hand with legal recognition of the Catholic and Protestant churches and is the basis not just of giving considerable social welfare presence to them but of large-scale state funding for their autonomously regulated welfare activities. We might want to express these four different national manifestations of secularism as in Table 6.1.

So, what are the appropriate limits of the state? Everyone will agree that there should be religious freedom and that this should include freedom of belief and worship in private associations. Family, too, falls on the private side of the line but the state regulates the limits of what is a lawful family – for example, polygamy is not permitted in many countries – not to mention the deployment of official definitions of 'family' in the distribution of welfare entitlements. Religions typically put a premium on mutuality and on care of the sick, the homeless, the elderly and so on. They set up organisations to pursue these aims, but so do states. Should there be a competitive or a cooperative relationship between these religious and state organisations, or do they have to ignore each other? Can public money – raised out of taxes on religious as well as non-religious citizens – not be used to support the organisations favoured by some religious taxpayers? What of schools? Do parents not have the right to expect that schools will make an effort – while pursuing broader educational and civic aims – not to create a conflict between the work of the school and the upbringing of the children at home but, rather, show respect for their religious background? Can parents, as associations of religious citizens, not set up their own schools and should those schools not be supported out of the taxes of the same parents? Is the school where the private (the family) meets the public (the state); or is it, in some Platonic manner, where the state takes over the children from the family and pursues its own purposes? Even if there is to be no established church, the state may still wish to work with organized religion as a social partner, as is the case in

Table 6.1.

	State	Religion in Civil Society
England/Britain	Weak establishment but churches have a political voice	Weak but churches can be a source of political criticism and action
United States	No establishment	Strong and politically mobilized
France	Actively secular but offers top-down recognition	Weak; rare for churches to be political
Germany	Secular constitution but massive funding for religious 'corporations'	Churches are important social partners of the state

Germany, or to have some forum in which it consults with organized religion, some kind of national council of religions, as in Belgium. Or, even if it does not do that because it is regarded as compromising the principle of secularism, political parties, being agents in civil society rather than organs of the state, may wish to do this and institute special representation for religious groups as many do for groups defined by age, gender, region, language, ethnicity and so on. It is clear then that the 'public' is a multi-faceted concept and in relation to secularism may be defined differently in relation to different dimensions of religion and in different countries.

We can all be secularists then, all approve of secularism in some respect, and yet have quite different ideas, influenced by historical legacies and varied pragmatic compromises, of where to draw the line between public and private. It would be quite mistaken to suppose that all religious spokespersons, or at least all political Muslims, are on one side of the line, and all others are on the other side. There are many different ways of drawing the various lines at issue. In the past, the drawing of them have reflected particular contexts shaped by differential customs, urgency of need and sensitivity to the sensibilities of the relevant religious groups (Modood 1994; 1997). Exactly the same considerations are relevant in relation to the accommodation of Muslims in Europe today – not a battle of slogans and ideological over-simplifications.

MODERATE SECULARISM AS AN IMPLICATION OF MULTICULTURAL EQUALITY

Multicultural equality, then, when applied to religious groups means that secularism *simpliciter* appears to be an obstacle to pluralistic integration and equality. But secularism pure and simple is not what exists in the world. The country-by-country situation is more complex, and indeed, far less inhospitable to the accommodation of Muslims than the ideology of secularism – or, for that matter, the ideology of anti-secularism – might suggest (Modood and Kastoryano 2006). All actual practices of secularism consist of institutional compromises and these can, should be and are being extended to accommodate Muslims. The institutional reconfiguration varies according to the historic place of religion in each country. Today the appropriate response to the new Muslim challenges is pluralistic institutional integration, rather than an appeal to a radical public-private separation in the name of secularism. The approach that is being argued for here, then, consists of

1. a reconceptualisation of secularism from the concepts of neutrality and the strict public/private divide to a moderate and evolutionary secularism based on institutional adjustments;
2. a reconceptualisation of equality from sameness to an incorporation of a respect for difference;
3. a pragmatic, case-by-case, negotiated approach to dealing with controversy and conflict, not an ideological, drawing-a-'line-in-the-sand' mentality.

This institutional integration approach is based on including Islam into the institutional framework of the state, using the historical accommodation between state and church as a basis for negotiations in order to achieve consensual resolutions consistent with equality and justice. As these accommodations have varied from country to country, it means there is no exemplary solution, for contemporary solutions, too, will depend on the national context and will not have a once-and-for-all-time basis. It is clearly a dialogical perspective and assumes the possibility of mutual education and learning. Like all negotiation and reform, there are normative as well as practical limits. Aspects of the former have been usefully characterized by Bhikhu Parekh as 'society's operative public values' (Parekh 2000, 267). These values, such as equality between the sexes, are embedded in the political constitution, in specific laws and in the norms governing the civic relations in a society. Norms, laws and constitutional principles concerning the appropriate place of religion in public life generally and in specific policy areas (such as schools or rehabilitation of criminals) consist of such public values and are reasoned about, justified or criticized by reference to specific values about religion/politics as well as more general norms and values in a society, such as fairness, or balance or consensus and so on. I, therefore, recognise that the approach recommended here involves solutions that are highly contextual and practical but they are far from arbitrary or without reference to values. While the latter are not static because they are constantly being reinterpreted, realigned, extended and reformed, nevertheless they provide a basis for dialogue and agreement.

An example is the development of a religious equality agenda in Britain, discussed above. It also includes the recommendations of the Royal Commission on the Reform of the House of Lords (2000) that in addition to the Anglican bishops who sit in that House by right as part of the Anglican 'establishment', this right should be extended to cover those of other Christian and non-Christian faiths (see chapter 8). The same point can be made in relation to the fact that as early as 1974 the Belgian state decided to officially recognise Islam within its Council of Religions as a full member, or to the way that Muslims in the Netherlands have long had state-funded religious schools and television channels as a progressive step in that country's traditional way of institutionally dealing with organized religion – namely, 'mosques'.[5] Similarly, a 'Muslim community' is becoming recognized by public authorities in Germany by appealing to the historic German idea of a 'religious society' (*Religionsgesellschaft*). Again, a series of French Interior Ministers have taken a number of steps to 'normalise' Islam in France by creating an official French Islam under the authority of the state in ways that make it identical to other faiths (for more on these cases, see Modood and Kastoryano 2006; also Cesari 2004).

The recognition of Islam in Europe can take a corporatist form, can be led or even imposed by the state in a 'top-down' way and can take a church or ecclesiastical model as its form. This may be appropriate for certain countries or at certain moments and could be – usually is – consistent with the conception of multiculturalism I have outlined. However, it would not be my own preference for it would not represent the British multicultural experience and its potentialities at its best. A corporatist inclusion would require Muslims and their representatives to speak in one voice and to create a unified, hierarchical structure when this is out of character in Sunni Islam, especially the South Asian Sunni Islam espoused by the majority of Muslims in Britain, and of the contemporary British Muslim scene. Corporatism would very likely consist of state control of the French kind, with the state imposing its own template, plans, modes of partnership and chosen imams and leaders upon Muslims. One mode of recognition is for the new minority faiths like Islam to be represented in relation to the state by their spiritual leaders like the Anglican Church is by its bishops, or even, indeed, as the Catholic Church is in Britain. For while the Catholic Church is not an established church, it has a clear relationship with the British, especially English, state (e.g., it is the single biggest beneficiary of state funding of faith schools) and it is its ecclesiastical hierarchy that are taken to be speaking for Catholics.

My own preference would be for an approach that would be less corporatist, less statist and less churchy – in brief, less French. An approach in which civil society played a greater role would be more comfortable with there being a variety of Muslim voices, groups and representatives. Different institutions, organisations and associations would seek to accommodate Muslims in ways that worked for them best at a particular time, knowing that these ways may or ought to be modified over time and Muslim and other pressure groups and civic actors may be continually evolving their claims and agendas, constituting a democratic constellation rather than a corporate actor (Modood 2007/2013, 135/125). Within a general understanding that there had to be an explicit effort to include Muslims (and other marginal and underrepresented groups), different organisations – like my earlier example of the BBC – may not just seek this inclusion in different ways but would seek as representatives Muslims that seemed to them most appropriate associates and partners, persons who would add something to the organisation and were not merely delegated from a central, hierarchical Muslim body. The idea of numerical or 'mirror' representation of the population might be a guideline but it would not necessarily follow that some kind of quota allocation (a mild version of the corporatist tendency) would have to operate. Improvisation, flexibility, consultation, learning by 'suck it and see' and by the example of others, incrementalism and all the other virtues of a pragmatic politics in close touch with a dynamic civil society can as much, and perhaps better, bring about multicultural equality than a top-down corporatist inclusion. 'Representation' here would mean the inclusion of a diversity of backgrounds and sensibilities, not delegates or corporate structures (Modood 2007/2013, 135/125). Recognition, then, must be pragmatically and experimentally handled, and civil society must share the burden of representation.

While the state may seek to ensure that spiritual leaders are not absent from public fora and consultative processes in relation to policies affecting their flocks, it may well be that a Board of Jewish Deputies model of community representation offers a better illustration of a community-state relationship. The Board of Deputies, a body independent of, but a communal partner to, the British state, is a federation of Jewish organisations which includes synagogues but also other Jewish community organisations and its leadership typically consists of lay persons whose standing and skill in representing their community is not diminished by any absence of spiritual authority. It is most interesting that while at some local levels Muslim organisations have chosen to create political bodies primarily around mosques (e.g., the Bradford Council of Mosques), at a national level, it is the Board of Deputies model that seems to be more apparent. This is certainly the case with the single most representative and successful national Muslim organisation, the Muslim Council of Britain (MCB), whose office holders and spokespersons are more likely to be chartered accountants and solicitors than imams. Most mosques in Britain are run by local lay committees and the *mullah* or *imam* is a usually a minor functionary.[6] Very few of those who aspire to be Muslim spokespersons and representatives have religious authority and are not expected to have it by fellow Muslims. So the accommodation of religious groups is as much if not more about the recognition and support of communities rather than necessarily about ecclesiastical or spiritual representation in political institutions. The state has a role here which includes ensuring that Muslim civil society is drawn into the mainstream as much as it is to seek forms of representation within state structures.

In my preferred approach it would be quite likely that different kinds of groups – Muslims, Hindus and Catholics for instance, let alone women, gays and different ethnic minority groups – might choose to organise in different ways and to relate to key civic and political institutions in different ways. While each might look over its shoulders at what other groups are doing or getting and use any such precedents to formulate its own claims, we should on this approach not require symmetry but be able to live with some degree of 'variable geometry'. I am unable to specify what this degree of flexibility might be but it should be clear that sensitivity to the specific religious, cultural and socio-economic needs in a specific time and place and political context is critical to multiculturalism. This indeterminacy leaves something to be desired but I hope it is evident that it can be a strength too. It also underlines that multiculturalism is not a comprehensive political theory but can and must sit alongside other political values and be made to work with varied institutional, national and historical contexts.

CONCLUSION

The emergence of Muslim political agency threw British multiculturalism into theoretical and practical disarray. It has led to policy reversals in the Netherlands and elsewhere, and across Europe has strengthened intolerant, exclusive nationalism. We should, in fact, be moving the other way and enacting the kinds of legal and policy measures that are necessary to accommodate Muslims as equal citizens in European polities. These would include anti-discrimination measures in areas such as employment, positive action to achieve a full and just political representation of Muslims in various areas of public life, the inclusion of Muslim history as European history in school and university curricula and so on. Critically, I have been arguing that the inclusion of Islam as an organized religion and of Muslim identity as a public identity are necessary to integrate Muslims and to pursue religious equality. While this inclusion runs against certain interpretations of secularism, it is not inconsistent with what secularism means in practice in Europe. We should let this evolving, moderate secularism and the spirit of compromise it represents be our guide. Unfortunately, an ideological secularism is currently being reasserted and generating European domestic versions of 'the clash of civilisations' thesis and the conflicts that entails for European societies. That some people are today developing secularism as an ideology to oppose Islam and its public recognition is a challenge both to pluralism and equality, and thus to some of the bases of contemporary democracy. It has to be resisted no less than the radical anti-secularism of some Islamists.

NOTES

1. I borrow this term from Carens 2000.
2. The Crime and Disorder Act 1998 introduced the concept of a 'racially aggravated' offence which covers not just the intention of an act but also its consequences. It relates primarily to acts of violence but also in relation to amendments to the section of the Public Order Act 1986 that deals with threatening, abusive, or insulting behaviour. So, the latter

behaviour is not determined by intentions alone. Following 9/11, an Anti-Terrorism, Crime and Security Act was quickly passed and extended the phrase 'racially aggravated' to 'racially or religiously aggravated'. In 2003, the High Court upheld the conviction in the case *Norwood v. Director of Public Prosecutions (DPP)* 2003, arguing that displaying a British National Party poster bearing the words 'Islam out of Britain' and 'Protect the British People' accompanied by a picture of the 9/11 attack on the Twin Towers amounted to an offence of causing alarm or distress. As discussed in chapter 3, the High Court argued that evidence of actual alarm or distress was not necessary if it was determined that 'any right thinking member of society' is likely to be caused harassment, alarm or distress (for further details see *Norwood v. DPP* 2003, and CMBI 2004).

3. As pointed out in chapter 2, note 2, the large PSI Fourth Survey found that nominal Christians and those without a religion were more likely to say they were prejudiced against Muslims than those Christians who said their religion was of importance to them (Modood et al. 1997, 134).

4. For a good short introduction to secularism, Copson 2017.

5. This principle that recognized that Protestants and Catholics had a right to state resources and some publicly funded autonomous institutions officially ended in 1960. It is, however, still considered as a 'relevant framework for the development of a model that grants certain collective rights to religious groups' (Sunier and von Luijeren 2002, 151) in such matters as state funding of Islamic schools. So, the accommodation of Muslims is being achieved through a combination of mild pillarization and Dutch minority policies.

6. As mentioned in chapter 2, the MCB's pre-eminence began to suffer from the mid-2000s, as it grew increasingly critical of the invasions of Iraq and of the so-called war on terror. The government started accusing it of failing to clearly and decisively reject extremism and sought alternative Muslim interlocutors. With the realization that no simple Muslim organization was fully reflective of non-jihadi Muslims, New Labour readmitted MCB back into the fold but as only part of a plurality; subsequent governments, however, have preferred to work with other Muslim bodies.

REFERENCES

Carens, J. H. (2000). *Culture, Citizenship and Community: A Contextual Exploration of Justice as Evenhandedness*. Oxford: Oxford University Press.

CBMI (Commission on British Muslims and Islamophobia). (2002). *Response to the Commission on Racial Equality's Code of Practice*. London: CBMI, February.

Cesari, J. (2004). *When Islam and Democracy Meet*. New York and Basingstoke, UK: Palgrave.

Chittenden, M. (2004). 'Blackadder Fights Law That Could Catch Out Comedians'. *The Sunday Times*, December 5.

Copson, A. (2017). *Secularism: Politics, Religion, and Freedom*. Oxford: Oxford University Press.

FAIR (Forum against Islamophobia and Racism). (2002). *A Response to the Government Consultation Paper, 'Towards Equality and Diversity: Implementing the Employment and Race Directives'*. London: FAIR.

Greely, A. (1995). 'The Persistence of Religion'. *Cross Currents*, 45, 24–41.

Hamburger, P. (2002). *Separation of Church and State*. Cambridge, MA: Harvard University Press.

Long, R. and Bolton, P. (2018). 'Faith Schools in England: FAQs'. Briefing Paper No 06972. London: House of Commons Library.

Modood, T. (1994). 'Establishment, Multiculturalism and British Citizenship'. *Political Quarterly*, 65, 53–73.

Modood, T. (1997). *Church, State and Religious Minorities*. London: Policies Studies Institute.

Modood, T. (2005) *Multicultural Politics: Racism, Ethnicity and Muslims in Britain*. Minneapolis: University of Minnesota Press and Edinburgh: University of Edinburgh Press.

Modood, T. (2007/2013). *Multiculturalism: A Civic Idea* (2nd ed., 2013). Cambridge: Polity Press.
Modood, T. and Ahmad, F. (2007). 'British Muslim Perspectives on Multiculturalism'. *Theory, Culture & Society*, *24*(2), 187–213.
Modood, T., Berthoud, R., Lakey, J., Nazroo, J., Smith, P., Virdee, S. and Beishon, S. (1997). *Ethnic Minorities in Britain: Diversity and Disadvantage*. London: Policy Studies Institute.
Modood, T. and Kastoryano, R. (2006). 'Secularism and the Accommodation of Muslims in Europe'. In Modood, T., Triandafyllidou, A. and Zapata-Barrero, R. (eds.), *Multiculturalism, Muslims and Citizenship: A European Approach*, 162–178. London: Routledge.
Muslim Council of Britain (MCB). (2003). 'Response to the Home Office Paper on the Government's Race Equality Strategy'. http://archive.mcb.org.uk/wp-content/uploads/2016/02/racestrategy.pdf, last accessed 25/02/2019.
Parekh, B. (2000). *Rethinking Multiculturalism: Cultural Diversity and Political Theory*. Basingstoke, UK: Macmillan.
Royal Commission on the Reform of the House of Lords. (2000). *A House for the Future*. London: HMSO.
Sandel, M. J. (1994). 'Review of Rawls' Political Realism'. *Harvard Law Review*, *107*, 1765–1794.
Sunier, T. and von Luijeren, M. (2002). 'Islam in the Netherlands'. In Haddad, Y. Y. (ed.), *Muslims in the West: From Sojourners to Citizens*, 144–157. Oxford: Oxford University Press.
Young, I. M. (1990). *Justice and the Politics of Difference*. Princeton, NJ: Princeton University Press.

Chapter Seven

Multicultural Citizenship and the Shari'a Controversy in Britain

An intense public debate and media controversy was triggered in Britain after a lecture delivered by Dr. Rowan Williams during his tenure as the Archbishop of Canterbury in 2008. The lecture raised important questions of law, state, faith and citizenship in a modern, plural society; and its bitter, polarizing aftermath equally highlights the issue of what kind of civic discourse about these questions is necessary if they are to be properly addressed. This essay responds to the debate and controversy by viewing them in the perspective of 'multicultural citizenship', a concept which allows for nuanced understanding of the inter-relationship of 'secular' and 'religious' notions in civic life.

Archbishop Rowan Williams's careful address explored the 'growing challenge' presented by 'the presence of communities which, while no less "law-abiding" than the rest of the population, relate to something other than the British legal system alone'; raised the question of 'what degree of accommodation the law of the land can and should give to minority communities with their own strongly entrenched legal and moral codes'; and included a developed and highly sensitive reflection on the reality and potential of 'plural jurisdiction', particularly in relation to the experience of and discussions about 'Shari'a courts', their capacity to rule on such matters as family disputes and claims, and their relationship to the 'statutory law of the United Kingdom'.[1]

It may seem astonishing that a lecture at the Royal Courts of Justice in London, academic both in atmospherics and language, should generate such passionate denunciation. It is less so if seen in a context where the 'legal recognition of communal religious identities'[2] conjures the worst suspicions and prejudices of those already attuned by a hostile public discourse to regard Islam-based practices, codes or ideas as, by definition, extreme or dangerous. Such sentiments are reinforced by a situation where criticism of multiculturalism – often focusing on its alleged socially divisive tendencies and supposed empowerment of reactionary religious forces – has become both routine and (often) ill-informed. In turn, they fuel the argument that a turn towards a more or less rigorous secularism that would exclude recognition of religion in the public sphere is desirable. This line of argument, however, offers a false diagnosis and therefore a flawed prescription.

A particularly stark vision of these alternative social models was presented by David Hayes in the weeks after the terrorist attacks in London on 7 July 2005: the attacks, he argued, opened a new period in Britain's development where the choice was between 'radical multiculturalism' and 'radical secularism'.[3] But these are not the only choices; indeed they are not realistic choices at all, because they deny the complex but definite reality of a deep resonance between citizenship and multicultural recognition. Together, these elements presuppose complementary notions of unity and plurality, and of equality and difference; and they are further linked by the fact that central to citizenship is respect for the group self-identities that citizens value. This is the context, I suggest, within which this latest 'multiculturalism' versus 'secularism' storm can best be understood.

A. CITIZENSHIP AND MULTICULTURAL CITIZENSHIP

Multicultural citizenship is based on the idea that citizens have individual rights, but as individuals are not uniform, their citizenship contours itself around the specific individuals that make up a citizenry of a particular time and place. Citizenship is not a monistic identity that is completely apart from or transcends other identities important to citizens. Their group identities are ever-present, and each group has a right to be a part of the civic whole and to speak up for itself and for its vision of the whole.[4]

Hence citizenship is a continuous dialogue. As the parties to these dialogues are many, not just two, the process may be described as 'multilogical'. The 'multilogues' allow for views to qualify each other, overlap, synthesize, modify one's own view in the light of having to coexist with others', hybridize, allow new adjustments to be made, new conversations to take place. Such modulations and contestations are part of the internal, evolutionary, work-in-progress dynamic of citizenship. Thus, civic inclusion does not consist of an uncritical acceptance of an existing conception of citizenship, of 'the rules of the game' and a one-sided 'fitting-in' of new entrants (or 'new equals' – mostly ex-subordinates of the colonial experience). To be a citizen, no less than to have just become a citizen, is to have a double right: to be recognized and to debate the terms of recognition.

Citizenship consists of a number of coterminous processes: a framework of rights and practices of participation; discourses and symbols of belonging; ways of imagining and remaking ourselves as a country and expressing our sense of commonalities; differences in the ways in which these identities qualify each other and create inclusive public spaces. Change and reform do not all have to be brought about by state action, laws, regulation or prohibitions; they are also the result of public debate, discursive contestations, pressure-group mobilizations and the varied and (semi-)autonomous institutions of civil society.

Citizenship, then, is not confined to the state but dispersed across society, compatible with the multiple forms of contemporary group identity. It is sustained through dialogue, new and reformed national identities and plural forms of representation that do not privilege one group as the model to which all others have to conform.

The ideal of multicultural citizenship is a critique of the cultural assimilation traditionally demanded by nation-states of migrants and minorities, as well as of that liberal individualism that has no space for groups. Nevertheless, it is clearly grounded in and is a development out of the ideas of individual equality and democratic citizenship. It is not about pre-democratic arrangements such as the Ottoman accommodation of minorities through the *millet* system. It seeks to pluralize, and hence adapt, not undermine, the unity and equality of citizenship and national identity.

B. MULTICULTURAL CITIZENSHIP AND RELIGION

What implications does this have for religious groups? It means that secularism, pure and simple – the absolute and dogmatic separation of citizenship and religion – appears to be an obstacle to pluralistic integration and equality. This is a big implication but not as radical as it sounds. For secularism *simpliciter* is not what exists in Britain, nor indeed in any democratic country. Britain is a secular country and a version of secularism is indeed hegemonic; but it is of a moderate kind that accommodates organized religion, religious identities and conscience.

This is evident in many areas: constitutional arrangements, schools, government support for welfare by religious agencies, ministerial consultations with religious groups among them. These arrangements reflect a particular history to the point of idiosyncrasy, but moderate secularism is the secularism of all democracies (as opposed to, say, the Soviet Union or communist China) – even though each draws the religion-politics linkages and separations in its own way.

Multicultural citizenship's relation to the state, and to the varied areas of civil society and local government that shape and make meaningful our civic identities, is broad, rather than narrowly, defined. This means that a focus on legal provisions is not the beginning or end of multicultural citizenship. But it is an important area, and so everything that the archbishop said about the need to explore accommodating aspects of Muslim principles and laws (the heterogeneous collection of texts and forms of reasoning summed up as Shari'a) within United Kingdom law is relevant to the task of multiculturalizing citizenship. The archbishop was thinking about how the work of the existing Shari'a councils (which adjudicate on personal and civil matters such as divorce) could be extended and given legal recognition in the way that their Jewish equivalents have enjoyed for decades or longer.

He was quite clear that this was not a matter of separate or parallel legal systems, for the Shari'a tribunals would not be able to go against U.K. laws, both on specific areas or cases and on individual and human rights in general. The decision to go to such Muslim adjudication services has, of course, to be voluntary by both parties, and above all, the archbishop rightly emphasized the importance of gender equality in these contexts. These courts would not have the power to punish or fine individuals and so they concern only civil matters and have nothing to do with criminal justice. Many people, wilfully or otherwise, misunderstood Dr. Williams's position and thought (sincerely or otherwise) that he was sanctioning the stoning of adulterers, hands-chopping for theft and beheadings for apostasy. Even some of those who recognize that he was not doing so still argue that his intentions here are not relevant, for granting anything to Muslims in this area would encourage extremists and unreasonable demands and propel the entire society down a slippery slope to the 'Talibanization' of British law.

This is not an argument but scaremongering on a large scale. To avoid discussing and conceding what is reasonable because someone else might later demand something unreasonable is irrational. And to associate a whole group, in this case Muslims, with their extremist elements is a kind of political demonization that may appropriately be called anti-Muslim racism, as argued in chapter 4. Of course, some Muslims may, just as anybody may, make unreasonable demands; but to therefore dismiss all Muslim demands is surely to draw the line between what is acceptable and unacceptable in the wrong place. As a matter of principle, each proposal should be considered on its own merits; and there is wisdom in discussing and implementing proposals on a gradual basis so that their practical effects can be seen and lessons can be learned.

C. LEGAL POSITIVISM AND CRITICAL INTERPRETIVISM

This is not just a matter of pragmatism and practical wisdom. It flows out of the ethics of multicultural citizenship: the imperative to seek the inclusion of marginal groups through dialogue, a commitment to seek mutual understanding and find accommodation. There is a yet deeper philosophical basis for what I am advocating. We should not ideologize Shari'a and secular law into rival, exclusive and inflexible systems. They have much in common both at the level of principles as well the capacity to live together. Those who think the opposite are likely to be influenced by a form of reasoning I will call 'legal positivism'.

Positivists understand principles, bodies of thought and practice, and traditions as if they were self-evident, and that once learned all that is needed is to apply them in a legalistic way to a specific situation. Legal reasoning itself highlights the distortion of reasoning this view embodies. For laws are not self-evident; otherwise why are there enormous legal libraries that contain voluminous commentaries, analyses and interpretations, as well as stacks of case law and precedent?

Interpretation and sensitivity to context are always essential to the application of a rule or law to a specific case. Understanding the rule depends upon reading it with other rules and principles that illuminate and qualify it. These rules and principles are not self-evident but rationally provoke questions which have to be critically engaged with. If the situation to which the rule has to be applied is to be understood, a capacity must exist both to identify what is similar in that situation to all the other cases to which the rule applies and what is distinctive or new about the context and which may require a questioning or refinement of the relevant body of principles and rules. In short, it requires the critical reasoning that Muslim jurists call *ijtihad*. A simple illustration lies in the fact that at the time of the founding texts of Islam, there was no tobacco in Muslim societies. Hence the question of what attitude a believer should have to tobacco – its cultivation, trade and consumption – is a matter of identifying the relevant rules and principles and showing in what ways and to what extent and under what conditions they apply to tobacco. To do that is to critically interrogate the texts and to extend the structure of thought and practice built upon them. The conclusion of the process may entail more than simply reflecting on a new case: it may open the way to a new understanding of the principles involved, their interrelationships, ambivalences and contradictions – perhaps even to a reinterpretation of what had been considered settled. Some principles may thus be tightened and given greater definition, others loosened to widen their range of applicability; and there can thus be implications for other cases and questions of behaviour.

D. PRACTICAL MULTICULTURALISM

There are significant practical difficulties in giving public recognition and legal incorporation of Shari'a councils. They must of course work within U.K. law, only delivering judgements that are consistent with it, including human rights, gender equality and child-protection legislation. There must be no compulsion or social pressure to go to them in preference to civil courts or other lawful remedies. The adjudicators need to be properly trained and qualified, both in terms of Islamic knowledge and authority but also in terms of their understanding of U.K. law and society, the complex context in which the cases arise and within which they must be understood and resolved.

As there is no single ecclesiastical authority in Islam, certainly not in Sunni Islam, these problems cannot be addressed simply at the top and filtered down through a hierarchy. Yet it is a fact that Shari'a adjudication councils do exist and operate in Britain and so it is very likely that some of the problems just mentioned are problems that already exist. These must be addressed, but in sensitive and feasible ways – that is, not by picking a fight with Muslims but by bringing them deeper into British institutions and practice, and by equitable treatment that extends to Muslims the opportunities and resources that other groups enjoy.

This issue has some parallel with that of faith schools. In England there are thousands of Christian and Jewish schools largely funded by the public purse and which teach about a quarter of all pupils. So, when some private Muslim schools sought to enter this voluntary-aided sector, their inclusion was reasonable and just and an appropriate elaboration of multicultural citizenship. But the process has been neither simple nor automatic. The schools had to teach within a national curriculum; have competent teachers, appropriate facilities and governance; meet a local need and be open to professional inspection. Some private Muslim schools have been able to meet these criteria – indeed, they meet them better than many comprehensives; others are working to reach these standards and most are outside the system.

This is a good model for finding ways to respond to the existence of Shari'a adjudication panels. The principle of their incorporation as a feature of the developing multicultural citizenship should be accepted. The existence of comparable Christian and Jewish institutions (such as the *Beth Din*) should be used as a benchmark – though not inflexibly nor as a perfect model; then the practical issues can be considered, including the safeguarding of individual right – especially those of women and children – each application examined on its own merits. Some applications may not be able to meet the requisite standards, others may not seek this formalization (though that is not to say that they should be beyond all regulation and support if there is a cause for concern). A trial-and-error basis should operate with existing arrangements as a guide; yet out of this, the emergence of some institutional innovation is likely, so, as always, caution is needed. This would both be a pragmatic way to proceed and an appropriately British form of multicultural integration, something that works with the grain of what already exists (just as other countries may want to do it their own way).

The storm that the archbishop's views provoked is in many ways more instructive than what he himself said. The reaction was immediate and was wholly disproportionate. Part of the problem is language. The mere fact of saying something positive about Shari'a leads to knee-jerk hostility among many people. Regrettably, and in a similar fashion, the term 'secularism' is understood by some Muslims as a policy of atheism, colonialism or postcolonial despotism. The use of either of these terms can lead to the closing of minds, however reasonable and qualified what is being said.

Beyond this, it is clearly indicative of deep insecurities and fears about Islam among many non-Muslim British citizens. The resulting tendency to demonize and victimize Muslims is deeply regrettable; yet the ethic of dialogical citizenship offers Muslims a basis both to stand up for equal status in a dignified way and to seek to address these fears sensitively and in the spirit of mutual concern and solidarity. It is not easy to be sympathetic and considerate when under attack, but a shared future depends upon handling even Islamophobic hysteria in the spirit of common citizenship. For Britain belongs equally to all its citizens, its problems no less than its gifts. In mutual recognition of this shared ownership lies the hope of a secure and inclusive future.

E. RETROSPECTION

The foregoing was written (taking a couple of days out of a busy academic schedule) in the heat of the moment, when the furore over Archbishop Williams's lecture was still in the airwaves.[5] Yet there is nothing in it that with hindsight – enriched by further reading and reflection, as well as the knowledge of subsequent developments – I would wish to change. I continue to think that much of the 'debate' was driven by stereotypes and fear of Muslims, and some of it by wilful scaremongering. I maintain that what the archbishop argued was sensible as well as learned and not anything as radical as his critics thought. The latter is vindicated by the fact that journalists have now discovered that Shari'a councils already operate in England. These usually comprise informal bodies of local imams providing a mediation and arbitration service covering mainly marriage and divorce matters – though in the case of the most organized body, the Muslim Arbitration Tribunal (MAT), it also resolves disputes between business partners or mosques. The MAT currently only operates in five cities but it intends to expand to other cities and also to train imams from other bodies.[6] Shari'a councils are completely voluntary and operate within the law of England and Wales as an arbitration service under the Arbitration Act 1996 and their judgements are not legally binding without the support of a county court. That they are not a challenge to English law was made clear by the Chief Justice, Lord Phillips's endorsement of them as vehicles for alternative dispute resolution, the chief justice noting that 'our system already goes a long way towards accommodating the Archbishop's suggestion'.[7]

I would, however, point to a fact that was quite visible at the time and yet which some, including myself, failed to highlight. This is that the controversy was not started by Muslims. They, together with the archbishop, faced a barrage of criticism, for which they were completely unprepared as the controversy was sprung upon them out of the blue. Indeed, it was unclear to what extent the call for the legal incorporation of Shari'a councils was of importance to most Muslims. For British Muslims the issue aroused nothing like the passion that some controversies had. Think of *The Satanic Verses* uproar, the Danish cartoon affair, the international and domestic 'War on Terror', the Israeli attacks on Lebanon and Gaza, and ongoing debates about female dress. The passion unleashed by the archbishop's lecture was very largely one-way: it consisted of mainly non-Muslims expressing outrage at Rowan Williams and at things Islamic. In this context, while there seems to be a growing demand by some Muslims, not least women in relation to issues surrounding divorce, for *halal* conflict resolution and that this demand is being met by an expansion in the number of Shari'a councils in Britain, I want to acknowledge that not all Muslims fully agree with the kind of support I have given above to this development. At one level it is obvious that not all Muslims agree on this (or indeed any other) matter. But I am thinking of people with whom I normally have wide areas of agreement and so would have expected to have agreement on this issue.

For example, Samia Bano has pioneered systematic research on the use of Shari'a councils in Britain by women. In a thoughtful article she makes a number of cautionary points. Her research suggests that while some women want the provision of Shari'a arbitration, in many cases the actual practice of the arbitration services reflects patriarchical assumptions and power relations. She believes that the institutionalization of Shari'a bodies should not proceed without a proper examination of the position of women and without the involvement of women.[8] I think the difference between us is not very great. As I originally argued, the vulnerability of women (and children) in the process must be highlighted and their rights safeguarded. So I would fully support the involvement of women at every level of consultation and institutional design. I would perhaps hesitate to make that a necessary condition of approval of a Shari'a body. Requiring such bodies to publish their *fatwas* would go some way to alerting women's organizations, professional advisers and individual supplicants about the track record of a council and so enable women-friendly bodies to be selected and hopefully proliferate over time. For me, the bottom line is that if such bodies already exist and are growing in number and scale then it is better to bring them into the system and regulate them. Creating barriers to that by instituting a regulatory regime that deters bodies from making themselves fully public and legal, especially if it is perceived that greater demands are being made on Muslims than on others, will not protect the interests of Muslim women (nor would it be consistent with equity and multicultural citizenship). It will only lead to 'backstreet Shari'a councils' that may do more harm than recognized bodies whose processes then can be publicized and monitored.

Perhaps a more fundamental disagreement is with Tariq Ramadan. Even though he was quoted at length by Dr. Williams, Ramadan did not appreciate the archbishop's intervention on this issue. This was partly because he saw how the lecture – however far this was from Dr. William's intentions – whipped up fears among non-Muslims. But more fundamentally, Ramadan baulked because he believed that talk of Shari'a in Britain was steering Muslims away from the importance of abiding by a singular law of the land.[9] This is wholly consistent with his French republicanism, which has always made him warn against minority rights and 'victim mentality', be lukewarm about multiculturalism and consistently stress the importance of the shared rights and duties of common citizenship.[10] I believe, as argued above, that this is too simplistic a view of citizenship, especially in a context of ethno-religious diversity. Our common citizenship should not swamp our other identities (that is usually a recipe for cultural majoritarianism) but should allow difference to coexist with and interact with commonalities.[11] I suspect that Ramadan also feels that Shari'a currently is interpreted in too many different ways and often it is applied in ways that I above described as legal positivist and inconsistent with its core principles. For Ramadan, Shari'a needs serious scholarly reform and consensual modernization and without this it is in no fit state to be brought into contact with English law.

If so, I do not disagree with that description, but I do not draw the same conclusion. One of the ways forward can be through piecemeal application (say, in relation to marriage and divorce) and through engagement with the principles and practice of contemporary English law. I differ from Ramadan here. Such interaction – which can be influential in both directions – is part of my understanding of citizenship in a multicultural society.

NOTES

1. R. Williams, 'Civil and Religious Law in England: A Religious Perspective', *Guardian*, 7 February 2008: https://www.theguardian.com/uk/2008/feb/07/religion.world2 (last accessed 5 October 2018).

2. Ibid.

3. David Hayes, 'What Kind of Country?', *Open Democracy*, 7 February 2008: http://www.opendemocracy.net/conflict-terrorism/britain_2713.jsp (last accessed 5 October 2018).

4. For a fuller statement of this understanding of citizenship, see my *Multiculturalism: A Civic Idea* (Cambridge: Polity Press, 2007; 2nd ed., 2013).

5. T. Modood, 'Multicultural Citizenship and the Anti-Sharia Storm', *Open Democracy*, 14 February 2008: http://www.opendemocracy.net/article/faith_ideas/europe_islam/anti_sharia_storm.

6. 'Muslim Arbitration Tribunal', Wikipedia: https://en.wikipedia.org/wiki/Muslim_Arbitration_Tribunal. See also J. R. Bowen, *On British Islam: Religion, Law, and Everyday Practice in Shari'a Councils*, vol. 62 (Princeton, NJ: Princeton University Press, 2016); and S. Bano (ed.), *Gender and Justice in Family Law Disputes: Women, Mediation, and Religious Arbitration* (Waltham, MA: Brandeis University Press, 2017).

7. See 'Sharia Law "Could Have UK Role"', *BBC News*, 4 July 2008: http://news.bbc.co.uk/2/hi/uk_news/7488790.stm.

8. S. Bano, 'In Pursuit of Religious and Legal Diversity: A Response to the Archbishop of Canterbury and the "Sharia Debate" in Britain', *Ecclesiastical Law Journal*, 10, no. 3 (2008): 283.

9. W. Woodward and R. Butt, 'Williams Defiant over Islamic Law Speech', *Guardian*, 9 February 2008: http://www.guardian.co.uk/politics/2008/feb/09/uk.religion.

10. T. Ramadan, *Western Muslims and the Future of Islam* (Oxford: Oxford University Press, 2004). Unfortunately, some French intellectuals completely fail to see this. In a translation of a co-authored article of mine published in a book by Presses de Sciences Po, the publisher (despite the efforts of the French editors) refused to publish the original footnote. This read, 'It is sadly ironic that such an integrationist is reviled by many French intellectuals and has been denied entry into the US, and was the target of a boycott attempt by the National Union of Students, who tried to exclude him from the 2004 European Social Forum (see www2.mpacuk.org)'. Instead, the publisher suggested: 'It ought to be remembered that Tariq Ramadan is a controversial scholar, that he has been under a lot of criticism from French intellectuals, and that his participation in the European Social Forum (2003) generated a great deal of controversy too'. Such academic censorship is a reflection of the demonization of one of the leading European Muslim intellectuals.

11. For an elaboration of this view, see my *Multiculturalism: A Civic Idea* (2007/2013).

Chapter Eight

Moderate Secularism, Religion as Identity and Respect for Religion

One of the features of the 'cultural turn' in social studies and of identity politics is that, while many think one or both may have gone too far, it is now commonplace that the classical liberal separation of culture and politics or the positivist/materialist distinctions between social structure and culture are mistaken. Yet religion – usually considered by social scientists to be an aspect of culture – continues to be uniquely held by some to be an aspect of social life that must be kept separate from at least the state, maybe from politics in general and perhaps even from public affairs at large, including the conversations that citizens have among themselves about their society. This religion/politics separationist view, which is clearly normative rather than scientific, can take quite different forms, either as an idea or as practice, and can be more or less restrictive, I shall call 'secularism'. While acknowledging the variety of forms it can take, I want to argue that one of the most important distinctions we need to make is between moderate and radical secularism. The failure to make this distinction is not just bad theory or bad social science but can lead to prejudicial, intolerant and exclusionary politics. I am particularly concerned with the prejudice and exclusion in relation to Muslims recently settled in Britain and the rest of Western Europe, but the points I wish to make have much more general application.

The chapter has three parts. First, I argue at an abstract level that it is not necessary to insist on absolute separation between religion and politics, though of course it is a possible interpretation of secularism. Second, radical separation does not make sense in terms of historical actuality and contemporary adjustments. Third, given that secularism does not necessarily mean the absence of state-religion connections, I explore five possible reasons for the state to be interested in religion.

RADICAL AND MODERATE SECULARISM

If secularism is a doctrine of separation, then we need to distinguish between modes of separation. Two modes of activity are separate when they have no connection with each other (absolute separation); but activities can still be distinct from each other even though there may be points of overlap (relative separation). The person who denies that politics and religion are absolutely separate can still allow for relative separation. For example, in contemporary Islam there are ideological arguments for the absolute subordination of politics to religious leaders, as (say) propounded by the Ayatollah Khomeni in his concept of the vilayat-i-faqih, but this is not mainstream Islam. Historically, Islam has been given a certain official status and pre-eminence in states in which Muslims ruled (just as Christianity or a particular Christian denomination had pre-eminence where Christians ruled). In these states Islam was the basis of state ceremonials and insignia, and public hostility against Islam was a punishable offence (sometimes a capital offence). Islam was the basis of jurisprudence but not positive law. The state functions – legislation, decrees, law enforcement, taxation, military power, foreign policy and so on – were all regarded as the prerogative of the ruler(s), of political power, which was regarded as having its own imperatives, skills and so on, and was rarely held by saints or spiritual leaders. Moreover, rulers had a duty to protect minorities. Similarly, while there have been Christians who have believed in or practised theocratic rule (e.g., Calvin in Geneva), this is not mainstream Christianity – at least not for some centuries.

Just as it is possible to distinguish between theocracy and mainstream Islam, and theocracy and modern Christianity, so it is possible to distinguish between radical or ideological secularism, which argues for an absolute separation between state and religion, and the moderate forms that exist where secularism has become the order of the day, particularly Western Europe,

Table 8.1.

Religion-state	Radical secularism	Radical public 'religionism'	Moderate secularism	Moderate public 'religionism'
1. Absolute separation	Yes	No	No	No
2. No separation	No	Yes	No	No
3. Relative separation	No	No	Yes	Yes

with the partial exception of France. In nearly all of Western Europe there are points of symbolic, institutional, policy and fiscal linkages between the state and aspects of Christianity. Secularism has increasingly grown in power and scope, but a historically evolved and evolving compromise with religion is the defining feature of Western European secularism, rather than the absolute separation of religion and politics. Today secularism does enjoy a hegemony in Western Europe, but it is a moderate rather than a radical – a pragmatic, rather than an ideological – secularism. Indeed, paradoxical as it may seem, Table 8.1 shows that mainstream religionist views and mainstream secularism are philosophically closer to each other than either is to its radical versions.

IS THERE A MAINSTREAM WESTERN SECULARISM?

Having established at an abstract level that mutual autonomy does not require separation, I would like to take further the point I have already begun making that while separation of religion and state/politics is a possible interpretation of secularism, it does not make sense in terms of historical actuality and contemporary adjustments. Rajeev Bhargava argues that 'in a secular state, a formal or legal union or alliance between state and religion is impermissible' and that 'for mainstream Western secularism, separation means mutual exclusion' (Bhargava 2009, 88). What does he mean by 'mainstream Western secularism'? His argument is that the secularism in the West has best developed in the United States and France, albeit in different ways. Americans have given primacy to religious liberty and the French to equality of citizenship, but in their differing ways they have come up with the best thinking on secularism that the West has to offer. 'These are the liberal and republican conceptions of secularism. Since these are the most dominant and defensible Western versions of secularism, I shall put them together and henceforth designate them as the mainstream conception of secularism' (Bhargava 2009, 93). Bhargava is critical of this conception of Western secularism, which understands secularism in terms of separation and 'mutual exclusion'; this is common ground between us and so, in my terms, he is a 'moderate' not a 'radical' secularist. He has principled arguments about the nature of secularism and believes that the Indian polity today better exemplifies these arguments than any Western polity (points which I do not address here). My concern here is with his characterisation of Western secularism. I believe he is mistaken in arguing that the United States and France are the best that the West has got to offer; nor are they the dominant/mainstream conceptions. His argument is based on a poor understanding of the British experience (which I know best) and of the Western European experience more generally. Most of Western, especially north-western Europe, where France is the exception not the rule, is best understood in more evolutionary and moderate terms than Bhargava's characterisation of Western secularism. They have several important features to do with a more pragmatic politics; with a sense of history, tradition and identity; and, most importantly, there is an accommodative character which is an essential feature of some historical and contemporary secularisms in practice. It is true that some political theorists and radical secularists have a strong tendency to abstract that out when talking about models and principles of secularism. If this tendency can be countered, British and other European experience ceases to be an inferior, non-mainstream instance of secularism but becomes mainstream and politically and normatively significant, if not superior to other versions.

Accommodative or moderate secularism, no less than liberal and republican secularism, can be justified in liberal, egalitarian, democratic terms, and in relation to a conception of citizenship. Yet it has developed a historical practice in which, explicitly or implicitly, organised religion is treated as a potential public good, which the state can in some circumstances assist to realise and without state support it may not be so well realised. This can take not only the form of an input into a legislative forum, such as the House of Lords, on moral and welfare issues; but also to being social partners to the state in the delivery of education, health and care services; to building social capital; or to churches belonging to 'the people'. So, even those who do not attend these churches, or even sign up to their doctrines, feel they have a right to use them for weddings and funerals. All this is part of what secularism means in most West European countries and it is quite clear that this is often lost in the models of secularism deployed by some normative theorists and public intellectuals. This is clearer today partly because of the development of our thinking in relation to the challenges of multicultural equality and the accommodation of Muslims, which highlight the limitations of the privatisation conception of liberal equality, and which sharpen the distinction between moderate/inclusive secularism and radical/ideological secularism. As can be seen in this book, I have been engaged in relating the accommodative spirit of moderate secularism to the contemporary demands of multiculturalism.

I would argue that it is quite possible in a country like Britain to treat the claims of all religions in accordance with multicultural equality without having to abolish the established status of the Church of England, given that it has come to be a very 'weak' form of establishment and the Church has come to play a positive ecumenical and multifaith role (Modood 1997; Parekh 2000, 257–261). Some other relevant considerations are nicely captured by John Madeley in his characterisation of an important strand in contemporary antidisestablishmentarianism:

> [A] residual opposition to and prejudice against what is seen as the unnecessary destruction or removal of those sets of arrangements, which have been found in many parts of Europe to make for the accommodation of religious diversity. It is not a doctrinal or ideological '-ism', more a rationalisation for a particular brand of cultural conservationism, which does not like to see old landmarks unnecessarily done away with and claims they are not to be valued as mere heritage but because they actually serve useful purposes . . . virtual quasi-establishment. (Madeley 2006, 404)

There is nothing in this that necessarily jeopardises equality of respect. Indeed, in approaching the reform of institutions, multiculturalists should be particularly sensitive to the ways that the historical and the inherited can be valued in a variety of ways, including giving people a sense of belonging and national identity.

Faced with an emergent multifaith situation or where there is a political will to incorporate previously marginalised faiths and sects and to challenge the privileged status of some religions, the context-sensitive and conservationist response may be to pluralise the state-religion link rather than sever it. This indeed is what is happening across many countries in Western Europe despite critics on both the left and the right, especially among the radical secularists and the Islamophobic populists (Modood and Kastoryano 2006). In relation to the British case, one can see it in a lot of incremental, ad hoc and experimental steps. For example, some years ago Prince Charles, the heir to the throne and to the office of Supreme Governor of the Church of England, let it be known he would, as monarch, prefer the title 'Defender of Faith' to the historic title 'Defender of the Faith' (Dimbleby 1994, 528). In 2004 the Queen used her Christmas television and radio broadcast – an important national occasion, especially for the older generation, on one of the most important Christian days of the year – to affirm the religious diversity of Britain. Her message was, in the words of Grace Davie,

> Religious diversity is something which enriches society; it should be seen as a strength, not a threat; the broadcast moreover was accompanied by shots of the Queen visiting a Sikh temple and a Muslim center. It is important to put these remarks in context. The affirmation of diversity as such is not a new idea in British society; what is new is the gradual recognition that religious differences should be foregrounded in such affirmations. Paradoxically, a bastion of privilege such as the monarchy turns out to be a key and very positive opinion former in this particular debate. (Davie 2007, 232–233)

If such examples are regarded as merely symbolic, then one should note how British governments have felt the need to create multifaith consultative bodies. The Conservatives created an Inner Cities Religious Council in 1992, chaired by a junior minister, which was replaced by New Labour in 2006 with a body having a much broader remit, the Faith Communities Consultative Council. Moreover, the new Department for Communities and Local Government, which is represented in the Cabinet, has a division devoted to faith communities. Or better still, consider an example of a high-level proposal (not yet acted up on and which may not be acted up on) that combines the symbolic and practical at a constitutional level – namely, the recommendations of the Royal Commission on the Reform of the House of Lords (2000), as mentioned in chapter 2. It argued that the House of Lords, the U.K. upper chamber, should be 'a relatively non-polemical forum for national debate, informed by the range of different perspectives which its members should have'. Members should, among other things, have 'the ability to bring a philosophical, moral or spiritual perspective to bear' (Royal Commission on the Reform of the House of Lords 2000, 151). The Royal Commission believed that it was time to end the hereditary principle of membership of the House but it did not recommend a wholly elected chamber. It thought that its ideals would be better met if part of the House continued to be unelected. The latter includes one of the elements of 'establishment' – namely, the right of 26 Anglican bishops to sit in the Lords. The Royal Commission endorsed this principle but argued that the number of Anglican bishops should be reduced to 16 and that they should be joined by five representatives of other Christian denominations in England, five seats should be allocated to other Christian denominations in the rest of the United Kingdom and a further five should be used to include the presence of non-Christians. Hence, the Commission sought to make up the democratic deficit that arises when national fora are completely dominated by party politicians by proposing not just an increase in the width of religious representation but also in the numerical increase from 26 to 31 seats.

Such proposals might be regarded as a form of reforming or pluralising establishment without abolishing it. It suggests that 'weak establishment' can be the basis for moving towards 'multicultural equality' without constitutional disestablishment (cf. Bader 2007). I am not contending that some version of establishment (weak or plural) is the only way or the best way of institutionalising religious pluralism in Britain or similar countries. My point is that a reformed establishment can be one way of institutionalising religious pluralism. In certain historical and political circumstances, it may indeed be a good way: we should be wary of ruling it out by arguments that appeal to 'the dominant and defensible western versions of secularism' (Bhargava 2009, 93). Stronger still: such institutional accommodation of minority or marginal faiths runs with the grain of mainstream Western European historical practice.

WHY THE STATE MIGHT BE INTERESTED IN RELIGION

Having then established that the separation of state and religion is neither a necessary feature of secularism in terms of abstract logic nor in terms of mainstream practice, I would now like to consider some of the reasons why the state might be interested in religion. I leave aside state attacks on religion such as those by the Jacobins, Soviet Union or Communist China that are characteristic of totalitarian secularism. I shall confine myself to democratic examples and to affirmative reasons. I offer here five types of policy reasons in a typology of my own devising. The issue I am exploring is: What kind of reason is a particular proposal or institutional purpose appealing to, what distinguishes it and what kind of legitimacy might it have? I am not arguing that these lines of reasoning lead to obvious policy results – that would require a much greater degree of contextualisation than I offer here – and I am not trying to determine policies. While I appreciate, of course, that all actual cases can consist of a mix of reasons, my typology of reasons is as follows:

1. Truth
2. Danger
3. Usefulness
4. Identity
5. Worthy of respect

I shall discuss them in this order but will give most attention to the last two: religion as identity and respect for religion.

POLICY BASED ON RELIGION AS TRUTH

If we consider 'policy' here to mean the state as a whole (i.e., as a holistic structure), then the idea that it is based on a putative truth as understood by a religion is clearly not compatible with democracy and certainly not a democratic multiculturalism. This is not necessarily because it is religious but because it is a totalitarian ideology; the same would apply to totalitarian secularism. As is the case with Plato's ideal republic based on the truth as understood by a philosophical Guardian, such totalitarian states would also fail to respect the autonomy and integrity of politics and/or religion.

There is a real sense, as Plato noted, that democracy is based on opinions, not truth. Having said that, it does not follow that there may be no scope for truth. Consider the famous declaration from the U.S. Declaration of Independence: 'We hold these truths to be self-evident that all men are created equal, that they are endowed by their Creator with certain inalienable Rights, that among these are Life, Liberty and the pursuit of Happiness' ('Declaration of Independence' 1776). This truth, however, was not reiterated in the Constitution (1787) itself and so is at least one step removed from specific policies and laws; as I earlier suggested, this is similar to most Muslim-majority states, which do conceive of the relationship between Islam and the state – namely, as foundational rather than in terms of positive law.

What about specific policies that are alleged to be based on religious truth, such as policies relating to abortion or genetic engineering? I am not sure, but in principle I think such policies probably would be acceptable if the policy proposal was subject to a democratic process, implemented within a framework of individual rights and allowed for exemptions on grounds of conscience (Bader 2007).

So, specific policies based on religious truth are probably compatible with democracy and multiculturalism, but in any case some of the remaining ways in which policies relate to religion are compatible. Of any proposal based on religious truth, we might want to ask if it is justifiable by reference to any of the others below rather than dismiss it per se.

Just as we can study physics without having a view as to whether God exists, so the state may not have a view on whether God exists or whether any religion is true. But that does not mean that the state is not interested in religion.

POLICY BASED ON RELIGION AS DANGER

This might seem odd to include here as I had said I was only interested in 'affirmative' reasons. I include it because where religion in general, or a particular religion or aspect of a religion, is thought to be dangerous and in need of state control – for instance, because otherwise social peace or unity is at serious risk – control might mean supporting favoured religious institutions. We see this in the case of how one of the most intolerant (semi-)-democratic secular states, Turkey, has a whole government department devoted to propagating, funding and staffing a particular version of Islam.[1] The French state does something similar in relation to versions of Catholicism, Protestantism and Judaism and is trying to do the same with Islam (Bowen 2007). The British government has for some years been seriously considering whether and how it needs to be involved in the training of imams, and on a more dramatic scale, it had to work with Catholics and Protestants, clerics as well as others, in order to end political violence in Northern Ireland. Indeed, nowadays many governments' security services are involved in monitoring Muslims and Islamic organisations; and which one supposes are deeply infiltrated as the IRA once was. Just as the IRA's defeat was dependent on the government winning the trust and cooperation of the Catholics, so one supposes must be the case in relation to Muslim communities vis-à-vis jihadi terrorism.

So, you do not have to think religion is always benign in order to support it or interact with it; the pursuit of the public good may sometimes require constraining, and not just supporting, religion, or a judicious mix of the two. In any event, both support and constraining involve regulation.

POLICY BASED ON RELIGION AS UTILITY

Religion may be a very personal thing but it can produce social outcomes, some of which may be desirable or undesirable in the view of the state, and so the state might wish to encourage or discourage religion. For example, suppose it were true that religious people are less likely to commit crime or less likely to have a marriage breakdown, with all of its attendant problems; this may be regarded as a reason to encourage the relevant religion regardless of whether one believed in it or not oneself. Some people have believed that while adults can do without religion, it nevertheless is pedagogically important; that it may be a good way to inculcate morals because it provides an imaginative scaffolding for moral precepts, or assists the development of the imagination in general (Collingwood 1924, 124–125). A research project I was involved in shows that among young British Pakistani working-class males there are high dropout rates from school but the rates are lower among those who say they practise Islam (Dwyer et al. 2011; cf. Modood 2004). So, any of these may be, at least hypothetically, reasons for the state to support religious institutions in the hope that, however indirectly, certain outcomes would follow that would lessen the scale of certain social problems and reduce the cost of remedies to the public purse.

More directly, the state may observe religious organisations as serving the needy – the poor, the aged, the homeless and so on – either just within their own communities or more generally, and these may be economical ways of providing certain services which the market could not provide and which the state would provide less economically or with more political difficulties. So the state may choose to fund these religious organisations.[2]

POLICY BASED ON RELIGION AS IDENTITY

This may work in relation to identity at a number of levels.

1. Individual identity

For example: I am an X (e.g., a taxpayer) and so want Y (e.g., a certain kind of school). The same identity appeal can be generalised: We are X and so want Y.

2. Public or civic identity

This may refer to an identity as a polity or a country: We are a Christian country and so Christianity should be taught in schools or be referred to in the Constitution and so on. This does not have to be a particularly conservative argument. The same logic is present in the following: We are no longer a Christian country and have to remake the national identity to reflect new inclusions, or we need to have multifaith schools or a plurality of schools within the state system and reflected in the national curriculum.

3. Minority identity

The state may note that certain religious groups and identities are stigmatised. An example is the finding of a Pew Survey (2008) of public opinion that a quarter of Britons and Americans, nearly four in ten French, and half of the Spaniards, Germans and Poles surveyed displayed hostility to Muslims. As with other kinds of stigmatised, marginalised or oppressed minorities, there may be a project to turn these negative identities into positive ones. This would be particularly important if the minorities in question valued this aspect of their identity and especially if they valued it more than was the norm in that society. This is precisely the case in Britain, for example. The 2001 Home Office Citizenship Survey shows that while those who say they have no religion are disproportionately from the advantaged and the powerful (i.e., they are more likely to be white, male and middle class) and only 17 per cent of whites say that religion is important to their self-identity, the numbers for black and South Asian respondents are 44 and 61 per cent respectively (O'Beirne 2004, 18). Religion, then, is clearly an ethnic feature of Britain, not just in the sense that most whites are Christians and most non-whites are not, but also in terms of the personal, social and political salience and significance of religion, as in the concept of ethno-religious, as discussed in chapter 5.

State action in this context could include the following:

a. Anti-discrimination measures in relation to religious groups (as discussed in chapter 6)

b. Even-handedness in relation to resources

Where one or some religions, perhaps for historical reasons, have a certain status, these may need to be made available to the previously absent or excluded minority faiths too. This can be done without strict 'equality'. For example, as the leading Anglican prelate, the Archbishop of Canterbury crowns the British monarch. Other faiths could be invited to share in this ceremony in some way without necessarily all having the same grand role (and even if they did, the question would be in what order). In other cases, one might judge that even-handedness required granting a special status to some religious groups but not to the population in general. This could be an exemption such as those enjoyed by the male, turban-wearing Sikhs in Britain in relation to the laws on motorcycle/bicycle helmets and 'hard hats' on building sites. Moreover, one can imagine that some special provisions may be created for a minority as a disadvantaged group, perhaps even without there being a corresponding provision for the majority faith. For instance, in Britain certain advisory and consultative bodies have been created in relation to Muslims but not other religious groups because it is perceived that Muslims have certain problems (e.g., 'radicalisation') that others do not have. This is comparable to the fact that we have a Minister for Women but not a Minister for Men. Another example would be that in March 2008, Britain repealed the blasphemy law, which related only to Christianity, because of the general feeling, shared by many Christians, that it did not need this protection, while an offence of religious hatred has been created because of, as discussed in chapters 3 and 6, a perception of vulnerability on the part of some minorities (though technically Christians are covered by it).

It should be noted that minority identity protection or recognition can apply not just where the majority is of one religion but also where it is non-religious. Some people seem to think that if there is not one populous religion, then there is an absence of hegemony or domination, but there could be a secularist or even an anti-religion hegemony in relation to which a minority provision may be sought.

c. Criterion of inclusivity

Just as we sometimes use gender, race and ethnicity as criteria to test the inclusivity of an institution (e.g., a workplace, a university or a legislature), so it may be thought appropriate to use religious identity. Just as a civil service under-represented by female managers might need a remedial policy, so similarly it might need a policy to address the under-representation of Muslims in senior posts. The issue is not confined to numerical presence but crucially extends to the symbolic remaking of public/common/national identities. Minority religious identities may need to be explicitly recognised in our sense of what the country is and will be in the future (see chapter 5). This is about minorities such as Muslims as co-citizens and worthy of respect as co-citizens; it is not in any way an endorsement of a particular religion such as Islam (that would be the first case: policy based on religion as truth).

d. Dialogue/Multilogue

The whole process of minority identity recognition should be dialogical, or more precisely, multilogical, because there are many parties and all are entitled to speak. That is the way of finding out about identities, negotiating compromises, the remaking of new identities and so on, but also of identifying the problems and discussing and finding solutions (as discussed in chapter 12).

Someone might be opposed to minority identity and recognition for a number of reasons and I would like to address one – namely, that minority identities are decomposing and becoming privatised so the kind of identities needed for recognition or accommodation are not available. Actually, I draw on this sociology myself and, while I think it complicates recognition, I don't believe it kills it off (Modood 2007/2013).

In his seminal essay, 'New Ethnicities', Stuart Hall argued that there has been a shift from taken-for-granted, singular cultural, ethnic and collective identities to self-conscious identities – the 'innocent black subject' is a thing of the past (if that) (Hall 1992, 252–259). People are active in identity formation; indeed, racial and ethnic identities are not merely ascribed, they are a form of agency in all senses of the term. Interestingly, this means, though Hall did not draw this implication, that a commonly drawn contrast between race as ascription and religion as choice no longer holds.

Not only are these identities impure, hybridic, fluid and varied but for some their significance will also be associational rather than merely or primarily behavioural. For example, in the Fourth National Survey of Ethnic Minorities, virtually everybody with an ethnic minority background said their ethnic identity was important to them and large majorities said their religious identity was important to them, but some of these individuals did nothing distinctively 'ethnic' in behavioural or 'religious' terms (Modood et al. 1997). This can have policy implications; for example, while about 50 per cent of Muslims wanted Muslim faith schools within the state sector, only half of these individuals said they would send their own children to one if it was available locally (in 1994). This may not be just about abstract fairness (if Christians have state-funded schools so should Muslims). Some Muslims can see their own identities in some ways as negativised (i.e., there is something wrong with Muslims): perhaps some kind of sentiment such as 'Most Muslims are problematic but you are okay!' It blocks the way for the 'OK Muslims', too, for they may think, 'If that is the way you think about Muslims or if joining you is to accept that view then I cannot join you'.

Perhaps 'new ethnicities' identities are not so radically new. For example, participation in religious activities can be for a variety of reasons, including some that could be regarded as less than fully religious. For example, it is interesting that in describing how he came as an adult to embrace the Christian faith, President Barack Obama does not mention Jesus or the Resurrection but rather, the hope and dignity it has given to African Americans to survive their personal and social suffering, to find 'a way out of no way'. Or consider how some Jewish synagogue attendance or Hanukkah or Sabbath observation may be for family and community rather than faith reasons – and so may raise time off and bank holiday–type issues for someone who is not a deep believer. In any case, 'new ethnicity' associational identities have a particular political force at the moment with some minority identities.

Olivier Roy has applied this kind of sociology to Muslims internationally. He suggests that Muslims, especially younger Muslims and those in the West, are much less likely than their parents or previous generations to do or believe things just because it is the done thing in their faith community (Roy 2004). They are less likely to be customary or conventional or obedient Muslims and more likely to think about and question what it means to be Muslim and to come up with their own answers, which may radically vary among themselves as well as with customary or authoritative Islam. I think this is right, but calling it 'individualisation', as Roy does, is quite misleading, for in some contexts that is seen as a corollary of 'privatisation' and 'secularisation'. These identities are not private. Increased personal and associational agency is a constitutive feature of these identities but the questions being asked by the relevant individuals – What does it mean to be a Muslim? What kind of a Muslim am I? – typically are open to public projections of identity commitment and contestations. What are at stake are indeed public identities and so contemporary British and other Muslim assertiveness can at least partly be understood in terms of identity politics and accommodated within a civic multiculturalism and existing secularist institutional accommodation of religion.

POLICY BASED ON RESPECT FOR RELIGION

There is an image of religion as organisations or communities around competing truths, which are mutually intolerant, which perhaps even hate each other's guts. There is some truth in that, in some times and places, but the opposite is more important. Let me illustrate this by reference to the decision of my late father, a devout and pious Muslim, that I should attend the daily Christian non-denominational worship at my secondary school. When I told him that I could be exempted from it, like the Jewish children, if he sent in a letter requesting this, he asked what they did during this time each morning. When I told him that some read comics, some took the opportunity to catch up with homework and some even arrived late, he said I should join the assembly. He said that as Christians mainly believe what we believe, I should join in fully but whenever it was said that Jesus was the Son of God, I should say to myself, 'no, he is not'. It is a view that can perhaps be expressed as this: It is better to be in the presence of religion than not and so the value of religion does not simply reside in one's own religion. One's own religious heritage is to be cherished and honoured but so are those of others and the demise of any religion is a loss of some sort.

I would suggest that historically it has been a prevalent view in the Middle East and South Asia that respect for the religion of others has extended to joining in the religious celebrations of others, borrowing from others, syncretism and so on (e.g., Mazower 2006). Respect for religion does not, however, require syncretism and can be found among contemporary Muslims in the West. Reporting on a recent Gallup World Poll, Dalia Mogahed, and Zsolt Nyiri write of Muslims in Paris and London that their 'expectations of respect for Islam and its symbols extend to an expectation of respect for religion in general' and add that recently 'Shahid Malik, a [now, former] British Muslim MP, even complained about what he called the "policy wonks" who wished to strip the public sphere of all Christian religious symbols' (Mogahed and Nyiri 2007). It is an attitude that the West (where mono-religion has been the historical norm) can certainly learn from, as I think some people of my generation realised and which is evidenced in the interest in the spiritualities of 'the East'.[3] Respect for religion is clearly beyond mere toleration but also beyond utility, for this valuing of religion and respect for the religion of others, even while not requiring participation, is based on a sense that religion is a fundamental good in itself and part of our humanity at a personal, social and civilisational level: it is an ethical good and so to be respected as a feature of human character just as we might respect truth seeking, the cultivation of the intellect or the imagination, or artistic creativity or self-discipline, not just because of its utility or truth. We can think of religion as a good of this sort regardless of whether one is a believer or not, just as we can think of music or science as a good whether we are musical or scientific or not. A person, a society, a culture, a country would be poorer without religion. It is part of good living and, while not all can cultivate it fully, some do and they should be honoured and supported by others.

This view could be part of 'Religion as Truth' but is not dependent upon it or any kind of theism because it can be a feature of some form of ethical humanism. I think it can be justified within a philosophy of human plurality and multi-dimensionality of the kind to be found in, for example, R. G. Collingwood's *Speculum Mentis* (1924) or Michael Oakeshott's *Experience and Its Modes* (1933).

Respect for religion is, however, clearly more than respect recognition or recognition of religious minorities, and while I am mainly concerned to argue for the latter, I am open to the former, especially as I believe that respect for religion of others is quite common among religious believers (the mirror-image of Richard Dawkins's view of religious believers) and I worry about an intolerant secularist hegemony. There may once have been a time in Europe when a powerful, authoritarian church or churches stifled dissent, individuality, free debate, science, pluralism and so on, but that is not the present danger. Since the 1960s, European cultural, intellectual and political life – the public sphere in the fullest sense of the term – is increasingly becoming dominated by secularism, with secularist networks and organisations controlling most of the levers of power. The accommodative character of secularism itself is being dismissed as archaic – especially on the center-left. Thus, respect for religion is made difficult and seems outlandish but may be necessary as one of the sources of counter-hegemony and a more genuine pluralism. Hence, respect for religion is compatible with and may be a requirement of a democratic political culture.

I appreciate that this may seem to be, and indeed may be a form of, 'privileging' religion. For in this idea that the state may wish to show respect for religion, I am going beyond not just toleration and freedom of religion but also beyond civic recognition. Nor am I simply pointing to the existence of overlaps and linkages between the state and religion. The sense of 'privilege' may not, however, be as strong as it may seem. After all, the autonomy of politics is the privileging of the non-religious, so this is perhaps qualifying that secular privileging. Moreover, it is far from an exclusive privileging. States regularly 'privilege' the nation, ethnicity, science, the arts, sport, economy and so on in relation to the centrality they give it in policymaking, the public resources devoted to it or the prestige placed upon it. So, if showing respect for religion is a privileging of religion, it is of a multiplex, multilogical sort (as explained in the introduction, and see chapter 10); and it is based on the recognition that the secular is already dominant in many contemporary states.

In any case, I offer my comments on respect for religion more tentatively than in relation to some of the other elements of my typology. While each of them may have a place within a moderate secularism, we clearly need to separate the five positions and differentiate between their normative justifications and policy implications, but we may still wish to appeal to more than one of them at a time or for different policy measures; or perhaps to appeal to some of them without repudiating the others.

NOTES

1. Interestingly, under the rule of the Moderate Islamist Party, the Truth and Development Party (AKP), Turkey had started moving away from its intolerant state secularism towards a more Western European version at the time this chapter was first written (2009) but this trend lasted less than five years after that. Erdogan seems to have adopted an even more authoritarian form of government than that of the radical secularists.

2. Some of this thinking was part of Prime Minister Cameron's 'Big Society' idea which, ironically, by empowering and resourcing local neighbourhoods and religious communities,

seems to be an example of the 'state multiculturalism' policies he deplored (Modood 2007/2013).

3. Sadly one must also acknowledge that in recent decades, in 'the East' the respect for religion I speak of has been put under great pressure by various forms of majoritarian, often religious, nationalism.

REFERENCES

Bader, V. (2007). *Secularism or Democracy: Associational Governance of Religious Diversity.* Amsterdam: Amsterdam University Press.

Bhargava, R. (2006). 'Political Secularism'. In Dryzek, John S., Honig, Bonnie and Phillips, Anne (eds.), *The Oxford Handbook of Political Theory*, 636–655. Oxford: Oxford University Press.

Bhargava, R. (2009). 'Political Secularism'. Reproduced in Levey, G. B. and Modood, T. (eds.), *Secularism, Religion and Multicultural Citizenship*, 82–109. Cambridge: Cambridge University Press.

Bowen, J. (2007). *Why the French Don't Like Headscarves: Islam, the State and Public Space.* Princeton, NJ: Princeton University Press.

Collingwood, R. G. (1924). *Speculum Mentis, or The Map of Knowledge.* Oxford: Oxford University Press.

Davie, G. (2007). 'Pluralism, Tolerance, and Democracy: Theory and Practice in Europe'. In Banchoff, T. (ed.), *Democracy and the New Religious Pluralism*, 223–241. New York: Oxford University Press.

'Declaration of Independence'. (1776). National Archives: America's Founding Documents. https://www.archives.gov/founding-docs/declaration-transcript.

Dimbley, D. (1994). *Prince of Wales, A Biography.* London: Little Brown.

Dwyer, C., Modood, T., Sanghera, G., Shah, B. and Thapar-Björkert, S. (2011). 'Educational Achievement and Career Aspiration among Young British Pakistanis'. In Modood, T. and Salt, J. (eds.), *Global Migration, Ethnicity and Britishness*, Pt. III, 177–204. London: Palgrave.

Hall, S. (1992). 'New Ethnicities'. In Donald, J. and Rattansi, A. (eds.), *'Race', Culture and Difference*, 252–259. London: Sage.

Madeley, J. (2006). 'Religion, Politics and Society in Europe: Still the Century of Antidisestablishmentarianism?'. *European Political Science*, 5(4), 395–406.

Mazower, M. (2006). *Salonica, City of Ghosts: Christians, Muslims and Jews, 1430–1950.* New York: Alfred A. Knopf.

Modood, T. (ed.). (1997). *Church, State and Religious Minorities.* London: Policy Studies Institute.

Modood, T. (2004). 'Capitals, Ethnic Identity and Educational Qualifications'. *Cultural Trends*, 13(2), 87–105.

Modood, T. (2007/2013). *Multiculturalism: A Civic Idea.* Cambridge: Polity Press.

Modood, T. (2011a). 'Is There a Secular Crisis in Western Europe?'. *The Immanent Frame*, August 24. http://blogs.ssrc.org/tif/2011/08/24/is-there-a-crisis-of-secularism-in-western-europe/.

Modood, T. (2011b). 'Multiculturalism and Integration: Struggling with Confusions'. In Mahamdallie, H. (ed.), *Defending Multiculturalism.* London: Bookmarks.

Modood, T., Berthoud, R., Lakey, J., Nazroo, J., Smith, P., Virdee, S. and Beishon, S. (1997). *Ethnic Minorities in Britain: Diversity and Disadvantage.* London: Policy Studies Institute.

Modood, T. and Kastoryano, R. (2006). 'Secularism and the Accommodation of Muslims in Europe'. In Modood, T., Triandafyllidou, A. and Zapata-Barrero, R. (eds.), *Multiculturalism, Muslims and Citizenship: A European Approach*, 162–178. London and New York: Routledge.

Mogahed, D. and Nyiri, Z. (2007). 'Reinventing Integration: Muslims in the West'. *Harvard International Review*, 29(2), 14–18.

Nizami, K. A. (1974). *Some Aspects of Religion and Politics in India during the Thirteenth Century* (2nd ed.). Delhi: Idarah-i-Adbiyat-i-Delhi.

Oakeshott, M. (1933). *Experience and Its Modes*. Cambridge: Cambridge University Press.

Obama, B. (2007). *The Audacity of Hope: Thoughts on Reclaiming the American Dream*. Edinburgh: Cannongate.

O'Beirne, M. (2004). *Religion in England and Wales: Findings from the 2001 Home Office Citizenship Survey*. Home Office Research Study 274. London: Home Office Research.

Parekh, B. (2000). *Rethinking Multiculturalism: Cultural Diversity and Political Theory*. Basingstoke, UK: Macmillan.

Pew Global Attitudes Survey. (2008). *Unfavourable Views of Jews and Muslims on the Increase in Europe*. Pew Research Center: Global Attitudes & Trends, September 17. http://www.pewresearch.org/wp-content/uploads/sites/2/2008/09/Pew-2008-Pew-Global-Attitudes-Report-3-September-17-2pm.pdf.

Roy, O. (2004). *Globalised Islam*. London: C. Hurst.

Royal Commission on the Reform of the House of Lords. (2000). *A House for the Future*. London: HMSO.

Chapter Nine

Multiculturalism and the 'Crisis of Secularism'

One of the distinctive features of this book is its placing questions about the nature and reform of political secularism as central to multiculturalism today, at least in Western Europe. This is due to the triple contingency of the arrival and settlement of a significant number of Muslims; a multiculturalist sensibility which respects 'difference'; and a moderate secularism – namely, that the historical compromises between the state and a church or churches in relation to public recognition and accommodation are still in place to some extent. In chapter 6, I argued that radical secularism or *laïcité* seems to be struggling to cope but the dominant version of secularism, far from being in crisis, offers a resource – suitably multiculturalized – for accommodating the new religious plurality of the region. An increasing number of academics think that we are experiencing a crisis of secularism. Jürgen Habermas, who has Western Europe very much at the forefront of his mind, has famously announced we are currently witnessing a transition from a secular to a 'post-secular society' in which 'secular citizens' have to express a previously denied respect for 'religious citizens', who should be allowed, even encouraged, to critique aspects of contemporary society and to find solutions to its problems from within their religious views (Habermas 2006). Instead of treating religion as subrational and a matter of private concern only, religion is once again to be recognized as a legitimate basis of public engagement and political action.[1] Some have gone further and speak of a global crisis. Even quite sober academics speak of 'a contemporary crisis of secularism' (Scherer 2010, 4), claiming that 'today, political secularisms are in crisis in almost every corner of the globe' (Jakelić 2010, 3). Olivier Roy, in an analysis focused on France, writes of 'the crisis of the secular state' (Roy 2007), and Rajeev Bhargava of the 'crisis of the secular state in Europe' (Bhargava

2010; 2011).[2] I think, however, that as far as Western Europe is concerned, the 'crisis of secularism' is really the challenge of post-immigration multiculturalism.

There seems to be no endogenous slowing down in the decline of secularization in relation to organized religion, attendance at church services and traditional Christian belief and practice in Western Europe. For example, to illustrate with the British case, church attendance of at least once a month has steadily declined from about 20 per cent in 1983 to about 15 per cent in 2008 among white people and with each younger age cohort (Voas and Crockett 2005; BRIN 2011; Kaufmann, Goujon and Skirbekk 2012).[3] This is not to say that religion has disappeared or is about to, but for many it has become more in the form of 'belief without belonging' (Davie 1994), or spirituality (Heelas and Woodhead 2005), or 'implicit religion' (Bailey 1997). For example, while belief in a personal God has gone down from more than 40 per cent in the middle of the twentieth century to less than 30 per cent by its end, belief in a spirit or life source has remained steady at around 35–40 per cent, and belief in the soul has actually increased from less than 60 per cent in the early 1980s to an additional 5–10 per cent by 2008 (BRIN 2011). All these changes, however, are highly compatible with political secularism, if not with scientism or other rationalistic philosophies. Whether the decline of traditional religion is being replaced by no religion or new ways of being religious or spiritual, neither is creating a challenge for political secularism. Non-traditional forms of Christian or post-Christian religion in Western Europe are in the main not attempting to connect with or reform political institutions and government policies; they are not seeking recognition or political accommodation or political power.[4]

The challenge to political secularism in Western Europe lies not in any slowing down of secularization, but in the presence of Muslims.[5] With estimates of 12 to more than 17 million Muslims in Western Europe today, the Muslim population in the former E.U. 15 is only about 3–5 per cent and is relatively evenly distributed across the larger states (Peach 2007; Pew Forum 2017). In the larger cities, the proportion which is Muslim, however, is several times larger and, being young and fertile, is growing at a faster rate than most of the population (Lutz, Skirbekk and Testa 2007). In this context – with the riots in the *banlieues* of Paris and elsewhere, the Danish cartoon affair and other issues about offence and freedom of speech, and the proliferating bans on various forms of female Muslim dress just being a few in a series of conflicts focused on minority-majority relations – questions about integration, equality, racism and Islam, and their relation to terrorism, security and foreign policy, have become central to European politics.

The issue, then, driving the sense of a crisis of secularism in Western Europe is the place of Muslim identities, or identities that are perceived to be ethno-religious (such as British Asian Muslim or Arab Muslim in France).

This multicultural challenge to secularism is among the most profound political and long-term issues arising from the post-war Western European hunger for labour migrants and the reversal of the population flows of European colonialism. The challenge is far from confined to secularism. It is a broad one: from socio-economic disadvantage and discrimination in the labour markets at one end, to a constitutional status or corporate relationship with the state at the other. Moreover, the awareness of this challenge began to manifest itself and was perceived before events such as 9/11; nor is it due to the fact that some Muslims, unlike other post-immigration groups, may have been involved in rowdy demonstrations and riots, because others (such as African Caribbeans in Britain) are associated with these without raising such profound normative questions.

Nor is it due to (Muslim) conservative values, especially in relation to gender and sexuality, though it is related to it. The core element of the challenge is the primacy given to religion as the basis of identity, organization, political representation, normative justification and so on. These matters were thought to be more or less settled (except in a few exceptional cases like Northern Ireland) until some Muslims began asserting themselves as Muslims in the public sphere of various West European countries. Some have thought that primacy could be given to, say, gender, ethnicity or class; others that primacy should not be given to any one or even a few of these social categories as identity self-concepts, but very few thought that religion should be in the select set (Modood 2005; Modood, Triandafyllidou and Zapata-Barrero 2006).

The rising multicultural challenge and the gradual weakening of the political status of Christian churches – in particular, the national churches – has been taking place at the same time. The intersection of these two trajectories is nicely captured in two policy initiatives in the Netherlands in 1983. In that year, the national system of 'pillarization', which had made the country a bi-religious communal state, was formally wound up, while simultaneously a new Minorities Policy (*Nota Minderhedenbeleid*) was being announced (see Bader 2011; Lentin and Titley 2011, 107–108), which created post-immigration ethnic minorities (*allochtones*) as a mini-pillar, giving them state funding for faith schools, ethno-religious radio and TV broadcasting and other forms of cultural maintenance (Bader 2011). Some of that policy began to be reversed in the 1990s, but, looking beyond the Netherlands, the pivotal moment was 1988–1989 and was, quite accidentally, marked by two events. These created national and international storms, setting in motion political developments that have not been reversed, and reveal contrasting responses by the two Western European secularisms to the Muslim presence. The events were the protests in Britain against Sir Salman Rushdie's novel *The Satanic Verses*; and, in France, the decision by a school head teacher to prohibit entry to three girls unless they removed their headscarves in school premises.

MODERATE AND RADICAL SECULARIST RESPONSES TO MUSLIM ASSERTIVENESS

The Satanic Verses was not banned in the United Kingdom as the protestors demanded, and the conduct of some Muslims, especially those threatening the life of the author, certainly shocked and alienated many from the campaign. In that sense, the Muslim campaign clearly failed. In other respects, however, it galvanized many into seeking a democratic multiculturalism that was inclusive of Muslims. A national body was created to represent mainstream Muslim opinion, initially in relation to the novel (UK Action Committee on Islamic Action), but later, with some encouragement from both the main national political parties, especially New Labour, it led to the formation of a body to lobby on behalf of Muslims in the corridors of power. This new body, the Muslim Council of Britain (MCB), was accepted as a major consultee by the New Labour government of 1997, until about the middle of the next decade when it sought to diversify its Muslim interlocutors. The MCB was very successful in relation to its founding agenda (Modood 2010). By 2001, it had achieved its aim of having Muslim issues and Muslims as a group recognized separately from issues of race and ethnicity; and of being itself accepted by government, media and civil society as the spokesperson for Muslims. Another two achieved aims were the introduction of state funding of Muslim schools on the same basis as Christian and Jewish schools; and in getting certain educational and employment policies targeted on the severe disadvantage of the Pakistanis and Bangladeshis (who are nearly all Muslims) as opposed to on minority ethnicity generally. Additionally, it played a decisive role in Tony Blair's inclusion of a religious question in the 2001 census despite ministerial and civil service advice to the contrary (Sherif 2011). This laid the foundation for a possible later introduction of policies targeting Muslims to match those targeting groups defined by race or ethnicity – or gender. The MCB had to wait a bit longer for the legislative protection it sought. Laws against religious discrimination were introduced in 2003, strengthened in 2007 and again in 2010, making them much stronger than anything available in the rest of the European Union. Incitement to religious hatred, the legislation most closely connected to the protests over *The Satanic Verses*, was introduced in 2006, though there is no suggestion that it would have caught that novel. Indeed, the protestors' original demand that the blasphemy law be extended to cover Islam has been made inapplicable as the blasphemy law was abolished in 2008 – with very little protest from anybody. Moreover, even as the MCB, because of its views on the government's foreign and security policies, fell out of favour, local and national consultations with Muslim groups has continued to grow and under New Labour probably exceeded consultations with any Christian body and certainly any minority group. Inevitably, this has caused occasional friction between Christians and Muslims. But on the whole these developments have taken place not only with the support of the leadership of the Church of England, but in a spirit of interfaith respect.[6]

That, then, is one path of development from 1988–1989. It was a mobilization of a minority, with the extension of minority policies from race to religion in order to accommodate the religious minority. The other development – namely, the one arising from *l'affaire foulard* was one of top-down state action to prohibit certain minority practices. From the start, the majority of the country – whether it be the media, the public intellectuals, the politicians or public opinion – supported the head teacher who refused to have religious headscarves in school (Bowen 2007; Scott 2007).[7] Muslims either did not wish to or lacked the capacity to challenge this dominant view with anything like the publicity, organization, clamour or international assistance that Muslims in Britain brought to bear on Rushdie's novel.

The Conseil d'État, France's highest administrative court, emphasized freedom of religion as long as the religious symbols were not 'ostentatious', and so ruled that the issue should be treated on a case-by-case basis (Kastoryano 2006; see also Bowen 2007). This quietened things down till they blew up again in 1994 in relation to another state school. On that occasion, the Minister of Education forbade the wearing of any ostentatious symbols, which explicitly included the headscarf. The issue would not go away, however, and in 2003 President Chirac appointed a national commission, chaired by Bernard Stasi, to consider the issue. The Stasi Commission recommended the banning of the wearing of conspicuous religious symbols in state schools, and a law to this effect was passed with an overwhelming majority by Parliament in February 2004. A few years later, the target of secularist and majoritarian disapproval was the full face veil that revealed only the eyes (niqab; burqa), as favoured by a few hundred Muslim women. This was banned in public places in April 2011, with Belgium following suit in July. Meanwhile related bans have been enacted in Germany and Denmark, and other European states are considering doing the same (Ferrari and Pastorelli 2016). Even in Britain there is popular support for a ban, and though the major parties have no truck with it, UKIP adopted it as policy commitment in 2017 (Elgot 2017).

While the radical secularist (*laïcité*) trajectory of the banning of some headdress favoured by some Muslim women was taking place, another was simultaneously taking place in France and elsewhere, which is important to note as it does not so easily conform to the common understanding of French *laïcité*.[8] Since 1990 each French government, whether of the left or the right, has set about trying to create a national Muslim council that would be a corporate representative of Muslims in France and the official government consultee. It would be the state's recognition of Islam, comparable in some respects to its recognition of the Catholic Church, Protestant churches and the Jewish Consistory. After at least three abortive attempts by previous Interior Ministers, Nicholas Sarkozy, when in that post, inaugurated the Conseil Français du Culte Musulman in 2003 (Modood and Kastoryano 2006, 174–175). Even now, this council is not yet accepted by the majority of Muslims in France and has little influence with the French media, civil society or government. Its importance for my argument does not depend on its effectiveness or on whether it has support among Muslims in France. Rather, it exhibits how even a laicist, anti-multiculturalist state, which is supported by most citizens in attacking fundamental religious freedom, is creating institutional linkages to govern Muslims in a way which is prima facie contrary to *laïcité*. It is not, however, contrary to the Western European tradition of moderate secularism, and France is not alone in following a path of anti-multiculturalist rhetoric and refusal to offer accommodation on specifics[9] with a willingness to deal with Muslims not just as individual citizens, but also as a religious group. Chancellor Merkel's government in Germany assembled a group of Muslims in 2006 for an Islamkonfrenz at the highest level of government and this has been repeated every year. Interestingly, the secularist strand of opinion in Britain which looks to France as a model is opposed to special consultative status for Muslim organizations, and sees this as consistent with the older demand for the disestablishment of the Church of England, the removal of bishops from a democratized House of Lords and a reduction in the number of state-funded faith schools.[10] 'Corporatist' accommodation, as argued in chapter 6, is a form of multiculturalism, albeit less preferable than the bottom-up and civil-society-led approach that is more common in Britain, but clearly seems to be more in tune with certain European state models. British radical secularists fail to note that such corporatist accommodation is part of the statist traditions of France and Germany and is an aspect of continental multiculturalism that is growing. It falls short of the ideal of multicultural citizenship which draws on a concept of citizenship which extends into voluntary associations and community activism – such that neighbourhood voluntary work can be said to exemplify 'active citizenship' or 'a good citizen'.

ADDITIONAL RESPONSES: CHRISTIAN VALUES AND MUSCULAR LIBERALISM

So, two responses to Muslim action and claims making have manifested themselves: the accommodationist, which through dialogue, negotiation and adaptation has tried to find a space for Muslims within an older, broad, racial-equality and multiculturalist orientation; and a radical secularist approach. Two other sentiments can also be identified: a Christianist and an intolerant or 'muscular' liberalism (which is not to say that Christians and liberals were not party to the first two approaches). The churches, especially the Church of England, have been actively involved in supporting British multiculturalism and developing interfaith dialogue, networks and policy coalitions with Muslims and other minorities. Similarly, what I refer to as liberal intolerance overlaps with the secularist intolerance that has already been discussed. What is distinctive about the two responses to Muslims is that one makes an explicit appeal to Christianity, and the other makes an explicit appeal to the limits of the prized value of toleration (Dobbernack and Modood 2013).

The reference to Christianity can be quite distant from policy. For example, it seems that the presence and salience of Muslims can be a factor in stimulating a Christian identity. An analysis of the voluntary question on religion in the 2001 U.K. census shows higher 'Christian' identification in areas near large Muslim populations (Voas and Bruce 2004). The emergence of a new, sometimes politically assertive, cultural identification with Christianity has been noted in Denmark (Mouritsen 2006) and in Germany, Chancellor Merkel has asserted, 'Those who don't accept [Christian values] don't have a place here' (cited in Presseurop 2010, reported as 'Muslims in her country should adopt Christian values'). Since then, several senior Bavarian politicians have made the link between German nationalism and Christianity even more emphatically (Fekete 2011, 46).[11] Similar sentiments were voiced in the European Union Constitution debate and are apparent in the ongoing debate about Turkey as a future E.U. member (Casanova 2009). These assertions of public Christianity are not, as said earlier, accompanied by any increase in expressions of faith or church attendance, which continue to decline across Europe. What is at work is not the repudiation of a status-quo secularism in favour of Christianity, but a response to the challenge of multiculturalism (as Merkel made explicit by asserting that 'multi-kulti' had failed and was not wanted back). Giscard d'Estaing, the former President of France, who chaired the Convention on the Future of Europe, the body which drafted the (abortive) E.U. Constitution, expresses nicely the assertiveness I speak of: 'I never go to Church, but Europe is a Christian continent'.[12]

Such political views, however, are also being expressed by Christian organizations, especially by the Catholic Church. Early in his papacy, Pope

Benedict XVI, in a speech at the Bavarian Catholic University at Regensburg, suggested that while reason was central to Christian divinity, this was not the case with the God of Islam, which licensed conversion by the sword and was deeply antithetical to the European tradition of rationality (Pope Benedict XVI 2006). It has been argued that Pope John Paul II 'looked at the essential cleavage in the world as being between religion and unbelief. Devout Christians, Muslims, and Buddhists had more in common with each other than with atheists'. Pope Benedict, the same author contends, 'thinks that, within societies, believers and unbelievers exist in symbiosis. Secular Westerners, he implies, have a lot in common with their religious fellows' (Caldwell 2009, 151). The suggestion is that secularists and Christians in Europe have more in common with each other than they do with Muslims. That many secularists do not share Pope Benedict's view is evident from the fact that the proposed clause about Christianity was absent from the final draft of the abortive E.U. Constitution. Moreover, it is indicative of the place of Christianity in Europe relative to radical secularism, that it emerged as a third, not a first or second trend. That is to say, it joined a debate in which the running had been mainly made by an accommodationist multiculturalism and an exclusionist secularism allied with nationalism. Yet, while there is little sign of a Christian right in Europe of the kind that is strong in the United States, there is to some degree a reinforcing or renewing of a sense that Europe is 'secular Christian', analogous to the term 'secular Jew' to describe someone of Jewish descent who has a sense of Jewish identity but is not religiously practising and may even be an atheist.

A fourth trend focuses on Muslims' conservative or illiberal moral values and practices. These are likely to centre on issues of gender and sexuality and so this trend overlaps with that which has led to legal restrictions on the wearing of the headscarf and the face veil, but goes much further and can be independent of questions of religion-state relations. It is alleged that the state needs to take special action against Muslims because their attitudes to, for example, gender equality and sexual orientation, are threatening to reverse what has been achieved in Western countries. This argument is found across the political and intellectual spectrum in the region, but is particularly strong in the Netherlands, where Pim Fortuyn's call for a halt to Muslim immigration because of their views on sex and personal freedom achieved considerable electoral success at the turn of the century (*Economist* 2002). The Dutch government produced a video to be shown to prospective Muslim immigrants, which included a close-up of a topless woman on a beach and gay men kissing in a park, to assist in the process of assessing applicants for entry into the country (Monshipouri 2010, 51). In neighbouring Denmark, the newspaper *Jyllands-Posten* famously published satirical and irreverent cartoons of the Prophet Muhammad to, according to its cultural editor, assist Muslims to be acculturalized into Danish public culture (Levey and Modood

2009, 227).[13] Ayaan Hirsi Ali, a former Dutch MP of Somali Muslim origin, became an international figure through her argument that the subordination of women was a core feature of orthodox Islam. The position I am referring to could be called a form of liberal perfectionism – that is, the view, in contrast to a Rawlsian neutralism, that it is the business of a liberal state to produce liberal individuals and promote a liberal way of life (Mouritsen and Olsen 2013), perhaps what Charles Taylor once called, liberalism as 'a fighting creed' or what Prime Minister Cameron has called 'muscular liberalism'. Its actual political dynamic has been to create and lead popular anti-Muslim hostility as in the form of Geert Wilders's comparison of the Qur'an with *Mein Kampf* and campaign to ban the former as long as the latter is banned. His campaign against the 'Islamization of Europe' has many echoes across Western Europe and is not limited to the Netherlands, where the party he founded in 2005, the Party for Freedom, became the third largest in the 2010 elections and a negotiating partner in the formation of a government (Wikipedia 2011).

ISLAMOPHOBIA

This 'muscular liberalism' perhaps matches the radical secularism of the hijab and burqa bans – at least, that is how it has been interpreted by Joppke (2009) and Hansen (2011), who argue that a ban on ostentatious religious dress is liberal if it does not name any particular religion but is equally restrictive of all of them! But I mention it separately as it is intellectually distinct,[14] and, more importantly, because it reveals how the dynamic that political secularism – and, indeed, liberalism – is being subjected to and is being tested on is that of the presence of Muslims combined with anti-Muslim hostility from various intellectual and political directions. Another example of this broad, anti-Muslim coalition is the majority that voted in a referendum to ban the building of minarets in Switzerland in 2009. It has been analysed as including a wide range of motives – from those whose primary motivation is women's rights to those 'who simply feel that Islam is "foreign"', who may have no problems with Muslims per se but who are not ready to accept 'Islam's acquiring of visibility in public spaces' (Mayer 2009, 6) and who generally did not vote 'out of a desire to oppress anybody, but because they are themselves feeling threatened by what they see as an Islam invasion' (Mayer 2009, 8). So, prejudiced or fearful perceptions of Islam are capable of uniting a wide range of opinion into a majority, including those who have no strong views about church-state arrangements, as indeed has been apparent from the beginning that Muslim claims became public controversies.

This means that the current challenge to secularism in Western Europe is being debated not only in terms of the wider issues of integration and multiculturalism, but also in terms of a hostility to Muslims and Islam, based on stereotypes and scare stories in the media that are best understood as a specific form of cultural racism or 'Islamophobia' (as discussed in chapters 1 and 4; Meer and Modood 2010; Sayyid and Vakil 2010; Morey and Yaqin 2011),[15] and, as such, is largely unrelated to questions of secularism. A meta-analysis of opinion polls between 1998 and 2006 in Britain concluded that 'between one in five and one in four Britons now exhibits a strong dislike of, and prejudice against, Islam and Muslims' (Field 2007, 465). A Pew survey in 2008 confirmed the higher figure and found its equivalent in France to be nearly double (38 per cent) and just more than 50 per cent in Germany (Pew Research Center 2008). These views are growing, finding expression in the rise of extreme right-wing parties, and even in terrorism, as happened in Oslo and the island of Atoye in July 2011 (Bangstad 2011). This, to put it mildly, is not a favourable context for accommodating Muslims and underscores the point that the so-called crisis of secularism is really about the presence and integration of Muslims, which of course partly depends on the behaviour of some Muslims – for example, those who commit acts of terrorism or make declarations of disloyalty to the country.

TO PLURALISE OR ABANDON MODERATE SECULARISM?

So, looking at the four trends and the wider Islamophobic climate of opinion, it looks as if the radical secularist trend and the Christianist trend could unite through cultural nationalism or cultural Europeanism, animated by Islamophobia (Brubaker 2017). I hope not. I would like to think that the spectre of a populist, right-wing nationalism – not to mention racism – would make enough people rally around a moderate secularism, which they would recognize has to be pluralized. But, either way, what this analysis suggests is that the real choice is between a pluralist, multifaith nationality or Europeanism and a monoculturalist nationalism or Europeanism. Or, put another way, the crisis of secularism is best understood within a framework of multiculturalism. Of course, multiculturalism currently has few advocates and the term is highly damaged.[16] Yet the repeated declarations, such as from the senior politicians of the region, that 'multiculturalism is dead' (Fekete 2011) are a reaction to the continuing potency of multiculturalism which renders obsolete liberal takes on assimilation and integration in the face of new forms of public gender and public ethnicity – and now public religion. Muslims are late joiners of this movement, but once they join, it slowly becomes apparent that the secularist status quo, with certain residual privileges for Christians, is untenable as it stands.

We can call this the challenge of integration rather than multiculturalism, as long as it is understood that we are not just talking about an integration into the day-to-day life of a society but also into its institutional architecture, grand narratives, and macro-symbolic sense of itself (Modood 2012). If these issues were dead, we would not be having a debate about the role of public religion or proposals for dialogue with Muslims and the accommodation of Islam. The dynamic for change is not directly related to the historic religion or the historic secularism of Western Europe; rather, the novelty – which then has implications for Christians and secularists and to which they are reacting – is the appearance of an assertive multiculturalism which cannot be contained within a matrix of individual rights, conscience, religious freedom and so on. If any of these were different the problems would be other than they are. Just as today we look at issues to do with, say, women or homosexuality not simply in terms of rights but in a political environment influenced by feminism and gay liberation, within a socio-political-intellectual culture in which the 'assertion of positive difference' or 'identity' is a shaping and powerful presence. It does not mean everybody is a feminist now, but the heightened consciousness of gender and gender equality creates a certain gender-equality sensibility. Similarly, a multiculturalist sensibility is present in Europe and yet it is not comfortable with extending itself to accommodate Muslims, but nor able to find reasons for not extending to Muslims without self-contradiction.

The nature of the reform I proposed in chapter 6 is not one of abandoning or radically moving away from the status quo of the dominant moderate secularism of Western Europe. A parallel approach has been proposed for Quebec (Bouchard and Taylor 2008, chapter 7; see also Maclure and Taylor 2011). Without endorsing the specifics of their understanding of a Quebecan 'open secularism', I recognize that their strategy is similar to mine. Moderate secularism can play a similar role in (much of) Western Europe to the one that Bouchard and Taylor identify as open secularism in Quebec. Bhargava has mistakenly attributed to me the view the view that '[f]or [Modood], moderate secularism is a perfect ideal' (Bhargava 2011), but I do reject his analysis which leads him to conclude that moderate secularism is 'irretrievably flawed' and while it has accommodated Christians it will not be able to accommodate Muslims.[17] Despite his suggestion that crisis can mean a turning point to 'recovery or mortality', the crisis that he believes exists for European moderate secularism is not of the kind that can be resolved through reform (Bhargava 2011). For me, it is the proverbial case of the bottle being half-full or half-empty: half-empty because it needs reforming to accommodate Muslims and religious diversity more generally; half-full because it acknowledges a place for religion within the state and/or supported by the state. The latter enable the possibility of the former, as argued in chapter 4. It also explains why talk of 'post-secular society' (like postmodern or post-national before it) has come to be seen as rather exaggerated. There now seems to be a consensus that the term 'post-secularism' means 'rethinking secularism' without any implication of anti-secularism or that it is time to move beyond secularism. While for some this is enough to make the case for using the term 'post-secular' (McLennan 2010), for me it makes evident that it is not an accurate term for what it is meant to capture, and if it is not to be abandoned it should at least be qualified as 'post-radical, post-uncritical secularism'. So a rethinking and opening up of political secularism in the light of contemporary multiculturalism, especially the challenge of accommodating Muslims, is what I believe 'post-secularism' amounts to in Western Europe. In the next two essays I explore further this multiculturalist rethinking and opening up of political secularism.

NOTES

1. It is though doubtful whether Habermas has really abandoned his earlier reason-religion duality (Harrington 2007).

2. Bhargava has qualified what he means by crisis as 'only a critical turning point . . . to recovery or mortality' but continues to believe that secularism in some or all countries of Western Europe is 'irretrievably flawed' (Bhargava 2011).

3. Immigration may however be masking some elements of decline in religious belief among 'natives' in Western Europe and North America.

4. It may be the case that some government policies are seeking to delegate certain welfare responsibilities but that is not based on rethinking secularism or Christianity but on wishing to limit the scale of the state for revenue or other reasons.

5. Roald (2012) offers a discussion of the effects of secularisation on Muslims in Sweden: that most Muslims are 'privatising' their beliefs while simultaneously projecting a public ethno-religious Muslim group identity in the manner discussed in chapter 8.

6. A study of aspects of Muslim participation in new forms of governance in Britain is the subject of the project, Muslim Participation in Contemporary Governance. 'Muslim Participation in Contemporary Governance', University of Bristol: Centre for the Study of Ethnicity and Citizenship: http://www.bristol.ac.uk/ethnicity/projects/muslimparticipation/index.html.

7. The way that race, religion and ethnicity do not neatly align today is illustrated by the fact that the head teacher whose inflexibility created the national crisis was a black African; later, when the same issue flared up in 2003, two of the excluded girls at the centre of the national controversy were supported by a Jewish father (thanks to David Lehmann for sending me to http://news.bbc.co.uk/1/hi/world/europe/3149588.stm). It has in fact been argued with some justification that the post-1989 *laïcité* is actually a much stricter interpretation than what was in place since the 1905 law that established *laïcité*; and that those who reject the contemporary interpretation, which includes some Muslim activists, are not antisecularists but true to the spirit of the 1905 law (Bauberot 2012).

8. Of course neither does the idea that the French Republic subsidises religious schools as mentioned in chapter 6. In fact, in both the *laïcité* Republic and 'Establishment' England about a quarter of all pupils attend state-subsidised religious schools and the scale of subsidy is not very different.

9. Sometimes refusal at a national level is accompanied by local compromises (Bowen 2010).

10. See National Secular Society and Humanists UK websites; for similar views among centre-left Christians, see the website of the think-tank, Ekklesia.

11. An interesting cross-national contrast is that in Britain, Muslims (79 per cent) and Hindus (74 per cent) are more likely than Christians (70 per cent) to agree, 'Our laws should respect and be influenced by UK religious values' (Nick Allen, *The Telegraph*, 24 February 2009; see also the next note).

12. More recently, Prime Minister Cameron, who has confessed to not being a steadfast believer, made a major speech arguing that Britons should not be shy of asserting that Britain is a Christian country (Prime Minister's Office 2011). While many secularists protested, the speech was welcomed by the chair of the Mosque and Community Affairs of the Muslim Council of Britain, Sheikh Ibrahim Mogra (BBC 2011). See also the previous note.

13. Even though he, or at least his newspaper, took a different view of an anti-Christian cartoon earlier (Fouché 2006).

14. 'Perfectionist liberalism is not intolerant *per se*. . . . Intolerance (and conflict with traditional liberal pluralism) enters at the point where officially promoted ideals of good liberal citizenship come to be seen as so important, so threatened, and so much in conflict with specific *un-civic* (religious) practices and dispositions, concentrated in defined and targetable out-groups, that attempts to change, penalize or even outlaw them become legitimate' (Mouritsen and Olsen 2013, 149). Levey (2012) offers a sophisticated and complex framework for evaluating whether putative, non-liberal, minority practices violate the ideal of liberal autonomy, warranting state intervention.

15. Interestingly, in Britain the Christian media has been less hostile to Muslims than the mainstream media (Faimau 2010 and 2011).

16. Which does not mean subscription to the thesis that multiculturalism is dead (Modood 2007/2013).

17. For a fuller discussion of why I think Bhargava misunderstands Western European secularisms, see Modood 2010 and Modood 2011.

REFERENCES

Bader, V. (2011). 'Associational Governance of Ethno-Religious Diversity in Europe: The Dutch Case'. In Smith, R. (ed.), *Citizenship, Borders, and Human Needs*, 273–297. Philadelphia: University of Pennsylvania Press.

Bailey, E. I. (1997). *Implicit Religion in Contemporary Society*. Kampen, The Netherlands: Kok Pharos.

Bangstad, S. (2011). 'Norway: Terror and Islamophobia in the Mirror'. Open Democracy, 22 August: http://www.opendemocracy.net/sindre-bangstad/norway-terror-and-islamophobia-in-mirror.

Baubérot, Jean. (2012). *La laïcité falsifiée*. Paris: La Decouverte.

BBC. (2011). 'David Cameron on Christianity – Views'. BBC News, 18 December: http://www.bbc.co.uk/news/uk-16231223, last accessed 23/9/2018.

Bhargava, R. (2010). 'States, Religious Diversity, and the Crisis of Secularism'. *Hedgehog Review*, 12(3), 8–22.

Bhargava, R. (2011). 'States, Religious Diversity and the Crisis of Secularism'. Open Democracy, 22 March: http://www.opendemocracy.net/rajeev-bhargava/states-religious-diversity-and-crisis-of-secularism-0.

Bouchard, G. and Taylor, C. (2008). *Building the Future: A Time for Reconciliation*. Quebec: Consultation Commission on Accommodation Practices Related to Cultural Differences.

Bowen, J. R. (2007). 'Why the French Don't Like Headscarves: Islam, the State, and Public Space', *European Review*, 15(3), 397–400.

Bowen, J. R. (2010) *Can Islam be French? Pluralism and Pragmatism in a Secularist State*. Princeton, NJ: Princeton University Press.

British Religion in Numbers (BRIN). (2011). 'Religious Affiliation and Church Attendance in Britain, 1983–2008'. British Religion in Numbers: http://www.brin.ac.uk/figures/#AffiliationAttendance.

Brubaker, R. (2017). 'Between Nationalism and Civilizationism: The European Populist Moment in Comparative Perspective'. *Ethnic and Racial Studies*, *40*(8), 1191–1226.
Caldwell, C. (2009). *Reflections on the Revolution in Europe: Immigration, Islam, and the West*. London: Allen Lane.
Casanova, J. (2009). 'Immigration and the New Religious Pluralism: A European Union–United States Comparison'. In Levey, G. B. and Modood, T. (eds.), *Secularism, Religion and Multicultural Citizenship*, 139–163. Cambridge: Cambridge University Press.
Davie, G. (1994). *Religion in Britain since 1945: Believing without Belonging*. Oxford: Blackwell Publishers.
Dobbernack, J. and Modood, T. (eds.). (2013). *Tolerance, Intolerance and Respect: Hard to Accept?*. Basingstoke, UK: Palgrave.
Economist. (2002). 'A Wind of Change in the Netherlands – and across Europe'. 16 May: http://www.economist.com/node/1136775.
Elgot, J. (2017). 'Ukip to Campaign to Ban Burqa and Sharia Courts, Says Paul Nuttal', *Guardian*, 23 April.
Faimau, G. (2010). 'The Discursive Representation of Islam and Muslims in the British Christian Media: Socio-Cultural Construction of Recognition'. PhD thesis, University of Bristol, UK.
Faimau, G. (2011). 'Naming Muslims as Partners'. *Journalism Studies*, *12*(4), 474–489.
Fekete, L. (2011). 'Understanding the European-Wide Assault on Multiculturalism'. In Mahamdallie, H. (ed.), *Defending Multiculturalism*, 38–52. London: Bookmarks.
Ferrari, S. and Pastorelli, S. (eds.). (2016). *Religion in Public Spaces: A European Perspective*. London: Routledge.
Field, C. D. (2007). 'Islamophobia in Contemporary Britain: The Evidence of the Opinion Polls, 1988–2006'. *Islam and Christian-Muslim Relations*, *18*, 447–477.
Foner, N. and Alba, R. (2008), 'Immigrant Religion in the US and Western Europe: Bridge or Barrier to Inclusion?'. *International Migration Review*, *42*, 360–392.
Fouché, G. (2006). 'Danish Paper Rejected Jesus Cartoons'. *Guardian*, 6 February: http://www.guardian.co.uk/media/2006/feb/06/pressandpublishing.politics.
Guardian. (2011). 'Italy Approves Draft Law to Ban Burqa'. 3 August: http://www.guardian.co.uk/world/2011/aug/03/italy-draft-law-burqa.
Habermas, J. (2006). 'Religion in the Public Sphere'. *European Journal of Philosophy*, *14*(1), 1–25.
Hansen, R. (2011). 'The Two Faces of Liberalism: Islam in Contemporary Europe'. *Journal of Ethnic and Migration Studies*, *37*(6), 881–897.
Harrington, A. (2007). 'Habermas and 'the Post-Secular Society''. *European Journal of Social Theory*, *10*(4), 543–560.
Heath, A. F. and Roberts, J. (2008). *British Identity: Its Sources and Possible Implications for Civic Attitudes and Behaviour*. Research report for Lord Goldsmith's Citizenship Review: http://webarchive.nationalarchives.gov.uk/+/http:/www.justice.gov.uk/docs/british-identity.pdf [accessed 6/08/2012].
Heelas, P. and Woodhead, L. (2005). *The Spiritual Revolution: Why Religion Is Giving Way to Spirituality*. Malden, MA: Wiley-Blackwell.
Jakelić, S. (2010). 'Secularism: A Bibliographic Essay'. *Hedgehog Review*, *12*(3), 49–55.
Joppke, C. (2009). *Veil: The Mirror of Identity*. Cambridge: Polity.
Kastoryano, R. (2006). 'French Secularism and Islam: France's Headscarf Affair'. In Modood, T., Triandafyllidou, A. and Zapata-Barrero, R. (eds.), *Multiculturalism, Muslims and Citizenship: A European Approach*, 57–69. London: Routledge.
Kaufmann, E., Goujon, A. and Skirbekk, V. (2012). 'The End of Secularization in Europe? A Socio-Demographic Perspective'. *Sociology of Religion*, *73*(1), 69–91.
Kymlicka, W. (2009). 'Review Symposium: Historic Settlements and New Challenges: Veit Bader, Secularism or Democracy? Associational Governance of Religious Diversity, Amsterdam: Amsterdam University Press, 2008'. *Ethnicities*, *9*(4), 546–552.
Lentin, A. and Titley, G. (2011). *The Crises of Multiculturalism: Racism in A Neoliberal Age*. London: Zed Books.
Levey, G. B. (2012). 'Liberal Autonomy As a Pluralistic Value'. *The Monist*, *95*(1), 103–126.

Levey, G. B. and Modood, T. (2009). 'Liberal Democracy, Multicultural Citizenship, and the Danish Cartoon Affair'. In Levey, G. B. and Modood, T. (eds.), *Secularism, Religion and Multicultural Citizenship*, 216–242. Cambridge: Cambridge University Press.

Lutz, W., Skirbekk, V. and Testa, M. (2007). 'The Low-Fertility Trap Hypothesis: Forces That May Lead to Further Postponement and Fewer Births in Europe'. In *Vienna Yearbook of Population Research 2006*, 167–192. Vienna: Vienna Institute of Demography.

Mayer, J.-F. (2009). 'Analysis: A Majority of Swiss Voters Decide to Ban the Building of New Minarets'. Religioscope Institute: http://religion.info/english/articles/article_455.shtml.

McLennan, G. (2010). 'The Postsecular Turn'. *Theory Culture Society*, 27(4), 3–20.

Maclure, J. and Taylor, C. (2011). *Secularism and Freedom of Conscience*, trans. J. T. Todd. Cambridge, MA: Harvard University Press.

Meer, N. and Modood, T. (2010). 'The Racialization of Muslims'. In Sayyid, S. and Vakil, A. (eds.), *Thinking through Islamophobia: Global Perspectives*, 69–84. London: Hurst and New York: Columbia University Press.

Modood, T. (2005) *Multicultural Politics: Racism, Ethnicity and Muslims in Britain*. Minneapolis: University of Minnesota Press and Edinburgh: University of Edinburgh Press.

Modood, T. (2009). 'Introduction: Odd Ways of Being Secular'. *Social Research: An International Quarterly*, 76(4), 1169–1172.

Modood, T. (2010). *Still Not Easy Being British: Struggles for a Multicultural Citizenship*. Stoke-on-Trent, UK: Trentham.

Modood, T. (2011). 'Moderate Secularism: A European Conception'. OpenDemocracy, 8 April: http://www.opendemocracy.net/tariq-modood/moderate-secularism-european-conception [last accessed 5/08/2012].

Modood, T. (2012). *Post-Immigration 'Difference' and Integration: The Case of Muslims in Western Europe*. London: The British Academy.

Modood, T. and Kastoryano, R. (2006). 'Secularism and the Accommodation of Muslims in Europe'. In Modood, T., Triandafyllidou, A. and Zapata-Barrero, R. (eds.) *Multiculturalism, Muslims and Citizenship: A European Approach*, 162–178. London: Routledge.

Modood, T., Triandafyllidou, A. and Zapata-Barrero, R. (eds.) (2006). *Multiculturalism, Muslims and Citizenship: A European Approach*. London: Routledge.

Monshipouri, M. (2010). 'The War on Terror and Muslims in the West'. In J. Cesari (ed.), *Muslims in the West after 9/11: Religion, Politics and Law*, 45–66. London: Routledge.

Morey, P. and Yaqin, A. (2011). *Framing Muslims*. Cambridge, MA: Harvard University Press.

Mouritsen, P. (2006). 'The Particular Universalism of a Nordic Civic Nation: Common Values, State Religion and Islam in Danish Political Culture'. In Modood, T., Triandafyllidou, A. and Zapata-Barrero, R. (eds.), *Multiculturalism, Muslims and Citizenship: A European Approach*, 70–93. London: Routledge.

Mouritsen, P. and Olsen, T. V. (2013). 'Liberalism and the Diminishing Space of Tolerance'. In J. Dobbernack and Modood, T. (eds.), *Tolerance, Intolerance and Respect: Hard to Accept?*, 127–156. Basingstoke, UK: Palgrave.

Murray, C. (2011). 'Norwegian Killer Linked to Tea Party and EDL'. July 23: http://www.craigmurray.org.uk/archives/2011/07/norwegian-killer-linked-to-tea-party-and-edl/ [accessed 13/08/2012].

Nussbaum, N. (2012). *The New Religious Intolerance: Overcoming the Politics of Fear in an Anxious Age*. Cambridge, MA: Harvard University Press.

Peach, C. (2007). 'Muslim Population of Europe: A Brief Overview of Demographic Trends and Socioeconomic Integration, with Particular Reference to Britain'. In Angenendt, S., Barrett, P., Laurence, J., Peach, C. Smith, J. and Winte, T. (eds.), *Muslim Integration: Challenging Conventional Wisdom in Europe and the United States*, 7–32. Washington DC: Center for Strategic and International Studies.

Pew Research Center. (2008). 'Unfavorable Views of Jews and Muslims on the Increase in Europe'. Pew Research Center: http://pewglobal.org/2008/09/17/unfavorable-views-of-jews-and-muslims-on-the-increase-in-europe/.

Pew Forum. (2017). 'Europe's Growing Muslim Population'. http://www.pewforum.org/2017/11/29/europes-growing-muslim-population/ [accessed 27/02/2019].

Pope Benedict XVI. (2006). 'Faith, Reason and the University Memories and Reflections'. Regensberg Lecture: http://www.catholic-ew.org.uk/Home/News/2006/2006-Offline/Full-Text-of-the-Pope-Benedict-XVI-s-Regensburg-Lecture [accessed 27/02/2019].

Prime Minister's Office. (2011). 'Prime Minister's King James Bible Speech'. gov.uk, 16 December: http://www.number10.gov.uk/news/king-james-bible [accessed 21/04/2015].

Roald, A. S. (2012). 'Expressing Religiosity In a Secular Society: The Relativisation of Faith in Muslim Communities in Sweden'. *European Review*, *20*(1), 95–113.

Roy, O. (2007). *Secularism Confronts Islam*. New York: Columbia University Press.

Sayyid, S. and Vakil, A. (eds.). (2010). *Thinking through Islamophobia: Global Perspectives*. El Paso, TX: Cinco Puntos Press.

Scherer, M. (2010). 'Landmarks in the Critical Study of Secularism'. *The Immanent Frame*: http://blogs.ssrc.org/tif/2010/11/12/landmarks-secularism/.

Scott, J. W. (2007). *The Politics of the Veil*. Princeton, NJ: Princeton University Press.

Sherif, J. (2011). 'A Census Chronicle – Reflections on the Campaign for a Religion Question in the 2001 Census for England and Wales'. *Journal of Beliefs & Values*, *32*(1), 1–18.

Voas, D. and Bruce, S. (2004). 'Research Note: The 2001 Census and Christian Identification in Britain'. *Journal of Contemporary Religion*, *19*(1), 23–28.

Voas, D. and Crockett, A. (2005). 'Religion in Britain: Neither Believing nor Belonging'. *Sociology*, *39*(1), 11–28.

Wikipedia. (2011). 'Dutch General Election, 2010'. http://en.wikipedia.org/wiki/Dutch_general_election,_2010.

Chapter Ten

State-Religion Connexions and Multicultural Citizenship

While many liberals believe that the state should be neutral on matters of the good and culture, and above all on religion, multiculturalists hold that the state should not be blind to difference.[1] Indeed, it should actively play a role in constructing and promoting a multicultural polity and national identity in which minority identities are respectfully included. This first tension can lead to a second one. For, if multicultural recognition, respectful inclusion and the multiculturalizing of the public space and national identity were to include minority religious identities, then this can clash with those forms of secularism based on the radical interpretation that religion should play no or a highly restricted role in politics, or at least law and governance.[2]

This may seem to pit multiculturalists against secularism. This, however, is not the case where radical secularism is not the dominant mode of political secularism, such as in Western Europe, where all states support one or more version of Christianity. Some secularists, including prominent academics, as we noted in the previous chapter, do indeed speak of a 'crisis of secularism' but that is because they have an exaggerated view of the requirements of secularism or are mistaken about the kind of secularism practiced by Western European states. This gap between theories of secularism and actual secular states reminds me of one of the pioneering moments of multiculturalism. Will Kymlicka has rightly pointed out that while liberal political theorists were arguing that liberalism has no truck with group rights, several liberal states had by the 1980s begun to implement policies using notions of group identities and group rights. Kymlicka argued that the practice of the liberal state was superior to the theories of academics and so we needed to get theory to catch up with practice.[3] Similarly, I think it became apparent in the 1990s that some of the practices of some liberal states were, in respect of secularism, superior to the theories of academics and we needed to catch up with practice. (A small irony here is that Kymlicka himself is a secularist that has no patience for the kind of Western European state practice that I shall suggest is a resource for multiculturalism.)[4]

My way out of the tensions between multiculturalism and liberalism and between multiculturalism and secularism is to argue that the presence of state-religion connexions (SRCs) is not normatively problematic in itself. They can be consistent with liberal democratic constitutionalism and may be a means of including ethno-religious minorities within a multicultural citizenship. I seek to establish that in principle SRCs are integral to a historical and reasonable version of secularism and do not constitute an indefensible privileging of religion.

POLITICAL SECULARISM AND STATE-RELIGION CONNEXIONS

I am committed to political secularism in general, which I take to be the view that political authority does not rest on religious authority and the latter does not dominate political authority; each has considerable, though not absolute, autonomy. I believe this is the generic idea common to all versions of liberal democratic states. Note that it does not say anything about whether states may have an 'established' religion or whether there has to be 'a wall of separation' between organised religion and the institutions and resources of the state. It is part of my argument that some versions of 'establishment' as a subset of SRCs are compatible with some versions of political secularism. I take these versions of political secularism to be part of a broad historical movement within Western Europe (with France being a notable if partial exception), which I refer to as 'moderate secularism' (not a narrow status quo in a specific country at a specific time).[5]

The key feature of moderate secularism is that it sees organised religion as not just a private benefit but also as a potential public good or national resource, and which the state can in some circumstances assist to realise – even through an 'established' church. These public benefits can be direct, such as a contribution to education and social care through autonomous church-based organisations funded by the taxpayer; or indirect, such as the production of attitudes that create economic hope or family stability; and they can have to do with national identity, cultural heritage, ethical voice and national ceremonies. Note that the public good of religion, and therefore possible SRCs in moderate secularism, are not confined to the organised delivery of public services but include identity and recognition within their possible ambit. Of course religion can also be a 'public bad' – it can, for example, in some circumstances be a basis for prejudice, discrimination, intolerance, sectarianism and so on – and so, as argued in chapter 8, the state has a responsibility to check the bad as well as enhance the good. Moreover, if religious organisations are supported with public funds or tasked by the state to carry out some educational or welfare duties then they must be subject to certain requirements, such as equal access or non-discrimination.

It is clear then that in moderate secularism the state-religion entanglements do not just flow one way, can have various aspects, and are highly context dependent, not least on what kind of religion or religions is present. Moderate secularism, nevertheless, is consistent with my minimalist definition of political secularism as relatively autonomous forms of authority without an entailment of absolute institutional separation, though many political theorists would not accept that it is a form of secularism.[6] While I argue that a formal or legal or constitutional connexion is characteristic of north-western European secularism, it being the historical form that secular states have taken, an alternative view of secularism is encapsulated in Rajeev Bhargava's claim that 'in a secular state, a formal or legal union or alliance between state and religion is impermissible'.[7] Bhargava is best known for his view that the Indian polity has something to teach the West – namely, that it is possible for a secular state to have principled, secularist reasons for rejecting strict separationism. He argues that while India is one of the few states in the world to be defined as 'secular' by its constitution it has an active policy of supporting and interfering with the religions of India. He argues that such policy behaviour is consistent with secularism. His explanation is based on dividing the idea of a secular state into three levels: ends, institutions and laws/policies. At the third level the normative ideal is 'principled distance' – namely, that the state is bound to interact with religions but must do so without favouring any or some religions relative to others. These interactions should be governed not by religious principles but by the principles and policies that the state is independently committed to. So, if the state is committed to pursuing affirmative action to help disadvantaged and stigmatised minorities, then the state may choose to invest (disproportionate) resources in improving the educational standards of a disadvantaged religious minority if there is a sound analysis that doing so will help to meet its overall goal. This is not, Bhargava argues, to favour a religion; it just so happens that principled state policies and the state benefiting a religious group (temporarily) coincide. Hence, he is insistent that to rule out such policies in the name of secularism is dogmatic and mistaken. His argument that at this third level of policy the state may be flexible, pragmatic and religion friendly (as long as not biased in favour of any religion beyond where policy requires) is well made and convincing.

My disagreement with Bhargava is in relation to his analysis of secularism in relation to the other two levels, those of ends and, in particular, at the level of state structure. There he allows no flexibility and works with dichotomous distinctions: he forces, for instance, a choice between 'establishment' or secular as he argues that there can be no overlap or duality of function between state and religious personnel.[8] I think, however, that at this level too we need elasticity and this is what a number of European states have done historically and indeed continue to do even in the absence of formal establishment – for example, through corporatist state-church partnerships in relation to education and welfare as in Germany or a state-level consultative council of religions as in Belgium. Such European states certainly have the policy-level connexions with organised religions (principally churches) but the connexion is not confined to that, and even the latter has a long-term character such that it is more a part of the state structure (e.g., of the tax-funded education system), rather than of policies which change with governments or new programmes of action. To think of such long-term state-religion 'alliances' simply as a set of policies is to considerably understate them as they overlap with structures of governance and state agencies. With state-religion connexions present at more than one level, we have a more substantial connexion than Bhargava's and related theories can include within their conception of legitimate secular states.

Interestingly, Bhargava allows that 'weak establishment' of the kind that exists in England (and 'weaker' still in Scotland, with the Presbyterian Church recognised as a 'national' church) is more or less a secular state. That is politically sound but it is not clear how he can make this move within his theory; it seems to lack a theoretical rationale.[9] Cécile Laborde offers one rationale when she says there are liberal forms of establishment – which are such either because they are 'multi-faith', or because they are only purely symbolic and do not confer any substantive advantage on the publicly recognised religion'.[10] For Laborde, the United States seems to be an example of a 'modest separation', while Europe is mainly versions of 'modest establishment'. She gets some of her terminology from Ronald Dworkin, who thinks that there is some truth to the conservative reading of U.S. history – namely, that it was founded as a tolerant religious nation (tolerant of unbelief) but in the second half of the twentieth century unelected judges made it a tolerant secular nation (tolerant of belief).[11] He also thinks that while somewhat complex, Britain, too, is a secular nation whose toleration of religion is because 'its established church owes more to its love of tradition and ceremony, I think, than to any genuine shared national religious commitment'.[12] Dworkin is right that the British state and politics is a form of secularism[13] but I think the language of 'separation' is quite misleading, as is seeing departures from absolute separation as departures from political secularism. In any case, I want to defend the possibility of state-religion connexions (of which certain kinds of establishment may be one version) that go beyond what Bhargava and Laborde believe are consistent with liberal and/or secular principles.

My understanding of a SRC is this: some kind of relationship with the state such that a religious organisation participates in the functions of the state *or* is a partner in governance, helping the state to discharge some of its duties and implementation of policies, *or* it is continuously supported by public funds, *or* it is part of the symbolism of the state in a clearly non-neutralist way – some form of 'formal or legal union or alliance between state and religion' to use Bhargava's disapproving vocabulary. The example that I am most familiar with and exercised by is the Church of England's relationship with the Head of State (the monarch is the Supreme Governor of the Church and only assumes the throne after being anointed in oil by bishops); its position in the House of Lords (26 bishops sit in the upper house of the legislature by right and have full voting rights); has a role in the national system of education (several thousand church schools are nearly wholly dependent on state funding); and recently has come to see itself and to be seen by government to have a responsibility to promote multifaith harmony.[14] Whilst some aspects of this relationship are symbolic, it is evident that it goes beyond the symbolic. On the other hand, there is no pretending that the Church has a lot of power within the state and hence I think it may be characterised as a form of 'weak establishment'; and my argument is that such an arrangement is consistent with political secularism.[15]

The Church of England is not the only example I have in mind in relation to SRCs. The term is capacious enough to include the status of Catholic and Protestant churches as legal corporations with various rights and entitlements, including having the state collect a voluntary tithe through the tax system and receive large amounts of public funding in order to carry out various welfare functions autonomously or semi-autonomously – an arrangement that has been referred to as 'multiple establishments'.[16] As in Denmark, it also includes the presence of an established church together with other, lesser and varied forms of recognition of other churches and faiths by the state.[17] It includes also the Belgian state's recognition of several religions as national religions and the French state relationship with Catholics, Protestants, Jews and Muslims at the highest level of the executive.[18] Moreover, it should be clear that when I include 'weak establishment' within the category 'state-religion connexions' (SRC) that I believe are consistent with, indeed a part of, Western European moderate secularisms, I am not including what may be called 'full establishment' or a confessional state – Western European states may have been like this once, but they ceased to be some time ago and are not so today. I do, however, by SRC mean much more than what Laborde calls 'symbolic' establishment'[19] and also more than what some people mean by the 'post-secular' – namely, the allowing of the presence of religious views in political debate[20] as long as those views or those religions are never identified with the state.[21] Veit Bader has a helpful definition of weak establishment as 'constitutional or legal establishment of one State-

Church, and de jure and de facto religious freedom and pluralism', though we should not lose sight of the fact that the term 'weak' marks that power lies elsewhere.[22]

There is a view that while there may be something like moderate secularism present in Western Europe and elsewhere, in the twentieth century it has continually given way and become weaker – perhaps even that there is a historical process at work that will ultimately lead to the disappearance of SRCs and the triumph of full secularism. Actually, there are certain substantive policy areas where SRCs have grown. Moreover, this is not just in the last decade or so – that is to say, in the period identified as 'post-secular'. One of the biggest growth in SRCs in England and France has been in the area of education and took place around the middle of the twentieth century. The 1944 Education Act meant a big growth in state funding of church schools (mainly Anglican and Catholics, but in due course extended to some others too) such that by the end of the twentieth century about a quarter to a third of pupils in England and Wales were in state-funded church schools. Similarly, and somewhat unexpectedly, given how French *laïcité* is standardly and comprehensively contrasted with England, the 'Debré Law' of 1959 enabled church schools (nearly all Catholic) in France to be nearly wholly subsidised by the state (17 per cent of all pupils in 2011–2012).[23] Despite the emergence of a new, hardened laïcité in response to Muslims in the last few decades, this state-Catholic arrangement has not been reversed nor properly extended to Muslims.[24] Moreover, in the last couple of decades SRCs have formed in relation to 'community relations' or 'interfaith relations' (in relation to England, see endnote 16) and currently several states are exploring and enacting the transfer of the delivery of some welfare services from the state to civil society, including religious organisations.[25] So, whether we look at the matter in terms of the last century or just the last couple of decades, SRCs have both declined and have grown under various liberal democratic regimes.

Formal 'weak' establishment, informal establishment and SRCs in general, then, are not a primary issue of secularism but a secondary one to do with context, time and place, including, no doubt, the political as well as the economic costs and benefits of, for example, moving from one set of arrangements to another.[26] I acknowledge that the historical movement has been generally for SRCs to be thinned down, to be marginalised and to be pluralised, despite some of the strong counterexamples I have just offered. It does not mean, however, that we have to take the thinning down to its nth point if there is a good reason to slow down, halt or even reverse the process, and it is interesting that in few states, if any, have many legislators or publics considered totally severing the SCRs. The reasons for SRCs, as already indicated, can be several and my suggestion is one which egalitarians should consider, namely, that they can be a means to accommodate new, marginal and stigmatised groups – most notably, Muslims in Western Europe – in a spirit of multicultural citizenship.

MULTICULTURALISM, LIBERALISM AND STATE-RELIGIONS CONNEXIONS

As I have stated my view of multicultural citizenship in a number of places and space here is limited, I will restate it very briefly and concentrating on what is absolutely necessary for my argument here.[27] Our most fundamental concept of equal citizenship is that all citizens have the same rights and duties, are treated the same by the state and by each other qua citizens and there is no discrimination on grounds such as gender, ethnicity, race, religion, sexuality and so on. However, we also understand that these social dimensions are also bases of identity which are important to some of their bearers and who seek respect and 'recognition' from fellow citizens and the state, especially in conditions where these identities have been stigmatised or marginalised.[28] These identities are not straightforwardly chosen; people do not choose to be born male or female, black or white. On the other hand, there is some room for individuals to choose what kind of and how much of an identity to project publicly and to have others publicise. For example, some black people do not want their blackness to be noticed politically; others insist on it and demand, for example, the right to autonomous organisations within political parties and trades unions and for special rights of representation (e.g., a number of reserved places on a national committee). If a polity gives expression to respect for group identities and group representation, or even simply group equality of opportunity, then the principle of treating everybody the same, colour-blindness and so on has to be modified under certain circumstances.

Some people, including some multiculturalists, believe that while what I have described holds for all the other bases of identity that I have mentioned, religion is an exception as it is something chosen, while all the others are 'given'. This, however, as I argued in chapter 6, is a false distinction. One does not choose to be born a Muslim but being of a Muslim background or being perceived as such can be the basis for a diminished citizenship in just the same way as the other bases of identity. Of course, some Muslims may not want to project a religious identity and may believe that religion is a private matter. Yes, but other Muslims may not. This is the same point as I was making about blackness and it also applies to gender and sexuality: multicultural identities have an element of 'giveness', which is not only biological but is socially constructed and ascribed, and they have an element of choice about how one relates to that as a self-identity – in particular, in relation to issues of privacy and publicity. However, there is one important implication for religion that should be highlighted. Multiculturalist accommodation of groups is primarily as identity or community based on descent and only secondarily about faith; it is based on recognition and inclusivity, not the truth of doctrines. In so far as doctrine comes in, it does so indirectly. For example, protecting Jews from incitement to hatred may mean protecting them from certain insults to their religion (e.g., that they are Christ-killers or their rituals involve the sacrifice of Christian babies), or allowing the community to transmit its identity over generations may require public support for Jewish schools in which Judaism is taught and not just or in addition to the national religion or non-religious ethics.

The first and most basic argument, then, for including religious identities, and specifically for the multiculturalist accommodation of a religious minority, is not by a comparative reference to Christians, but by reference to equal respect. In so far as there is a comparative reference, the initial comparative reference is to the egalitarian accommodation of women, black people, gays and so on. Perhaps the most immediate implication for political secularism is that any political norm that excludes religious identities from the public space, from schools and universities, from politics and nationhood – what I call 'radical secularism', which tries to privatise religion – is incompatible with multicultural citizenship; and if religious identities face this kind of exclusion but not identities based on race, ethnicity, gender and so on, then there is a bias against religious identity and a failure to practice equality between identities or identity groups. When groups protest against such forms of exclusion, as Muslims have been doing, we should identify what they are asking for and consider whether it is reasonable, and here the argument has to soon become contextual. Do we normally grant such things? If we do, is there a reason to not continue to do so or to not pluralise it? Conversely, if we do not normally grant such things, is there a good reason to do so now? This is not merely about precedent or status quo; it is looking at precedents, the status quo and considerations about what will work and runs with the grain of familiar norms and practices from the point of view of multicultural inclusion.[29] Inclusion may be possible without using SRCs, but that may be one way to achieve it or is part of the way to do it.

I will consider an important objection to the SRCs that I am saying may be justifiable and may be of value in relation to the accommodation of minorities. The objection is that I am in breach of the liberal requirement of state neutrality, that the state should not be seen to be associating itself with a conception of the good and especially not a religion. I have a number of responses, the first of which is that if by 'neutral' is meant that a state should have no cultural or religious character, then that is an impossible condition to fulfil. There is no such thing as a culturally contentless state or public space. The state will always have some historical-cultural character. For example, there will be an official language(s) in which the business of the state is conducted in and which provides the rhetoric, the collective memories and cultural texture through which civic communication is achieved. Similarly, any state will draw on a specific set of ethical, political and legal traditions, and while they will have some element of universality, they will always have some particularity too. Moreover, this particularity extends to the ways in which the state-religion connexion is expressed. This will be true of its substantial aspects such as the presence of the bishops in the House of Lords as well as of its symbolic aspects such as the ways in which prayers are part of the parliamentary calendar in the United Kingdom or a large cross dominates the chamber of the Quebec Provincial Assembly. While it is true that language is essential to the functioning of a state and a religion is not, the question of, and therefore making a decision about, the state-religion question is not optional. In any case, in respect of being optional, religion is on a par with many things that are unproblematically supported by states. For example, the state supports non-essential but valued activities such as the motor industry or the Olympics. While each of these has its critics, few people hold the view that state support should be confined to only those features essential to the existence of a state.

If by 'neutrality' is meant not cultural contentless-ness but that the basic structure of the state and its laws and policies must not be derived from or only be justified by reference to a religion because, say, such justifications must be consistent with what Rawls called a 'political conception of justice', then bearing in mind that Rawls was ruling out not just appeals to religion but to all 'comprehensive doctrines',[30] SRCs can be consistent with neutrality albeit with two qualifications. First, we must not assume that political justice in this basic sense is cut and dried, that the principles are only consistent with a small set of comprehensive doctrines and susceptible to a narrow set of meanings. Charles Taylor usefully offers a capacious understanding of 'overlapping consensus' – namely, a flexible and dialogical way of (re)interpreting the core principles of political justice and of how they may be implemented.[31] We can take this one step further by not thinking of 'overlapping consensus' as simply an overlapping set of derivations from discrete comprehensive doctrines evaluated against an independent a priori standard of justice, but rather as an interactive, dynamic process of persuasion and mutual learning, which is always a work in progress, and we might better express by calling it 'consensus building'.[32] Rawls's political conception of justice is in effect, as Bader points out, best understood not as an epistemological filter of 'reasonableness' but politically as adherence to Liberal Democratic Constitutionalism (LDC) – which of course has a substantive political content and so is far from 'politically neutral' in the normal meaning of the term.[33]

Second, if we assume LDC as a baseline or a core that we want all politics and political institutions to work from, including SRCs, it means that the state cannot *subtract* from LDC; it cannot be less than LDC. It does not mean that the just state cannot build on LDC; indeed, that is exactly what it must do. On this understanding of 'neutrality', the state can pursue sociopolitical projects such as, say, the elimination of poverty, or to put a man on the moon, or to enhance interfaith understanding among citizens or in the world generally; and can even identify with one or more comprehensive doctrines, socialism or liberal perfectionism – as long as and to the extent that such state identification or projects are within the limits of LDC. A state can identify with a philosophical or religious doctrine but it cannot make citizens conform to this doctrine in ways that violate the norms of LDC. It can in principle declare 'In God We Trust' or 'Allahu Akbar', but all entailments must be acted upon in ways consistent with liberal democratic constitutional rights and processes. Moreover, there are limits to what we can hope for from the state. For example, religious truth can't *come from* the state/politics (as Locke pointed out); no more than scientific truth can come from the state/politics, or indeed art or healthy living. Yet that does not mean that the state cannot promote religion any more than it means that the state cannot fund science or art or health care.[34] It is true that the state cannot require any citizen to believe in the truth of any religious doctrine, but no more can it require a belief in any comprehensive or political doctrine. The state may fund science at universities or may fund church-run schools without requiring any citizens to believe in any scientific hypothesis or religious doctrine.

It may sound like I am saying that it is consistent with LDC (what others may choose to call the liberal neutral state) to privilege religion. Yes, a kind of 'privileging' of religion is permissible. For example, a particular state may fund church schools teaching the national curriculum but not schools organised around atheism or 'race'. Such funding is a kind of privileging of religion but in a multiplex way. 'Multiplex' is a word that conjoins 'multiple' and 'complex'. The *Oxford English Dictionary* defines it as an adjective describing the 'involving or consisting of many elements in a complex relationship'. The state typically engages in not merely multiple cases of privileging but, moreover, the cases of privileging are not all of one basic kind. The state may legitimately choose to give funding and prestige to banking, to opera, to the Olympics and to 'blue skies' scientific research but without using the same arguments or the same metrics of calculation. So similarly, with the funding and bestowing of prestige on faith schools within a state-regulated system of schooling.

The liberal state may recognise that religion is special[35] and may honour and support it in special ways but this is not necessarily equivalent to simple 'privileging'. So you could say there is a multiplex privileging or a multiplexity of privileging and that there is no special or unique privileging of religion. What this shows is that the concept of 'neutrality' is not very helpful over and beyond a requirement not to subtract from LDC.

So far I hope I have shown that the 'privileging' of religion is not in principle inconsistent with LDC. This leaves unresolved many questions about what shape this privileging should take. I cannot resolve them but I would like to identify some of them and offer a few comments. There are in fact three separate issues of 'privileging':

1. Religion relative to non-religion (e.g., ethnicity or nation or economics): The multiculturalist view should be that no one type of identity or social dimension (e.g., religion, ethnicity, gender, class) should be privileged at the expense of the others. Moreover, there is no single measure of importance and so a variable geometry is inevitable: how a state will promote the Olympics will be different from how it will promote religion.
2. Religion relative to no-religion: This is the most difficult issue but not really specific to this case. The same applies, for example, to sport and no-sport, for just as there are people who think that religion should not be privileged and paid for out of taxes, so people hold the same view about sport (or opera or university scholarship etc.). Hence, I suggest 'multiplex privileging' may not be a kind of second best; there may be no other way of resolving a 'bias'.
3. One religion relative to another: This is not easy either and I do not have a fully worked out view on this but I think some important considerations are as follows: We should equalise upwards, not downwards.[36] That is to say, the presumption is that if there is a benefit that one party has and the other does not (to the same extent), then the party with the lesser benefit or without the benefit, should be brought closer to the level of the other party, rather than the other way round. We should not, for example, ask schools or other public institutions to stop celebrating Christmas because of the presence of Muslims or Hindus; rather, we should extend the public celebrations to include Eid and Diwali.[37] All the evidence suggests that this is what most minorities, especially Muslims, want – certainly in Britain. It is not the case that 'accommodating Muslims in the political sphere, certainly requires abandoning a commitment to the Christian norms that have, historically, defined European states'.[38] The challenge is not how to fully de-Christianise our states but how to appropriately add the new faiths alongside the older ones. This indeed is what is happening across much of Western Europe. What is interesting is that those most uncomfortable with this are not Christians or churches, but ideological secularists.

It may be useful for readers, especially for American readers, to see how distant my views are from First Amendment disputations in the United States. So, let me very briefly say how the position I am arguing for sits in relation to the five-part *Private Choice Test* that has been developed by the U.S. Supreme Court in relation to whether an educational voucher programme that benefits religious schools is constitutional:

- The program must have a valid secular purpose.

    Yes, but it may at the same time have some sort of religious purpose or endorsement.
- Aid must go to parents and not to the schools.

    In Western Europe nearly all states subsidise faith schools and this is part of my understanding of moderate secularism.
- A broad class of beneficiaries must be covered.

    Not necessarily. Sometimes religious groups may be targeted in an affirmative action manner if multicultural equality is best promoted that way in the specific circumstances.
- The program must be neutral with respect to religion.

    I offer an understanding of 'neutrality' based on LDC and multiplex privileging.
- There must be adequate nonreligious options.

    Yes, where this is applicable – for example, in relation to schools, health services and so on.[39]

My response, then, to the objection that SRCs are a violation of liberal neutrality is that if we mean cultural neutrality, that is a condition impossible to satisfy; if we mean something like LDC, then it is not inconsistent with respecting that to have what I call multiplex privileging and which I suggest can take many forms, of which SRCs are one. While SRCs like the current Anglican 'establishment' are unsatisfactory in terms of multicultural citizenship, it may be the case that, in a pluralised form, they offer a basis for the multicultural inclusion of religion, which would be blocked if they were to be abolished without alternative SRCs to be put in their place. It has, however, been argued that the Anglican establishment (and similar SRCs in other countries) alienates those who are outside the established Church,[40] in contrast to the inclusionary effects of a 'separation' regime – namely, U.S. denominationalism.[41] I shall consider this objection in the next chapter.

I believe that multicultural equality requires some kind of public multifaithism in an SRC way. In relation to Britain, for example, it does not have to be within an Anglican establishment, nor its equivalent in other countries; but that it, pluralised in some way, does offer one way forward and we should consider it as a practical proposition – especially if it is the least disruptive and if it allows those for whom establishment is important, or who are uncomfortable with multiculturalism, a relatively unthreatening way forward. At least I hope I have raised the challenge of how are we to give appropriate recognition to ethno-religious groups if it is not in part by pluralising existing SRCs? By 'existing SRCs' I mean the context of moderate secularism within LDC, where religious authority does not dominate political authority; where when religious organisations are publicly funded to deliver social services, citizens have options to receive the same services by non-religious organisations; and where, more generally, there is multiplex privileging and religion is not privileged in a unique and special way and a large range of non-religious activities also are privileged.

NOTES

1. I am grateful for written comments, on a previous draft, from Cécile Laborde, Jean Cohen, Matteo Bonotti and Sune Laegaard.
2. Tariq Modood, *Multiculturalism: A Civic Idea*, 2nd ed. (Cambridge: Polity Press, 2013).
3. Will Kymlicka, *Multicultural Citizenship* (Oxford: Oxford University Press, 1995).
4. Will Kymlicka, 'Historic Settlements and New Challenges', *Ethnicities*, 9, no. 4 (2009): 546–552.
5. Cécile Laborde, *Critical Republicanism* (Oxford: Oxford University Press, 2004) has argued that in doing so I am guilty of 'status quo partiality'. My commitment to political secularism as practiced in Western Europe is comparable to a commitment to democracy as practiced in those states: it is not a commitment to an existing set of institutions or to one particular time – namely, to a narrow status quo.
6. Though, see Alfred Stepan, 'Religion, Democracy, and the "Twin Tolerations"', *Journal of Democracy*, 11, no. 4 (2000): 37–57.
7. Rajeev Bhargava, 'Political Secularism: Why It Is Needed and What Can Be Learnt from Its Indian Version', in G. B. Levey and T. Modood (eds.), *Secularism, Religion and Multicultural Citizenship* (Cambridge: Cambridge University Press, 2009), 88. In chapter 8, I critique his understanding of secularist conceptions in the West as not being able to include West European versions.
8. Bhargava 'Political Secularism', 88.
9. Bhargava's theoretical position has become more difficult as while still holding on to his tripartite analysis of the secular state (ends, institutions, laws/policies), he has come to accept moderate secularism as a distinct West European form of secularism (Rajeev Bhargava, 'Can Secularism be Rehabilitated?', in Bruce J. Berman, Rajeev Bhargava and Andre Lalliberte [eds.], *Secular States and Religious Diversity*, 69–93 [Vancouver: University of British Columbia Press, 2013]; Rajeev Bhargava, 'Is European Secularism Secular Enough?' in Jean L. Cohen and Cécile Laborde [eds.], *Religion, Secularism, and Constitutional Democracy*, 157-181 [New York: Columbia University Press, 2016]) even though moderate secular states cannot be analysed in terms of state-religion *institutional* separations.
10. Cécile Laborde, 'Political Liberalism and Religion: On Separation and Establishment', *Journal of Political Philosophy*, 21, no. 1 (2013): fn. 3, 2.
11. Ronald Dworkin, *Is Democracy Possible Here? Principles for a New Political Debate* (Princeton, NJ: Princeton University Press, 2006), 62.
12. Dworkin, *Is Democracy Possible Here?*, 57.
13. I assume that is what he means by saying that Britain is a secular nation. Nevertheless, he simultaneously thinks of Britain as an ambiguous example of a 'moderate religious state', while for me Britain is a primary example of a moderate secular state.
14. In relation to the last point, I would point to how, for example, the Bishop of Bradford played a leading role in leading a local dialogue with Muslims who angrily burnt copies of the novel *The Satanic Verses* in 1989; since then this interfaith role has come to have government

involvement, especially through the creation of a new government department, the Department of Local Government and Communities, and one of its most developed recent manifestation is the policy of 'Near Neighbours', in which central government funds are distributed to local community initiatives, but applications have to be initially validated by a local priest of the Church of England.

15. 'Weak establishment' is not a flattering term and perhaps 'thin' or' minimal' might be substitutes for 'weak', but I continue to use the latter as it refers to power and it is clear that secularism is about relations of power.

16. Joel S. Fetzer and J. Christopher Soper, *Muslims and the State in Britain, France, and Germany* (Cambridge: Cambridge University Press, 2004).

17. Sune Laegaard, 'Unequal Recognition, Misrecognition and Injustice: The Case of Religious Minorities in Denmark', *Ethnicities*, 12, no. 2 (2012): 197–214.

18. Tariq Modood and Riva Kastoryano, 'Secularism and the Accommodation of Muslims in Europe', in T. Modood, A. Triandafyllidou and R. Zapata-Barrero (eds.), *Multiculturalism, Muslims, and Citizenship: A European Approach*, 162–178 (London: Routledge, 2006).

19. 'Symbolic establishment' is discussed by Daniel Brudney, '*On Noncoercive Establishment*', *Political Theory*, 33, no. 6 (2005): 812–839; and Laborde, 'Political Liberalism and Religion', and allowed as consistent with liberalism.

20. Cf. John Rawls, 'The Idea of Public Reason Revisited', *The University of Chicago Law Review*, 64, no. 3 (1997): 765–807; and Jurgen Habermas, 'Religion in the Public Sphere', *European Journal of Philosophy*, 14, no. 1 (2006): 1–25.

21. Charles Taylor, 'The Meaning of Secularism', *The Hedgehog Review*, 12, no. 3 (2010): 23–34; Gérard Bouchard and Charles Taylor, *Building the Future: A Time for Reconciliation*, Abridged Report (Quebec: Gouvernement du Québec, 2008); and Jocelyn Maclure and Charles Taylor, *Secularism and Freedom of Conscience*, trans. J. T. Todd (Cambridge, MA: Harvard University Press, 2011).

22. Veit Bader, 'The Governance of Religious Diversity: Theory, Research and Practice', in Paul Bramadat and Mathias Koenig (eds.), *International Migration and the Governance of Religious Diversity*, 43–72 (Montreal: McGill-Queen's University Press, 2009): 52.

23. Jean Baubérot, 'The Evolution of Secularism in France: Between Two Civil Religions', in Linnel E. Cady and Elisabeth Shukman Hurd (eds.), *Comparative Secularisms in a Global Age*, 57–69 (Basingstoke, UK and New York: Palgrave, 2012).

24. Murat Akan, 'Laïcité and Multiculturalism: The Stasi Report in Context', *The British Journal of Sociology*, 60, no. 2 (2009): 237–256.

25. In relation to Finland, see Tuomas Martikainen, 'Muslim Immigrants, Public Religion and Developments towards a Post-Secular Finnish Welfare State', *Studies in Contemporary Islam*, 8, no. 1 (2014): 98–105.

26. In chapter 8 I offer five different reasons why the state may be interested in religion, of which truth is just one, and, of course, is one that lost considerable legitimacy in the 20th century in Western Europe.

27. See Modood, *Multiculturalism*. I am presenting a conception of multiculturalism that is based on the pioneering work of Will Kymlicka, Bhikhu Parekh, Charles Taylor and Iris Marion Young, without being identical to the views of any one of them.

28. Cf. Charles Taylor, 'Multiculturalism and "The Politics of Recognition"', in Amy Gutmann (ed.), *Multiculturalism and 'The Politics of Recognition'*, 25–74 (Princeton, NJ: Princeton University Press, 1994) with Maclure and Taylor, *Secularism and Freedom of Conscience*. The latter's focus on conscience and protection of negative liberty, of exemptions from the state, seems to supplant the ideas of recognition and the harms of misrecognition, of alienation and symbolic equality, which are central to Taylor's famous earlier work. My own view is much closer to the 'non-procedural liberalism' that Taylor argues for in *Multiculturalism*, centred on recognition and that 'judgement about the good life can be enshrined in laws and state action' as long as they are consistent with liberal democratic constitutionalism (LDC) without being confined to LDC.

29. Cf. the discussion on the role of 'operative public values' in Bhikhu Parekh, *Rethinking Multiculturalism: Cultural Diversity and Political Theory* (Basingstoke: Macmillan, 2000/2006), as referred to in chapter 6.

30. Rawls, 'The Idea of Public Reason Revisited'.
31. Taylor, 'Meaning of Secularism'.
32. I owe this point to a discussion with Sune Laegaard.
33. Veit Bader, *Secularism or Democracy? Associational Governance of Religious Diversity* (Amsterdam: Amsterdam University Press, 2007).
34. After years of arguing that the appropriate liberal response to diversity is neutrality, Christian Joppke now argues that a liberal state may have a Christian identity, though he restricts this to a Christian cultural heritage identity, but interestingly believes it may be more inclusive of religious diversity than a narrowly 'liberal' state identity. Christian Joppke, 'A Christian Identity for the Liberal State?', *British Journal of Sociology* 64, no. 4 (2013): 597–616; Christian Joppke, 'Pluralism vs. Pluralism: Christianity and Islam in the European Court of Human Rights' in J. L. Cohen and C. Laborde (eds.), *Religion, Secularism, and Constitutional Democracy*, 89–111 (New York: Columbia University Press, 2015).
35. Dworkin, *Is Democracy Possible Here?*, denies that religion is special in the 'moderate secular state's view of religion' (62), which is odd because the whole point of secularism is that religion has to be treated specially and as a unique problem.
36. It is specifically in relation to my advocacy of 'equalising upwards' that Laborde, *Critical Republicanism*, believes I fall into the error of 'status quo partiality'.
37. Similarly, in the case of how to extend equality to gays and lesbians in relation to marriage, few have suggested that it should be done by abolishing the institution, one way of placing heterosexual and homosexuals on the same level.
38. P. T. Lennard, 'What Can Multicultural Theory Tell Us about Integrating Muslims in Europe?', *Political Studies Review*, 8 (2010): 317.
39. As established in *Zelman v. Simmons-Harris* (2002). '*Zelman v. Simmons-Harris*', Wikipedia: http://en.wikipedia.org/wiki/Zelman_v._Simmons-Harris [accessed 9/01/2014].
40. Rajeev Bhargava, 'States, Religious Diversity, and the Crisis of Secularism', *Open Democracy*, 22 March, 2011: http://www.opendemocracy.net/rajeev-bhargava/states-religious-diversity-and-crisis-of-secularism-0; 'Is European Secularism Secular Enough?'; Laborde, 'Political Liberalism and Religion'.
41. José Casanova, 'Immigration and the New Religious Pluralism: A European Union–United States Comparison', in G. B. Levey and T. Modood (eds.), *Secularism, Religion and Multicultural Citizenship*, 139–163; Kymlicka, 'Historic Settlements'; Nancy Foner and Richard Alba, 'Immigrant Religion in the US and Western Europe: Bridge or Barrier to Inclusion?', *International Migration Review*, 42 (2008): 360–392 .

Chapter Eleven

Multiculturalizing Secularism

Two states that most people will agree are secular states are the United States and the USSR (when it existed).[1] Of course they are very different states; one was a Communist Party dictatorship; the other, a liberal democratic enablement of capitalism. Moreover, they have very different relations with religion. The USSR had a self-declared atheist philosophy and actively suppressed religion, while the United States, a country with vigorous and publicly active Christian churches, has a constitutional 'wall of separation', which is actively, if variably, enforced by its Supreme Court.

What is it that makes these two states exemplars of political secularism? It clearly cannot be the separation of religion and state (the USSR was active in controlling and persecuting churches, mosques, etc.), and for the same reason it cannot be about freedom of conscience, nor can it be the idea that religion is a matter of personal, private belief (religion in the United States is a very public matter).

WHAT IS POLITICAL SECULARISM?

I suggest that the core idea of political secularism is the idea of political autonomy – namely, that politics or the state has a raison d'être of its own and should not be subordinated to religious authority, religious purposes or religious reasons. This is a one-way type of autonomy, where secularism can be supportive of autonomy of organized religion and freedom of religion too, as in the United States, but it does not have to be. Autonomy does not mean strict separation of the U.S. type. It is consistent with some government control of religion, some interference in religion, some support for religion and some cooperation with (selected) religious organizations and religious purposes. These are prominent forms of state-religion connections. By 'state-religion connections' (SRCs), as per the last chapter, I am referring to moderate secularism's presence within liberal democratic constitutionalism (on the latter, see Bader 2007), where religious authority does not dominate political authority, religious organizations are publicly funded to deliver social services, citizens have options to receive the same services by non-religious organizations, religion is not privileged in any uniquely special way and a large range of non-religious activities such as sport, opera and banking may also be privileged, albeit each in a different way. Such connections are present in every single Western European state, which after all is the seedbed for modern, Western political secularisms. Nevertheless, state control and support of religion must not compromise the autonomy of politics and statecraft: it must be largely justifiable in political terms, not just religious reasons, and must not restrict (but may support) political authority and state action.

Political secularism is then a value in itself. It is not some kind of 'neutrality', nor is its place above the fray of politics. It is something that one can be for or against, or for it under certain conditions, or for certain variations of it. It has no special connection with democracy, which it predates. In the West it has mainly been conjoined with liberal democracy (but not necessarily, as the USSR illustrates), when, among other features, it becomes two-way mutual autonomy: the autonomy of both the state and religion is valued and protected in constitutional arrangements. This is a mutual autonomy that Stepan (2000) calls 'twin tolerations'. Mutual autonomy – but not strict separation – has historically emerged as the liberal democratic version and the one that is most widespread today. For such secularists, religious freedom is one of the most essential and cherished political values. This commitment sometimes blinds them to the fact that religious freedom is not an unlimited good within all versions of secularism – as the examples of how the French and Turkish states control aspects of Islam vividly reminds us. New thinking about political secularism has suggested that secularism is, in its essentials, really about 'managing diversity' (Taylor 2010; also Taylor 2014; discussed by Bilgrami 2014). This has a contemporary pertinence – indeed it emphasizes what is central yet underappreciated today – but it cannot be right as a definition of political secularism. If there was no religious diversity in a country or in the world, if only one religion was present, there would still be a question about the relationship between religion and politics, and 'political autonomy' would still be a suitable answer.[2]

Moreover, secularism is not an answer to questions about any kind of diversity (such as linguistic diversity). It arises specifically in relation to religion, the power and authority of religion and the challenge it may pose to political rule or, say, equality among citizens (Bilgrami 2014). Indeed, one can go further and say that the secular and religion are correlative concepts.

If there was no religion in the world, not merely that it had passed away but if it had never existed in the first place so that there was no concept of religion, then secularism would have no reference point and there would be no concept of political secularism. In that sense, secularism is a secondary concept, dependent on the concept of religion. However, once there is a concept of secularism – with advocates, promoters, supportive monarch, armed militants and so on – then it has a dialectical relationship with religion. Secularism is not merely being defined by engagement with religion. Secularism also intellectually and politically redefines religion to suit secularist values and purposes (Asad 1993; 2003). In this way, in secularist countries, what we regard as religion today (an 'inner life', a 'belief', a private matter) is a much more socially restricted set of activities, relationships and forms of authority than was the case before secularism's rise to power, or than what prevails in nonsecularist countries today. Once an outgrowth of religious arrangements ('secular' orders of monks were those unconfined to monasteries), secularism has come to define or redefine religion and its proper place in many countries in the world.

This chapter is confined to Western Europe (west of what used to be called the Iron Curtain). This region is not typical, and perhaps even exceptional (Berger 1999; Berger et al. 2008). It is the one region in the world in which participation in religious activities (even private prayer) is a minority pursuit as a result, not of state ideology or state action, but of social change, education, political argument and the working of liberal democracy. Throughout the 20th century there has been a process of 'secularization', including a decline in religious worship and belief. This process has accelerated over time and across generations and has spread outwards from urban centres to rural areas, from Protestant countries to Catholic countries, and from north-western Europe to southern Europe. Moreover, the present century has seen limited reversal of this trend; indeed, in many places there has been acceleration. Yet, political secularism and its relation to religion has become a vibrant topic, and some scholars and public intellectuals even speak of a 'crisis of secularism'. What is the character and cause of this agitation and alarm? I contend that it is a product of a concatenation of three independent factors that have contingently come together.

WESTERN EUROPEAN MODERATE SECULARISM

For many intellectuals, especially political theorists, secularism or Western secularism is understood in terms of the religious-liberty secularism of the United States and/or the equality of citizenship secularism or *laïcité* of France. An example of this approach is Bhargava's, where these two secularisms are described as 'the most dominant and defensible western versions of secularism' and taken jointly are designated 'as the mainstream conception of secularism' (Bhargava 2009, 93). As a matter of fact, neither of these models approximates particularly closely to church-state relations among West European countries beyond France. In Germany, the Catholic and Protestant Churches are constitutionally recognized corporations for whom the federal government collects voluntary taxes and grants large amounts of additional public monies so that between them, they have a larger public welfare budget than the federal state. Belgium officially recognizes many religions (as well as non-religious philosophies). Norway, Denmark and England each have an 'established' church; Sweden had one until 2000; and Finland has two (Stepan 2011; cf. Koenig 2009). (The United Kingdom also has two state-recognized national churches, the Church of England and the Church of Scotland, but the latter is independent of the U.K. state, including of the Scottish state in which it plays no formal role.) Yet, it would be difficult to dispute that these states are not among the leading secular states in the world – more precisely, one could only dispute that if one had some narrow, abstract model of secularism that one insisted on applying to the varieties of empirical cases. So, the question is: How are we to characterize the secularisms of Western Europe? I have argued that despite their distinctive histories and institutional diversity that I have referred to, these states can be understood as having evolved what I have called 'moderate secularism' (Modood 2007; and chapter 8 above). I sketch this conception in terms of five features:

1. Mutual autonomy, not mutual exclusion or one-sided control. This is not distinctive to 'moderate secularism', as it is central to U.S. liberal secularism too, and to some extent France as well, although it leans more towards one-sided control.
2. Religion is a public good, not just a private good. Organized religion can play a significant role in relation to ethical voice,[3] general social well-being, cultural heritage, national ceremonies and national identity. This can take various forms, such as having input into a legislative forum on moral and welfare issues; being social partners with the state in the delivery of education, health and caring services; or, more intangibly, building social capital and the production of attitudes that create, for example, family stability or economic hope. Of course the public good that religion contributes is contextual; religion can, in other contexts, be socially divisive and can lead to civil and international wars. Hence religion can also be a public harm. The point is that religion's contributions are not confined to private lives; they are socially and politically significant in many different ways.

3. The national church or churches (organizers of this public good) belongs to the people and the country, not just to its religious members and clergy. All citizens, regardless of membership, can feel that the national church should meet certain national standards not expected of religious organizations in general. For example, when the Church of England's ruling body, the Synod, failed in 2012 to achieve the two-thirds majority necessary to permit female bishops, many secular commentators felt that the Church of England had let the country down, while the absence of female Catholic priests or female imams is not part of a national conversation. The loud criticism by those who are not active Anglicans played a part in the Church's reversal of its decision in 2014. The Lutheran Church in Denmark, as another example, is almost universally thought by Danes to be a central element of Danish national identity, even though only a minority say they believe in its doctrines and even fewer worship in the church. In these and other 'moderate secular' countries, even atheists feel that they have a right to use the national church for weddings and funerals.
4. It is legitimate for the state to be involved in eliciting the public good that comes from organized religion and not just to protect the public good from dangers posed by organized religion. If recognized as public goods, then, depending on the circumstances, it may be decided that they are best achieved through some state-religion connections rather than strict separation. This is a contingent matter, but the experience of Western Europe is that some connections are better than none. Of course, as was said in chapter 8, religion can also be a 'public harm', since it may serve as a basis for prejudice, discrimination, intolerance, sectarianism, social conflict, violence and so on, so the state has a responsibility to prevent harm as well as enhance the good. As with public goods, so with public harms. The interest of the state will not be primarily theological or taking preferential sides for or against one religion regardless of consequences; the state will be motivated by fostering and maintaining tangible and intangible public – or 'secular' – goods. The key consideration for the state will not be secular 'purity'. Instead, the state shall ensure that the means and ends are consistent with, and effectively serve, secular rationales, without constraint by a fetish for 'separation'. In recent years, concerns about Islamist terrorism and 'radicalization' have led states to extol and condemn certain kinds of Islam, to co-opt certain Muslim groups into governance and to engage in matters of imam training and the schooling of Muslim children.[4] Moreover, if religious organizations are supported with public funds or tasked by the state to carry out some educational or welfare duties, then the state will want to ensure that they do not compromise key policy goals. That is why religious organ-

izations are increasingly subject to certain legal requirements, such as equal access or non-discrimination – at least in some European states such as Britain, more so than others such as Germany (Lewicki 2014).

5. Moderate secularism can take different forms in different times and places, and not all forms of religious establishment should be ruled out without attending to specific cases. State-religion connections take different forms in different Western European countries depending on their histories, traditions, political cultures and religious composition, which all may change over time.[5] One of the forms it may take is 'establishment'. Formal establishment is only found in a minority of countries, yet nevertheless it is one of the forms that moderate secularism takes.[6] Even when it does so, I call this complex of norms and practices 'moderate secularism' rather than 'moderate establishment' (as Dworkin [2006] labels Britain; see also 'modest establishment' of Laborde 2013), as secularism is and should be in charge: the place for religion and establishment is dependent on secularist institutions and decision makers referring to secularist values and principles and pragmatic considerations. Moreover, moderate secularism really exists in practice; it is not just an ideal. Both in relation to the church-state relations narrowly conceived and in terms of an expansive sociological analysis, governing power lies with secularist institutions, networks and individuals employing secular identities, interests and goals. Moderate secularism is not something to contrast with religion; religion is already a component of it. Moderate secularism is a particular way of relating religion with state power and politics.

MULTICULTURALISM

Since the 1960s, in a number of countries a new way of thinking and organizing minority-majority relations has emerged. Initially associated with the new social movements and identity politics of gender, race, and sexuality, it is identified in Western Europe with the institutional accommodation of post-immigration ethno-religious minorities, which I call 'multiculturalism' (Modood 2007/2013). It marks a new conception of equality. Multiculturalism is not just anti-discrimination, the sameness of treatment and the toleration of 'difference', but also a respect for difference. This respect is not simply about equal rights despite differences but also about equality as the accommodation of difference in the public space, which is shared, rather than dominated, by the majority. Instead of creating a sharp distinction between the public sphere of rights and civic relations and a private sphere (of male-female relations, sexual orientation or religious belief), the public sphere reflects various norms and interests of all.

This genuine equality requires dropping the pretence of 'difference blindness' and allows marginalized minorities to also be visible and explicitly accommodated in the public sphere. This equality will sometimes require enforcing uniformity of treatment and eliminating discrimination against (for example) religious affiliation, and it may also require the recognition of distinctive disadvantages (such as measures to increase the number of women in a legislature) or special needs (such as the provision of halal meat in state schools). Finally, multiculturalism as a mode of post-immigration integration involves not just the reversal of marginalization but also a remaking of national citizenship, so that all can enjoy a sense of belonging. In the case of France, there should be a way of being French that Jews and Muslims, as well as Catholics and secularists, can possess (Modood 2007/2013).

The new ethno-religious diversity presented by Muslims and other post–World War II groups settling in Western Europe, should be mentioned here. This is not just about demography but also about claims made concerning shared public spaces, keeping in mind that initial claims were made within newly instituted discourses and policy frameworks of race (Britain), ethnicity (Netherlands) and guest workers (Germany). The majority of this post-immigration, ethno-religious population is Muslim, although the shift toward Muslimness was partly facilitated by an evolving and expansive set of identity politics and equality discourses in several countries and multiculturalism in particular, along with the way that Muslim populations are growing and settling down in their countries of migration (and birth, for the second generation). These trends could be said to be part of a more or less global rise in Muslim consciousness, both in relation to religiosity (including public religiosity) and the rise of Muslim identity or Islamist politics. In Western Europe, events of 1988–1989, the Salman Rushdie Affair in Britain and *l'affaire du foulard* in France were particularly pivotal, as explained in chapter 9.

This is an all-too-brief account of a complex set of concepts. While across the world – but especially in Western Europe and especially since the emergence of international Islamist networks of terrorism and increasing attacks in the West – multiculturalism has become an unpopular idea with politicians and publics. Nevertheless, there is good evidence that multiculturalist policies and accommodations are not being reversed (Kymlicka 2012). Also, a 'multiculturalist sensibility' (Kivisto 2012) is growing, as an approach is extended from what we might call ethno-racial diversity to ethno-religious pluralism. The important point is that despite the unpopularity of the term 'multiculturalism', as doubts about certain policies and anxieties about certain minorities continue, mainstream public discourses are also conceiving of this diversity not merely in terms of toleration (putting up with something negative), but in terms of the positive inclusion for minorities who do not have to assimilate or conform to the norms and attitudes of the majority. This multiculturalist sensibility did not arise in the context of religious difference, where various regimes of governance, including moderate secularism, have accommodated religious pluralism in limited ways and with limited reference to a concept of equality. Yet this multiculturalist sensibility – the idea that 'difference' is not an unfortunate fact to be put up with but a difference worthy of equality and respect – has travelled in different directions from its origins, so that many, not excepting Muslim minorities, now view the field of religious diversity differently.

My argument, then, in relation to the contingencies considered so far, is that current debates about the accommodation of Muslims and Islam in Western Europe must be viewed in terms of two conceptual-political complexes: moderate secularism and multiculturalism. Of course my argument is not that this is the only relevant way in which Muslims' claims upon the public sphere are being responded to, as was made clear in chapter 9. One way forward, particularly favoured by liberal political theorists and commentators, would be to move toward the 'separation' of religion and the state on the grounds that the state should be neutral in relation to 'conceptions of the good' (Rawls 1971; 1993). This position would be a departure from, rather than a continuity with, traditions of European moderate secularism, yet it can be seen as an extension of trends within European countries in the 20th century (see previous chapter). Another option would be to reassert that Europe is a Christian continent (as Pope Benedict XVI affirmed) or to claim that specific countries such as Germany or Britain are 'Christian countries'. Interestingly, some religious minorities prefer the latter options to what has come to be called 'aggressive secularism',[7] but they are not necessarily the first choice of groups agitating for accommodation. My interest is in a third option, one based on the multiculturalist sensibility of taking difference seriously. This, however, is a sensibility that is open to a number of interpretations. This chapter next considers three alternative interpretations and points out some of their shortcomings. The common problem turns out to be that they have an unsatisfactory conception of multiculturalism and/or moderate secularism.

RELIGION IS NOT PART OF MULTICULTURALISM?

Will Kymlicka rightly argues that the 'state unavoidably promotes certain cultural identities, and thereby disadvantages others' (1995, 108), but he excludes religion and ethno-religious groups from 'cultural identities'. While his interpretation of multicultural citizenship is primarily directed toward justifying special support or differential rights in relation to language and indigenous people, meeting needs of religious minorities seem to fall within the ambit of the traditional freedoms of worship, association and conscience. The only additional questions that his political multiculturalism considers in relation to religious minorities are exemptions (such as allowing Sikh men to wear turbans when others have to wear motorcycle helmets), rather than, as in the case of other cultural groups, minority demands for democratic participation, public resources or greater institutional representation. Kymlicka thinks that the integration of religious migrants such as Muslims has been best achieved in the United States, where no religion enjoys state support but all denominations are allowed to flourish in equality with the rest (Kymlicka 2009, 548).

This last point has also been said by some sociologists to be generally historically true: 'Without the separation of church and state, we believe, the religions imported by past immigration streams could not have achieved parity with Protestant versions of Christianity' (Foner and Alba 2008, 379). Whether this is true regarding Muslims in the United States and Western Europe is not obvious. On the one hand, anti-Muslim hostility is comparable in both regions – for example, the Pew Research Center (2011) found that only 57 per cent of Americans have a favourable view of Muslims compared to 64 per cent of Britons and French (Putnam and Campbell 2010). Furthermore, the levels of national identification and patriotism among immigrants and the second generation is far higher than often assumed (Reeskens and Wright 2014). Interestingly, as is discussed later in the chapter, national identification and patriotism among Muslims in Britain are higher than the population as a whole, despite the fact that Britain has a state church (Wind-Cowie and Gregory 2011).

Regardless of whether U.S. denominationalism or European moderate secularism is better at integrating religious groups, the more fundamental question remains: Why should language be appropriate for multiculturalism but not for religion? Is there some categorical difference between religion and language? A state must, it is argued, use at least one language, and so choices must be made. Which language(s)? How many languages? Complete state neutrality about language is impossible. Fairness therefore dictates that the state does not pretend to be neutral, so it should pursue an alternative strategy. Religion, on the other hand, is optional. It is not necessary to the functioning of the state, and this critique of neutrality does not extend to it. Moreover, citizens can learn several languages, but one would not be a member of several religions at the same time, so a multilingual state is an option while a multireligious state is not. That supplies a further reason why state neutrality in relation to language implies the addition of linguistic options but state neutrality concerning religion only implies disestablishment (Baubock 2003, 43–44).

These arguments fail to save Kymlicka's theory from the charge of an antireligion bias, nor do they make practical sense. First, although Kymlicka's theory does center on language, it extends well beyond language to cover 'cultural identities'. His theory is meant to protect and empower ethnocultural groups and not merely languages; all cultures contain elements that are no more necessary than religion, and some cultures are centred around religion. Moreover, the idea that a multireligious state is impossible is a misunderstanding. Countries as diverse as Germany and India could be described as being quasi-multi-establishment states. The German state has various institutional and fiscal ways of supporting and working corporately with the Roman Catholic Church and the Lutheran Churches. The Indian state regulates several organized religions and incorporates their principles into law. This state recognition of faith communities is a granting of political or legal status, without meaning that state officials or citizens have to believe in any or all of these faiths. Indeed, consider an even more fundamental case of an either/or exclusivity than the case of religion as presented by Baubock. One cannot be of more than one sex (extreme exceptions prove the rule), but it does not follow that a state in all its laws and policies must be gender-blind. Rather, the state should promote the interests of all genders, ensuring that differential treatment, where appropriate, can be justified by reference to differential needs while staying consistent with a suitably differentiated concept of equality. States do support much that is not essential to the state's existence, and a multiculturalist state surely is no exception.

IS MULTICULTURALISM ABOUT 'ANTISECULARIZATION', NOT ACCOMMODATION?

In contrast to Kymlicka's satisfaction with a pre-multiculturalist position on religious diversity, Yolande Jansen (2014) explicitly defends a multiculturalist secularism. With a focus on French laïcité, she shows how even in a context of republican universalism, the process of incorporating Jews led French society and the French state to demand that the Jews surrender their communal lives, an extraordinary pressure not experienced by most other French people in the nineteenth or early twentieth century – but faced by Muslims today. On her interpretation, Jansen's solution is a multiculturalism opposing the ascriptive and stereotypical images that French society creates for groups such as Jews and Muslims, while demanding of individual Jews and Muslims that they publicly distance themselves from these imagined undesirable groups by distancing themselves from their communities.[8] Opposition to such demands upon minorities about how they should live is the multiculturalist opposition to what Jansen calls 'secularization'. I endorse

Jansen's conclusion that such secularization is a form of coercive assimilation incompatible with multiculturalism. This pressure to secularize ethno-religious identities, however, takes an extreme form in republican secularism; and moreover there may be no remedies to it within that form of secularism. Yet moderate secularism, even where it may be susceptible to similar stereotypings of Jews and Muslims, is not intrinsically fearful of religious communities and religion in public life, so it can endorse state support for religious plurality and for resisting assimilation in favour of accommodating minorities. Moreover, a multiculturalism consisting of anti-ascription and anti-assimilation is too modest; a positive, institutional accommodation is crucial to multiculturalism – in just the same way that accommodation is a defining feature of moderate secularism. So, a project of multiculturalizing secularism cannot take its lead from what is possible within republican secularism, and the scope and ambitions of multiculturalism cannot be confined within even a reformed version of this unaccommodating secularism.

IS MODERATE SECULARISM PART OF THE PROBLEM, NOT PART OF THE SOLUTION?

Unlike those who think that secularism is inadequately dealing with multiculturalism because it is not similar enough to United States and/or France, Rajeev Bhargava believes that Europe is not sufficiently like India. He argues that religious diversity has been central to Indian secularism, unlike Europe's tradition. Now that Europe is compelled to adjust to religious diversity, it can learn much from India. While this is a useful recommendation, his analysis of European secularism is somewhat problematic. One of his long-standing positions has been that the mainstream conception of political secularism in the West consists of two, and only two, opposed models: the U.S. model and the French model (see chapter 8). However, as argued in chapter 6, this position is inaccurate since most of Western Europe consists of secular states that do not resemble either of those models, because they display their own distinctive model. Bhargava now accepts this view (Bhargava 2013, 77; Bhargava 2014a), while continuing to hold the view that European secularism is not sufficiently secular (Bhargava 2014a; also 2014b, 44.)

Bhargava's interpretation of a multiculturalist sensibility has judged that what I have labelled as moderate secularism is 'irretrievably flawed': while it has accommodated Christians, it will not be able to accommodate Muslims.[9] For Bhargava, moderate secularism is part of the problem, not the solution, since it cannot be reformed; specifically, it cannot be multiculturalized (Bhargava 2013, 78), and he adds that this marks a profound disagreement between us (Bhargava 2014b, 45). He offers several arguments, but only one can be discussed here. Bhargava claims that the Christian bias inherent to any established religion, something akin to the Anglican Church's establishment in Britain, indicates that even a reformed version will alienate British Muslims.

Cécile Laborde makes a similar argument. She recognizes how the Anglican establishment has relatively little power and holds a largely symbolic significance. Nevertheless, she argues that even when

> establishment is mostly symbolic and cannot be said to put anyone at a serious disadvantage, symbols do matter when the basic identification of citizens with their institutions is concerned . . . [therefore] Muslims are likely to be alienated by the distinctively Christian religiosity permeating public institutions. (Laborde 2008, 90–91)

She evokes a conception of citizenship that I share – namely, that 'all citizens should be able to not to feel alienated by their political institutions in light of their deepest beliefs, and that institutions should consequently be framed with that aim in mind' (Laborde 2013, 84). I actually hold a stronger version of this duty of symbolic recognition: not only must the state not alienate, the state must make positive efforts to ensure that all citizens are able to feel a sense of belonging.

Leaving that aside, I want to stress that Bhargava and Laborde are not simply making a conceptual point about civic status, as their positions are also about how citizens feel about citizenship. That is a valid concern, but they offer no evidence that British Muslim citizens feel alienated by the Anglican establishment. Indeed, they ignore evidence about the strong sense of British identification and national pride among Muslims in Britain. An analysis of two Citizenship Surveys has concluded, 'We find no evidence that Muslims or people of Pakistani heritage were in general less attached to Britain than were other religions or ethnic groups' (Heath and Roberts 2008, 2). This has in fact been the finding of many surveys, including one which concluded that

> Our polling shows that 88 per cent of Anglicans and Jews agreed that they were 'proud to be a British citizen' alongside 84 per cent of non-conformists and 83 per cent of Muslims – compared with 79 per cent for the population as a whole (Wind-Cowie and Gregory 2011, 39). . . .
> . . . This optimism in British Muslims is significant as – combined with their high score for pride in British – it runs counter to a prevailing narrative about Muslim dissatisfaction with and in the United Kingdom. While it is true that there are significant challenges to integration for some in the British Muslim community – and justified concern at the levels of radicalism and extremism in some British Muslim communities – overall British Muslims are more likely to be both patriotic and optimistic about Britain than are the white British community. (Wind-Cowie and Gregory 2011, 41–42)

British Muslims do include many vociferous political groups, and they have mounted many arguments, not to mention campaigns, in relation to socio-economic deprivation, religious discrimination, incitement to religious hatred, various foreign policies, antiterrorist policies and so on (as discussed in chapters 2 and 6). So it is the case that Muslims in Britain do seem to feel excluded and alienated by certain aspects of British society and indeed European society in general. Yet there is no record of any criticism by a Muslim group against the Anglican Church's establishment. On the other hand, many Muslims complain that Britain is too unreligious and anti-religious, too hedonistic, too consumerist, too materialist and so on. Muslims protest far more vigorously about secularist bans on modest female clothing, such as the headscarf (banned in French state schools since 2004) and the face veil (banned in public places in France and Belgium and perhaps in other European countries soon) than they do about 'establishment' or Christian privileges.

Muslims and other religious minorities appreciate that establishment is a recognition by the state of the public and national significance of religion. That recognition holds out the prospect of extending state-religion connections. Disestablishment, by contrast, would foreclose that prospect without conferring any benefits to religious minorities. This appreciation of establishment by religious minorities is partly the result of the fact that the Church of England takes its mission to serve the country quite seriously, including the goal of incorporating new minority faith communities into its vision for the country and for the Church's own sense of its responsibilities (Modood 1997). When Prime Minister David Cameron, during the 2011 Christmas season, said that it should be asserted that Britain is 'a Christian country' (Prime Minister's Office 2011) – the first time a British prime minister had spoken like that in a long time – it was welcomed by Ibrahim Mogra, the then chairman of the Mosque Committee of the Muslim Council of Britain and later the Assistant Secretary General.[10]

These matters do not argue for the mistaken view that Islamophobia is not an issue in Britain or that Muslims do not feel alienated in Britain, but only point to the way that these concerns make very little reference to Christianity, let alone the Anglican establishment. My own suspicion is that religious minorities such as Muslims are more likely to be alienated by the kind of secular state that Laborde argues for, one that she thinks is unavoidably more suited to non-religious citizens than religious citizens (Laborde 2013, 88) and equally alienated by the kind of secular state that actively seeks to reform aspects of Islam as Bhargava advocates (Bhargava 2014b). Bhargava thinks that moderate secularism, which is supposedly unreformable, should be replaced by the diversity-friendly secularism that developed in India. Interestingly, he does not discuss how the Indian state has failed to eradicate the high levels of religious violence in India and failed to protect Muslims from massacres and systematic discrimination (Bajpai 2017; Sutton 2014; Black, Hyman and Smith 2014, 2).

To better support the interpretation undergoing criticism in this section, an alternative understanding of alienation may try to appeal not simply to the experiences of religious minorities but also to 'objective alienation'.[11] This objective alienation would be something that can be said to exist even if the sufferers of the alienation were not themselves aware of it. I suppose that this idea parallels something that Karl Marx had claimed about alienation, that it is not simply an experience but a degraded condition of humanity in which the labouring class has no possibility of creativity or self-expression (Marx 1988). The danger – not at all hypothetical – to resorting to a concept of objective alienation involves how it could be used. For example, it could be raised (by French republicans or other secularists) in order to deny the need for confirming evidence that women wearing the Muslim headscarf are oppressed and dominated even when they themselves insist they are not and where no evidence shows that coercion or intimidation is taking place. In practice, that kind of denial can serve as the basis for the civic domination of Muslims through 'state paternalism' or at least 'educational paternalism' (de Latour 2013). A satisfactory account of objective alienation must explain how to properly handle evidence (and counterevidence), yet those explanations have not been provided by any interpretations I have examined.

Those who argue for U.S. or French types of disestablishment by claiming that contemporary Christian state-religion connections only alienate groups such as Muslims are relying heavily on certain secularist assumptions and not enough on evidence. Secularists concerned with minimizing alienation would do well to first focus on how their secularism results in alienation. This suggests that the significant difficulty in Britain of integrating Muslims concerns more what Casanova identifies as the more important factor – namely, what he calls 'recent trends towards drastic secularization' (Casanova 2009, 141). Hence, if the United States is better at integrating post-immigration religious minorities, this may not be due to its lack of an establishment but to the greater presence of religion and, in particular, the greater social status of religion and its closeness to the mainstream of society (a point recognized by Casanova (2009) and offered as a factor by Foner and Alba (2008). In this respect, it is important to note that while the United States may be more of a secular state than Britain, the latter is more of a secular society and has an increasingly secularist political culture (see chapter 6). It is as if two quite different social compacts were at work: in the British case, the deal is that the religious majority can have state recognition at the highest level but must exercise self-effacement in relation to the democratic process, if not public culture as well. The deal in the United States, however, is that if all churches can agree to allow a certain limited area of public life as 'religiously neutral' and 'beyond religion', the rest of public life is an open field for religion. In the United States, all religious groups are free to *lead the nation*, to seek to make the nation in their own image – as long as it is not through Establishment. It is not that politics is a no-go area, but Establishment is not considered an appropriate means to further religious ends (Modood 2009). While this may work well for the United States, it is far from stress-free, as we have seen with the rise of an embittered Christian Right, alongside support for aggressive foreign policies with Islamophobic politics as extreme as those in Europe, but more conspicuously led by Christians.[12] Indeed, initially the U.S. Tea Party, and more recently President Trump's former alt-right strategist Steve Bannon, have forged links with Islamophobic groups such as the English Defence League, and some of its luminaries are a source of nourishment for the mass murderer, Anders Breivik (Murray 2011). In this situation, where U.S. state secularism sits alongside Christianist anti-Muslim political campaigns as aggressive as any found in Europe (except that, as we have seen, in Europe they are not primarily Christianist), it is unfortunate that admirers of U.S. state secularism express pessimism regarding the capacity of moderate European secularism to reform and evolve.

Moreover, if I am correct to suggest that Muslims and other religious minorities are seeking equality through their accommodation within something resembling the status quo in Europe, rather than a disestablishment of Christian churches, then we are talking about an additive view of inclusivity, not a subtractive view. Typically, recognition or accommodation for minorities implies that particular social dimensions important to those minorities become more, not less, politically significant. Equality movements do not usually pursue diminished political importance for their social subgroups. This is the case with regard to equality movements about race, gender, nationality, sexual orientation, class and so forth. It is difficult to see why equality concerning religion has to be treated differently. Therefore, the multicultural challenge for secularism is not how to de-Christianize Western states but how to appropriately include newly arriving faiths alongside older faiths.

CONCLUSION

I hope I have offered some reasons for at least some Europeans to be more optimistic about their capacity to multiculturalize their own institutions in ways faithful to their own logic. This will certainly mean that there will be no singular European solution – the countries of Europe are too different for that. But one of the sources of hope is the moderate secularist legacy, with its varied forms in different states providing a plural set of resources, some of which may be more suitable for certain polities but from which there can be mutual learning and borrowing in the crafting of the multifaith and multicultural citizenships that are not so much dead as struggling to be born.

NOTES

1. For the rather Eurocentric view that the Soviet Union was not a secular but only a quasi-secular state because it did not implement religious freedom, see Berman, Bhargava and Laliberté (2013, 8).
2. I owe this point to Bhikhu Parekh.
3. Habermas (2006) suggests that this is imperative in the twenty-first century. He is, however, mistaken in suggesting that the perception that this is desirable is new to European publics. It may, however, be a relatively new idea for some secularist intellectuals.
4. For a study of various aspects of this in England, see O'Toole et al. (2013).
5. Despite this statement, I have been criticized by Bader and others for lumping together different models of religious governance into one conception of moderate secularism. He, however, is close to my approach when he says that 'the most important dividing line may be between religious institutional pluralism recognizing some forms of selective cooperation between state and organized religions . . . and strict separationism' (Bader 2017).
6. The Western European countries that I say can be characterized in terms of 'moderate secularism' are in constitutional-political terms characterized as 'selective co-operation' by Ferrari (1995) but are separated by Stepan into the 'Established Religion' and 'Positive Accommodation' models (2011).
7. Baroness Warsi's speech at The Vatican, 'Baroness Warsi Decries Europe's "Aggressive Secularism"', *Telegraph*, 14 February 2012: http://www.telegraph.co.uk/news/religion/9083045/Baroness-Warsi-decries-Europes-aggressive-secularism.html. See Modood (1997).
8. See Laborde (2008): 'What defines a minority is precisely its vulnerability to "identity assignation" by the majority' (10; see also 24). Like Jansen, Laborde, too, thinks that undoing this domination is not about accommodation but, unlike Jansen, she thinks what is involved is not a critical multiculturalism but a 'critical republicanism'.
9. For a fuller discussion of why I think Bhargava misunderstands Western European secularisms, see chapter 8 and Modood (2011), though I note that in 'Can Secularism Be Rehabilitated?' (Bhargava 2013), he accepts that Western European moderate secularisms are distinct from and additional to his contention that the American and the French models are the mainstream Western models.
10. 'David Cameron on Christianity – Views,' *BBC News*, 18 December 2011: http://www.bbc.co.uk/news/uk-16231223.
11. Laegaard (2017) has usefully made a distinction between alienation and symbolic inequality and argued that it is the latter that is at stake.
12. In relation to inflammatory politics around the 'Ground Zero Mosque', 'Shariah Law' and public burnings of the Qur'an, and how these controversies should be dealt with, see Nussbaum (2012).

REFERENCES

Asad, T. (1993). *Genealogies of Religion: Discipline and Reasons of Power in Christianity and Islam*. Baltimore, MD: Johns Hopkins University Press.
Asad, T. (2003). *Formations of the Secular: Christianity, Islam, Modernity*. Stanford, CA: Stanford University Press.
Bader, Veit. (2007). *Secularism or Democracy? Associational Governance of Religious Diversity*. Amsterdam: Amsterdam University Press.

Bader, Veit. (2009). 'The Governance of Religious Diversity: Theory, Research and Practice'. In Bramadat, P. and Koenig, M. O. (eds.), *International Migration and the Governance of Religious Diversity*, 43–73. Montreal: McGill-Queen's University Press.
Bader, Veit (2017). 'Secularisms or Liberal-Democratic Constitutionalism?' In Zuckerman, P. and Shook, J. R. (eds.), *The Oxford handbook of secularism*, 333–353. Oxford: Oxford University Press.
Bajpai, R. (2017). "Secularism and Multiculturalism in India: Some Reflections'. In Triandafyllidou, Anna and Modood, Tariq (eds.), *The Problems of Religious Diversity: European Challenges, Asian Approaches*, 204–227. Edinburgh: Edinburgh University Press.
Baubock, R. (2003). 'Public Culture in Societies of Immigration'. In Sackmann, R., Peters, B. and Faist, T. (eds.), *Identity and Integration: Migrants in Western Europe*, 37–57. Aldershot, UK: Ashgate.
Berger, Peter L. (1999). *The Desecularization of the World: Resurgent Religion and World Politics*. Washington, DC: Ethics and Public Policy Center.
Berger, Peter, Davie, Grace and Fokas, Effie. (2008). 'Religious America, Secular Europe?' In *Religious America, Secular Europe? A Theme and Variations*, 9–21. Aldershot, UK: Ashgate.
Berman, B. J., Bhargava, R. and Laliberté, A. (eds.). (2013). *Secular States and Religious Diversity*. Vancouver: University of British Columbia Press.
Bhargava, Rajeev. (2009). 'Political Secularism: Why It Is Needed and What Can Be Learnt from Its Indian Version'. In Levey, G. B. and Modood, T. (eds.), *Secularism, Religion and Multicultural Citizenship*, 82–110. Cambridge: Cambridge University Press.
Bhargava, Rajeev. (2011). 'States, Religious Diversity, and the Crisis of Secularism'. Open Democracy, 22 March: http://www.opendemocracy.net/rajeev-bhargava/states-religious-diversity-and-crisis-of-secularism-0.
Bhargava, Rajeev. (2013). 'Can Secularism Be Rehabilitated?' In Berman, B. J., Bhargava, R. and Lalliberte, A. (eds.), *Secular States and Religious Diversity*, 69–97. Vancouver: University of British Columbia Press.
Bhargava, Rajeev. (2014a). 'How Secular Is European Secularism?' *European Societies*, 16(3), 329–336.
Bhargava, Rajeev. (2014b). 'Should Europe Learn from Indian Secularism?' In Black, Brian, Hyman, Gavin and Smith, Graham M. (eds.), *Confronting Secularism in Europe and India*, 39–58. London: Bloomsbury.
Bilgrami, Akeel. (2014). 'Secularism: Its Content and Context'. In Stepan, Alfred and Taylor, Charles (eds.), *Boundaries of Toleration*, 79–129. New York: Columbia University Press.
Black, Brian, Hyman, Gavin and Smith, Graham M. (eds.). (2014). *Confronting Secularism in Europe and India*. London: Bloomsbury.
Casanova, José. (2009). 'Immigration and the New Religious Pluralism: A European Union–United States Comparison'. In Levey, G. B. and Modood, T. (eds.), *Secularism, Religion and Multicultural Citizenship*, 139–163. Cambridge: Cambridge University Press.
de Latour, Sophie Guérard. (2013). 'Is Multiculturalism Un-French? Towards a Neo- Republican Model of Multiculturalism'. In Balint, P. and de Latour, S. G. (eds.), *Liberal Multiculturalism and the Fair Terms of Integration*, 139–159. Basingstoke, UK: Palgrave.
Dworkin, Ronald. (2006). *Is Democracy Possible Here? Principles for a New Political Debate*. Princeton, NJ: Princeton University Press.
Ferrari, Silvio. (1995). 'Emerging Pattern of Church and State in Western Europe: The Italian Model'. *The Brigham Young University Law Review*, 2, 421–437.
Foner, Nancy and Alba, Richard. (2008). 'Immigrant Religion in the U.S. and Western Europe: Bridge or Barrier to Inclusion?'. *International Migration Review*, 42(2), 360–392.
Habermas, Jurgen. (2006). 'Religion in the Public Sphere'. *European Journal of Philosophy*, 14(1), 1–25.
Heath, Anthony and Jane Roberts. (2008). *British Identity, Its Sources and Possible Implications for Civic Attitudes and Behaviour*. London: Department of Justice, HMSO.
Jansen, Yolande. (2014). *Secularism, Assimilation and the Crisis of Multiculturalism: French Modernist Legacies*. Chicago: University of Chicago Press.

Kivisto, P. (2012). 'We Really Are All Multiculturalists Now'. *Sociological Quarterly*, 53(1), 1–24.

Koenig, M. (2009). 'How Nations-States Respond to Religious Diversity'. In Bramadat, P. and Koenig, M. (eds.), *International Migration and the Governance of Religious Diversity*, 293–322. Kingston, ON: School of Policy Studies, Queens University.

Kymlicka, Will. (1995). *Multicultural Citizenship*. Oxford: Oxford University Press.

Kymlicka, Will. (2009). 'Historic Settlements and New Challenges: Review Symposium'. *Ethnicities*, 9(4), 546–552.

Kymlicka, W. (2012). *Multiculturalism: Success, Failure, and the Future*. Washington, DC: Migration Policy Institute.

Laborde, Cécile. (2008). *Critical Republicanism*. Oxford: Oxford University Press.

Laborde, Cécile. (2013). 'Political Liberalism and Religion: On Separation and Establishment'. *Journal of Political Philosophy*, 21(1), 67–86.

Lægaard, S. (2017). 'What's the Problem with Symbolic Religious Establishment? The Alienation and Symbolic Equality Accounts'. In Laborde, Cécile and Bardon, Aurelia (eds.), *Religion in Liberal Political Philosophy*, 118–131. Oxford: Oxford University Press.

Lewicki, Aleksandra. (2014). *Social Justice through Citizenship? The Politics of Muslim Integration in Germany and Great Britain*. Basingstoke, UK: Palgrave Macmillan.

Marx, Karl. (1988). *The Economic and Philosophic Manuscripts of 1844 and the Communist Manifesto*. Buffalo, NY: Prometheus Books.

Modood, Tariq. (1997). *Church, State and Religious Minorities*. London: Policy Studies Institute.

Modood, Tariq. (2007/2013). *Multiculturalism: A Civic Idea* (2nd ed., 2013). Cambridge: Polity Press.

Modood, T. (2009). 'Introduction: Odd Ways of Being Secular'. *Social Research: An International Quarterly*, 76(4), 1169–1172.

Modood, Tariq. (2011). 'Moderate Secularism: A European Conception'. *Open Democracy*, 8 April: http://www.opendemocracy.net/tariq-modood/moderate-secularism-european-conception.

Modood, Tariq. (2016). 'State-Religion Connexions and Multicultural Citizenship'. In Cohen J. and Laborde C. (eds.), *Religion, Secularism and Constitutional Democracy*, 182–203. New York: Columbia University Press.

Murray, C. (2011). 'Norwegian Killer Linked to Tea Party and EDL'. July 23: http://www.craigmurray.org.uk/archives/2011/07/norwegian-killer-linked-to-tea-party-and-edl/ [accessed on 13/8/2012].

Nussbaum, N. (2012). *The New Religious Intolerance: Overcoming the Politics of Fear in an Anxious Age*. Cambridge, MA: Harvard University Press.

O'Toole, T., DeHanas, D. N., Modood, T., Meer, N. and Jones, S. (2013). *Taking Part: Muslim Participation in Contemporary Governance*. Bristol, UK: Centre for the Study of Ethnicity and Citizenship, University of Bristol: http://www.bristol.ac.uk/media-library/sites/ethnicity/migrated/documents/mpcgreport.pdf.

Pew Research Center. (2011). 'Muslim-Western Tensions Persist'. Pew Research Center: Global Attitudes & Trends: http://www.pewglobal.org/2011/07/21/muslim-western-tensions-persist/.

Prime Minister's Office. (2011). 'Prime Minister's King James Bible Speech'. gov.uk, 16 December: http://www.number10.gov.uk/news/king-james-bible [accessed 21/04/2015].

Putnam, Robert D. and Campbell, David E. (2010). *American Grace: How Religion Divides and Unites Us*. New York: Simon & Schuster.

Rawls, J. (1971). *A Theory of Justice*. Oxford: Oxford University Press.

Rawls, J. (1993). *Political Liberalism*. New York: Columbia University Press.

Rawls, John. (1997). 'The Idea of Public Reason Revisited'. *University of Chicago Law Review*, 64, 765–807.

Reeskens, Tim and Wright, Matthew. (2014). 'Host-Country Patriotism among European Immigrants: A Comparative Study of Its Individual and Societal Roots'. *Ethnic and Racial Studies*, 37(14), 2439–3511.

Stepan, Alfred. (2000). 'Religion, Democracy, and the "Twin Tolerations"'. *Journal of Democracy*, *11*(4), 37–57.
Stepan, A. (2011). 'The Multiple Secularisms of Modern Democratic and Non-Democratic Regimes'. In Calhoun, C., Juergensmeyer, M. and VanAntwerpen, J. (eds.), *Rethinking Secularism*, 114–144. Oxford: Oxford University Press.
Sutton, Deborah. (2014). 'Secularism, History and Violence in India'. In Black, Brian, Hyman, Gavin and Smith, Graham M. (eds.), *Confronting Secularism in Europe and India*, 113–128. London: Bloomsbury.
Taylor, Charles. (1994). 'The Politics of Recognition'. In Gutmann, Amy (ed.), *Multiculturalism* (2nd ed.), 25–75. Princeton, NJ: Princeton University Press.
Taylor, Charles. (2010). 'The Meaning of Secularism'. *The Hedgehog Review*, *12*(3), 23–34.
Taylor, Charles. (2014). 'How to Define Secularism'. In Stepan, Alfred and Taylor, Charles (eds.), *Boundaries of Toleration*, 79–129. New York: Columbia University Press.
Wind-Cowie, Max and Gregory, Thomas. (2011). *A Place for Pride*. London: Demos.

Chapter Twelve

Intercultural Public Intellectual Engagement

DIALOGUE AND REASON IN POLITICAL THEORY

I would like to conclude this collection of essays on secularism and multiculturalism with some reflections on aspects of dialogue and public intellectual engagement on these topical themes. A good place to begin the topic of dialogue and the contribution of intellectuals, and especially of political theory, is with Socrates. Not only does he, as he appears in the works of his student Plato, take us to what may iconically represent the founding moment of Western philosophy and political theory, he also takes us to the most basic meanings of the term 'dialogue' – namely, focused oral communication between at least two interlocutors or its portrayal as a literary genre. Socrates was famous for endlessly questioning individuals in the public square, the *agora*, and Plato wrote dialogues. Plato's dialogues take two forms. Most of the early dialogues, referred to as *eristic*, take the form of an interrogation. Socrates is portrayed engaged in a hostile series of questions aimed to show that his interlocutor, often a well-known 'sophist', does not know what he is talking about.[1] Socrates sets out to destroy the argument of his interlocutor and to discredit him as either a teacher, a learned person or an authority on wise conduct. These dialogues typically end in a breakdown with Socrates's opponent alleging that Socrates is constantly twisting his words for his own self-aggrandisement, so there is no point carrying on. The other kind of dialogue, of which the *Republic* is the most famous example, is more like an interview and consists of rational cooperation to discover the Truth.

While both these kinds of oral exchanges have lived on and are central to the disciplines of philosophy and political theory – as in the 'Q and A' after a lecture, at a seminar or tutorial – the dialogue as a literary form is the exception rather than the norm in any academic discipline. While the oral exchanges, principally of the adversarial kind, do have a lively presence in certain democracies, not to mention in courts of law, the dominant mode of reasoning together that modern theorists have conceived as appropriate for the most fundamental questions of political life is altogether different. The dominant tradition in modern Western political theory is that of the 'social contract'. When theorists like Thomas Hobbes, John Locke or Jacques Rousseau pose questions about why polities exist and what gives rulers the right to rule, they assume that the question is posed of individuals who can be hypothesised to give their free consent. This assumes that the individuals know what they want. They negotiate among themselves to get the best deal for oneself or for all parties, yet they reason about the founding of states and coercive laws on the basis of pre-existing desires and preferences, which are already known to them. There is, however, one line of continuity with Socrates. While it is assumed that individuals will vary in their desires, it is further assumed that there is a single truth, a single set of principles or correct answer to be discovered by Reason.

While Hobbes postulated that all would rationally choose to subject themselves to absolute authority because the alternative, the 'state of nature', was permanent insecurity and constant likelihood of death (Hobbes 1968 [1651]). Locke thought all persons had certain natural rights that could not be overridden and so individuals would only give their consent to be ruled by a state which had a mechanism for self-limiting its power by, for example, having an independent judiciary to check that the government respected the rights of each individual (Locke 1966 [1690]). Rousseau took this idea of individuals' contracting to obey a common authority further by conceiving it as not just a foundational act but also as a process of democratic lawmaking by citizens. For him, this meant that the conditions for the emergence of law in an assembly had to be of a particular kind. Above all, they should be such that the citizens should not be thinking in terms of their personal desires or gain, their class interests or political party membership, but should think in terms of what was best for the republic. Only then would their 'general will' as opposed to a collection of personal wills manifest itself (Rousseau 1920 [1762]).

John Rawls is the most important recent theorist in this tradition. He too looks to found politics and social justice on what free, rational individuals would collectively agree to after discussion. As Rousseau, Rawls thinks that the conditions or circumstances in which such dialogue takes place are critical. The discussants should be able to focus on what is good for individuals in general, or to put it differently, what all individuals would want after reflection, not on what individuals like themselves would want. They must think selflessly – literally. Rawls designs a thought experiment, the centrepiece of which is what he calls 'the Veil of Ignorance' (Rawls 1971). For the deliberation of individuals to lead to the discovery of social justice or 'fair terms of social cooperation' (Rawls 1985, 232) they must be made ignorant – stripped – of their specific identities such as their gender, their class, their nationality, culture, religion and so on. So none of the reasoners knows for example whether they are rich or poor, black or white, Christian or Muslim and so on. So no one will risk favouring laws and policies that unduly favour a particular class, race or religion in case when – at the end of the deliberation, the Veil of Ignorance is lifted and they (re)learn who they are – it turns out they are not of the group they favoured.

Rawls's claim is, then, that the principles of social justice can only be worked out by individuals, intellectuals, lawmakers, benign governments and so on to the extent that they approximate to being self-less or identity-less reasoners. That, however, means that dialogue among such individuals is not necessary because, stripped of all their differences, such reasoners are identical. One reasoner can in theory come up with the just solution without there having to be a dialogue among all the citizens. Moreover, behind the Veil of Ignorance, the debate makes no difference to what is valuable in the product of the debate. The product – the principles that a diverse society should live by – are not influenced by who is or is not included in the debate, and so they remain the same however the debate goes. That is to say, they are not influenced by the debate and the principles could indeed have been known without any dialogue having taken place. More precisely, they are known by *reason*, not by dialogue or by who participates in the dialogue.

DIALOGUE AS USED BY MULTICULTURALISTS

This is not, however, how multiculturalists have approached political theory. Dialogue, rather than abstract reasoning by a sole reasoner or identical identity-less individuals, has motivated multiculturalists. They assume that the context for politics is already thoroughly imbued with dominant ways of thinking and doing – with cultural orientations such as national history and language, with religious and/or secular perspectives, with institutional norms and so on – and that these contextual factors cannot be abstracted out so as to identify a set of culture-free problems. Moreover, the relationship between the relevant parties is likely to involve domination-subordination, or inclusion-exclusion and that the weaker or newer party is likely to lack recognition or be misrecognised (Taylor 1994). Dialogue rather than identity-less reasoning will be relevant here for at least three reasons. First, the solution to the problem, or the arriving of a principle by which to address the problem, needs an effort at cross-cultural understanding. It is not just a question of taking material interests into account, but a matter of (re)designing the shared public space and rules of conduct so diverse cultural commitments and needs are explicitly taken into account – so that the public space does not simply reflect the dominant culture, but is opened up to accommodate new or marginalised minorities. Second, this means that the solution is genuinely open. By this I do not mean that 'anything goes'. Rather, that the solution cannot be predicted in advance in the way that, say, the final step of a piece of mathematical reasoning can, of which we say the answer was there all along waiting to be discovered. The dialogue makes a difference: it contributes to a growth of understanding that genuinely is novel or additional to what was present before and the quality or character of the dialogue is dependent on the participants – not simply in terms of their power of reasoning but also in terms of 'where they are coming from' – so that with different parties a different outcome would have been reached. Third, the dialogue is important not just in discovering an outcome, but also in building a *relationship* of trust, of co-operation and ultimately of belonging together between parties to the dialogue. These three reasons makes the dialogue very different from the 'behind the veil' reasoning of identity-less reasoners.

The multiculturalist political theorists I have in mind include Iris Young, who assisted people to understand themselves as oppressed and to discover themselves in collective identities such as black or gay and to thus develop a liberatory identity and group politics and using it to engage with other groups to institute a new form of democratic politics (Young 1990). Charles Taylor's idea of a dialogical ethics and politics based on 'recognising' those whose distinct cultural identities have been dismissed or held in contempt – such as the identities of African Americans in the United States or francophone Quebecers in Canada – too is an example (Taylor 1994). Interestingly, in his more recent work Taylor relates his approach to diversity to a Rawlsian idea, that of 'an overlapping consensus' (Rawls 1987; Taylor 2009).[2] For Rawls, this referred to the body of laws and policies that those with different religious and cultural perspectives could all agree on by focusing on politics rather than their full set of religious and value commitments. Taylor rejects the idea of the identityless self (sometimes referred to as 'the unencumbered self') and abstract reasoning as the method for arriving at a consensus. He borrows and adapts 'overlapping consensus', but makes the process of arriving at it much more expansive and dynamic so that it in fact is best understood as consensus building – something not given but to be worked at, including through new interpretations of actors' points of views, one of the things that one might expect from a dialogue (Taylor 2009). James Tully has continually emphasised that cooperation under conditions of deep diversity or 'multiplicity' requires a 'multilogue' (Tully 1995), and has proposed the idea of 'public philosophy', the questioning of society's dominant assumptions in order to expose their contingency – their lack of necessity – and so open the way to identifying other possible ways of thinking and living (Tully

2008). Bhikhu Parekh explicitly makes intercultural dialogue central to his conception of multiculturalism. His interventions in relation to *The Satanic Verses* affair, in which he argued against a freedom-of-speech absolutism and argued that angry Muslims must be given a sympathetic hearing, are exemplary (Parekh 1989).[3] While fully recognising that in such public controversies, the majority dominate public discourse, and often in a manner that is not conducive to dialogue or mutual learning, he argues that multiculturalism is not about allowing each minority to-live-as-it-wishes relativism (Parekh 2000/2006). Rather, it is about ensuring that there is a genuine dialogue and that the minority is allowed to express its point of view. While such dialogues inevitably have a majoritarian or status quo starting point, because even while wanting to express unfamiliar sensibilities and bring in new arguments, minorities are primarily trying to persuade the majority. This often takes the form of a minority arguing that what it is seeking is not so different from what the majority, at one time or another, has sought for itself. In so arguing the minority must justify itself by appealing to – even while seeking to modify – the existing 'operative public values' which structure public debate and what is thought to be legitimate or reasonable in that polity at the time (Parekh 2006, 267).[4]

For such multiculturalists the principles of social justice are not known in advance or simply by reason, but are arrived at by conflict and *learning*, by dialogue and negotiation in circumstances of inequality and minority–claims making. Admittedly, in Rawls's methodology, there is a to-ing and fro-ing from principles and experience/particularities/context – what he calls 'reflective equilibrium' (Rawls 1971). But it can be done by an isolated reasoner or an assembly of identity-less, selfless reasoners, because at its best, it is disinterested, selfless reasoning carried on far away from conflict. For the multiculturalists, the dialogue is claims based and contentious, and based on identity assertion (relative to other identities), not identity effacement. It seeks to get beyond – even if it never gets there – the conflict or challenge to which it gives rise by urging the recognition of the excluded, the inferiorised and the misrecognised, and by the formation of new, inclusive, hyphenated and multiple overlapping identities. The dialogue comes into being because of identity-based claims; it proceeds by recognising identities; and its goal, its teleology, is the construction of new identities and new relationships, which are not reducible to redistribution.

MULTICULTURALISM AND INTERCULTURALISM

The kind of public intellectual engagement or multiculturalist dialogue I am arguing for here needs to be contrasted with other conceptions of intercultural dialogue. It can, for example, be contrasted with a philosophical multiculturalism which is concerned to develop a frame in which different cultures and religions can come to an understanding of each other and, therefore, to a richer understanding of humanity. Taylor, for example, sees the ultimate frontier of the politics of recognition as being the development of sensibilities and ways of thinking so that we can understand cultures radically different from our own and thereby evaluate their contribution to human civilisation (Taylor 1994). He, though, sees this frontier far from contemporary capacities. Similarly, Parekh, emphasises that the ultimate value of multiculturalism lies in cross-cultural and cross-civilisational understanding through which we simultaneously appreciate the varied ways to be human, while more profoundly understanding one's own distinctive location (Parekh 2000). While my own formulation of multiculturalism is built on a reading of Taylor and Parekh (among others), the philosophical views which I have just ascribed to them carry important and controversial philosophical theses, which I can leave to one side – for example, Taylor's suggestion that different cultures can be evaluated and ranked by and against each other; or Parekh's moral intersubjectivism: the view that values and morality, while grounded in a conception of human nature, ultimately have no foundations independent of reasoning selves (Parekh 2006, 128). These are debates that I do not need to enter. My interest and advocacy is confined to political multiculturalism. While Parekh and Taylor locate their political multiculturalism within a wider, philosophical multiculturalism, I am not locating political multiculturalism in anything bigger than itself, or, more precisely, in nothing bigger than contemporary ideas of democratic citizenship and belonging (Modood 2013, 60–61).

Relatedly, I leave to one side how what I am presenting as multiculturalist dialogue relates to identity groups at an international or global level, as in the idea of a 'dialogue of civilizations'. I will confine myself to an intranational context; and more specifically to liberal democratic contexts. Within such contexts there has been a reaction to multiculturalism that relates to the question of dialogue, specifically to intercultural or interfaith dialogue. Multiculturalism has been criticised at many levels and across the political and intellectual spectrums, but I am referring to one specific position that goes under the name of 'interculturalism'. To be more precise, there are at least two reactions that use the same self-label. One reaction is specific to Quebec and is very much connected to Quebec nationalism (Meer and Modood 2012; Modood 2014). This interculturalism, however, is not a rejection of dialogical or identity politics. On the contrary, it conceives of the multiculturalism of Canadian federal government as not sufficiently dialogical, but as being too based on justiciable individual rights and judges rather than on political dialogue (Gagnon and Iacovino 2006). The other interculturalism is associated with the Council of Europe (2008) and UNESCO (2008). These bodies have produced a critique of multiculturalism, which, with Nasar Meer, I have examined and rebutted elsewhere (Meer and Modood 2012).[5] Our argument was that this interculturalist critique is of a caricature without any significant reference to the views of any multiculturalist authors, theorists and advocates, or even to policies advanced in the name of multiculturalism, say, in the United Kingdom, Canada, United States or Australia. It simply associated multiculturalism with separatism, ghettoisation and anti-integration (Meer and Modood 2012; see Meer, Modood and Zapata-Barrera 2016 for a multi-sided debate; and the Levreau and Loobuyuk [eds.] online symposium [2017–2018] for a considerable contraction of the claims of interculturalism). My point of interest here is on only one aspect of the interculturalist critique and the corresponding positive recommendation. This is the argument that multiculturalists have been too focused on general public discourses, especially at a macro national level, whereas the real work of social acceptance, equality and living in diversity is at the level of everyday life in one's neighbourhood, school, workplace and so on (Loobuyck 2016). At the level of the latter, people rub along without major value conflicts; but nevertheless, intercultural encounters, rather than avoidance of contact, is essential for a multicultural society and so it is at these micro levels that the techniques for intercultural dialogue need to be learnt and practiced (Wise and Velayutham, 2009). Multiculturalism, it is alleged, is too focused on the macro and the conflictual and dialogue should be redirected to the micro and the cooperative.[6] My response to this critique is to accept it as a correction to an exclusively macro and political focus but to reject it as presenting an either-or choice. One can welcome the interculturalists' focus on micro-relations, but this does not require abandoning the idea of dialogue at the level of political controversies and public discourses. Groups and inter-group problems exist in society and cannot be simply handled at a micro-level of contact, interaction and sociability (as is made apparent in the Levreau and Loobuyuk [2017–2018] online symposium).[7]

PUBLIC INTELLECTUAL ENGAGEMENT

The kind of macro-level dialogue that I am speaking of can also be understood as a form of public intellectual engagement. One of the best known statements on the nature of public intellectuals in recent times is that by Edward Said (Said 1996). Following Gramsci, he drew a contrast between traditional intellectuals, who here we might understand as academics, and 'organic intellectuals' – namely, those who serve particular organisations, such as journalists, or lobby for particular interests for a fee, or have an expertise, such as an economist or a scientist working for a government (Said

1996, 4, 13). Derived from a characterisation by Julien Benda, Said writes of a third kind of intellectual, 'of the intellectual as a being set apart' (Said 1996, 8), angry and oppositional, a critic of all worldly powers. They have the academic's commitment to intellectual values, but combine it with a critique of injustice, which is aimed, not just at fellow specialists, but also at as wide a public audience as they can manage. I can offer my understanding of public intellectual engagement by relating it to Said's idea of a public intellectual, which I find too one-sided and painted too starkly (Modood 2019).

An example of the one-sidedness I mean is the detachment from society that Said attributes to public intellectuals. He argues that their aim is to uphold universal 'standards of truth about human misery and oppression . . . despite the individual intellectual's party affiliation, national background, and primeval loyalties' (Said 1996, xii). Of course this kind of integrity is what one requires not just from public intellectuals but also from all professionals, such as academics, doctors, judges, engineers and so on. It is neither distinctive of public intellectuals, nor does it mean that those with such responsibilities have to be less members of their society; that they share less understanding and concerns with their co-ethnic, co-religionists or co-nationals; or do not care for the well-being of their groups (including protesting when they think injustice is being done by their groups). Yet, Said describes public intellectuals as – indeed exhorts them to be – 'outsiders and exiles' (Said 1996, 51) and admiringly quotes Adorno: '*It is part of morality not to be at home in one's home*' (Said 1996, 57; italics in original). Said notes that '[b]ecause the exile sees things both in terms of what has been left behind and what is actual here and now, there is a double perspective that never sees things in isolation' (Said 1996, 60). Thus, despite presenting a self-image of the intellectual as standing outside or above the society s/he is engaging with, Said recognises there actually has to be a – or more typically, multiple – commitment to a people(s) or concrete institutions and practices, not just to abstract principles like Truth or Justice or Humanity. My point is that commitments to groups, people, causes, institutions, one's country and so on are not incidental to an engaged public intellectual or a nuisance it would be best did not exist. They are as essential to the public intellectual as the commitment to intellectual integrity. The public intellectual has to care about a people, a place or a cause and not just about being an intellectual (brought out nicely in relation to George Orwell and Albert Camus in Walzer 2002). The public intellectual has to have a home, but this commitment must not be blind or incompatible with an equally strong commitment to intellectuality. Just as, of course, there must not be a blind commitment to certain intellectual points of view and theories, including those which have the prefix of 'critical'; a prefix that seems to some to be a badge of adherence rather than something to deconstruct. The public intellectual endeavour is to engage in and lead the moral, ethical and political conversation that any society has with itself, and while some 'outsider' features can offer some epistemological advantages (and no doubt some blind spots), one needs to be part of the society that one seeks to engage.

Said cites the African Americans James Baldwin and Malcolm X as exemplars of public intellectuals (Said 1996, xvii). Yet they were individuals who knew which side they were on. They were outsiders to certain structures of power but not outsiders to groups, to belonging and commitment to the well-being of the groups they (thought) they belonged to. It is most unlikely that they endorsed Said's motto of 'Never solidarity before criticism' (Said 1996, 32). In Said's own case there was a passionate lifelong commitment to the Palestinian people. Moreover, when it comes to multiculturalist public intellectuals they are likely to belong to more than one group and so are unlikely to be either wholly insiders or outsiders – again something that describes Said as an eminent American. The public intellectual, then, has to negotiate critical outsiderness and epistemological insiderness and belonging, solidarity and rootedness. S/he does not need to give up entirely on her social roots, indeed to do so is to risk losing an important understanding and sympathy for her group or society as well as trust and standing with the group and/or society. So, it is to cultivate not a blind loyalty but nor to go into exile; much better it is to develop multiple belongings and possibilities of dialogue rather than exile or aloofness from the concerns of one's group or society.

A similar one-sidedness characterises Said's distancing of public intellectuality from 'specialisation' and 'expertise', overlooking that a public intellectual has to be in one or some intellectual discipline(s). He argues that '[t]he particular threat to the intellectual today . . . [is] an attitude that I will call professionalism' (Said 1996, 76, 77, 73), which he describes as treating intellectual work as just a job, on a nine-to-five basis, the demotion of an intellectual vocation to what today is likely to be called 'work-life balance'. Said also worries about intellectuals seeking acceptance, prestige and honours (Said 1996, 100–101). I agree that some university institutional cultures – such as that of Britain, say, during 1990–2010 – encourage a narrow scholasticism, typified by the high esteem bestowed on disciplinary jargons and low esteem on clarity, but Said is too dismissive of expertise (Modood 2009). Much scientific expertise improves material living standards, public services and personal well-being. It is about engaging with the pressing needs of individuals and communities, such as seeking a cure for cancer, reducing world poverty or contributing to the advancement of 'the knowledge society' with a view to improving regional and national productivity and promoting technological innovation. We may agree with Said, however, that such activity is not public intellectual engagement, which is about an intellectual speaking in their own voice to a public; not about research teams, new techniques and purely material concerns. And as for an intellectual not seeking honours, yes, that can't be the primary motive, but it is the case there is – and should be – honour and recognition, social status in public intellectual engagement, and it is odd that Said, who received much such acclaim (including being chosen by the BBC to deliver the prestigious Reith Lectures, in which he presented the views I am discussing), should fail to mention it. A better understanding of how the professional and the personal, and of what one might call honourable ambition interplay is captured in this description of public intellectuals as 'those who live with the tensions generated by the contrasting pulls of specialist focus and peer recognition, on the one hand, and on the other, the risks and thrills associated with being known as someone who addresses a much wider range of publics on issues of general concern' (Kenny 2008, 7). Of course these different elements are not always in harmony, but it is not a betrayal of vocation to recognise the fact of and the dangers of competing motives and purposes than to define public intellectuals in ascetic and purist terms.

Despite Said's tendency to sometimes express himself in a one-sided way, he also offers a more complex characterisation and is closer to the mark when he does so – for example,

> There is therefore this quite complicated mix between the private and the public worlds, my own history, values, writings and positions as they derive from my experiences, on the one hand, and on the other hand, how these enter into the social world where people debate and make decisions about war and freedom and justice. (Said 1996, 12)

There is, however, one issue on which I do not simply think Said has a preference, albeit exercised inconsistently, for one-sidedness but where our views collide. In earlier talking of Parekh as a multiculturalist public intellectual, I evidenced his interventions in relation to the crisis around Salman Rushdie's novel, *The Satanic Verses*. It happens that Said, too, refers to this crisis and states that to have failed to have defended this novel is 'to betray the intellectual's calling'. This is because 'uncompromising freedom of opinion and expression is the secular intellectual's main bastion' (Said 1996, 89). In addition to what I have already said in relation to Parekh, in the interview below I give my own reasons for my own intervention in this crisis and so will not add anything more here (but see also chapter 3). It may be that by 'secular' Said does not mean non-religious, but as someone who does not have a 'belief in a political god' (ibid., 109) or 'a total dogmatic system' (ibid., 113). If so, I share that view and have warned of 'the danger of ideology' in discussions of multiculturalism (Modood 2007/2013, 128–132/ 118–122). I suspect, however, that in at least one respect I take the freedom owed to public intellectuals further than Said, who so passionately defines the latter in anti-establishment and anti-national terms. Michael Burawoy, who initiated a major, international debate about the nature of public sociology, offered the same kind of political restrictedness, arguing that it 'defends the interests of humanity', which he interpreted to mean standing up for civil society against the market and the state (Burawoy 2005, 24). My colleague Gregor McLennan has added that if one can impose political tasks on sociology then his own list includes resistance to 'the encroachments of religiosity' (McLennan 2007, 859). In contrast, I think a public intellectual must be politically free to be left-wing, right-wing, centrist, religious, secular and so on – and of course to argue for her point of view by attending to other, especially dissenting, voices and respond to objections and critiques. Public intellectual engagement is of course political, not neutral, but it is a dialogue or a multilogue of complementary and contending intellectual-political positions and one cannot appropriate a whole discipline such as sociology or political theory for one's own normative position or against a colleague's (as Burawoy 2005 also, if inconsistently, argues). Or, as Hashemi argues, by juxtaposing the theorist of the Iranian Revolution, Ali Shariati, with Burawoy, 'public sociology can work as a frame of debate about the priority of each battlefield. Otherwise, it can be easily turned into a target for the criticism of those who do not share the interest in Burawoy's preferred struggle' (Hashemi 2016, 474). The field outside the academy that public intellectuals are committed to is not civil society but the home of 'the public', which we may call 'the public sphere' following this excellent quote from Andrew Gamble which sums up in what way intellectuals are public or political:

> The political theorists of multiculturalism such as Bhikhu Parekh . . . have been active participants in politics in the sense that they seek to advance the political education of citizens, by articulating choices, framing questions, offering alternatives, and challenging orthodoxies and entrenched attitudes. They address themselves to the public, not to [just] coteries of experts, or office holders. They are essential builders of the public sphere. (Gamble 2015, 297)

One of the ways, then, that intellectuals can contribute to societal dialogues is through what I will call 'public intellectual engagement'. As an exemplification of what I have in mind as an aspiration and in relation to multiculturalism, I offer in Part II the interview I gave to Simon Thompson (Modood 2016a). It refers to my own engagement with some of the challenges which the presence of British Muslims as British citizens creates for British public culture and the national citizenship. In relation to this theme I have already mentioned Bhikhu Parekh above and my appreciation of him as an outstanding British public intellectual.[8]

PART II

On Being a Public Intellectual, a Muslim and a Multiculturalist[9]

Tariq Modood interviewed by Simon Thompson

What does it mean to be a public intellectual?
Intellectual or academic life is usually organised in disciplines, and intellectuals' questions come out of those disciplines. But in public intellectual engagement the question does not primarily come out of a discipline. It comes from the public. It concerns our relations with each other as members of a society and especially as citizens of a polity. A public intellectual is a concerned citizen who accepts responsibility for their society and brings to its understanding insights of their discipline.

Most of what salaried academics do is contribute to their disciplinary community or to a broader academic community. So, a political theorist may say, 'Hannah Arendt was engaged with this question. This is a question that is still alive and her thought on this is strangely lucid. I want to revisit it and perhaps recover neglected aspects of it'. These questions all arise organically from thinking about Hannah Arendt.

But we also at times think about questions that don't just arise from the discipline. So, for example, we think about the relationship between religious identity and political equality. Is there any relation? Does political equality simply mean we are not interested in anybody's religious identity? We simply don't suppress or promote any such identities? Sounds plausible. But then if we think about it, we realise that in fact, some people's religious identity tells them to have an ethical orientation which is clearly social *and* political – to do with questions like what kind of economic relations to have or not have, to be hospitable to refugees or not. Whereas for other people their religious identity is an entirely private matter.

So if political equality means merely ignoring religious identities, we are favouring religious identities that are purely private, and *not* treating all religious identities equally. We're *preferring* a particular kind of religious identity. So now we are not just talking about, say, Hannah Arendt's ideas. We're thinking about our existing political arrangements in light of the claims that some Muslims or some Christians or – for that matter – some 'new atheists' are making about political life and equality. We are engaged in public questions. But we are still drawing on academic conversations, academic tools, academic perspectives.[10]

Do you think we've resolved this question – about how to square equality for all religious identities with political equality – in Britain?
I think we have entered a period where we are rethinking the place of religion in relation to equality and the public sphere. But there's a deep

antipathy to treating religious identities on a par with others. A good measure of this is how in the Labour Party or in a major trade union there can be a women's section, an LGBT section, a black or ethnic minorities section, but we can all imagine the consternation if and when Muslims ask for a Muslim or a religious minorities section!

Should all intellectuals or academics be public intellectuals?

Intellectual life, like society, has a division of labour. I'm not saying, 'All academics or sociologists or political theorists must engage in intellectual activity of just one kind'. The pursuit of knowledge for its own sake is a good, though it's not the only good we should be concerned with. We need a certain amount of publicly supported fundamental or 'blue skies' or pure academic research, because who knows what will come from it? Even the publicly engaged intellectual working on political theory will still get a lot of value from the person who says 'I really want to understand Arendt'.

Public engagement is desirable rather than essential for individual academics. But when it comes to the collective – a department of politics or a school of sociology – I think it is essential for at least some of its members to be engaged. And what I mean by desirable is not simply 'optional'; public engagement is something that should be pursued if possible.

Do you see yourself as bringing a specifically Muslim voice to public debate?

To answer this we need to go back to the Rushdie Affair. The Rushdie Affair was a pivotal intellectual and biographical moment for me, because in some ways I came to *be* a Muslim at that time. It would have been quite straightforward for me to walk away from all these angry, aggressive Muslims and simply say: *They have nothing to do with me*. But I thought instead: *These people* are *something to do with me*. I was working in racial equality and community relations, I had a sense of belonging, solidarity, with a community of suffering. I was aware of and proud of my Pakistani roots. I thought of myself as British Asian, so to extend that to think of myself as a British Asian Muslim didn't seem such a leap. But it wasn't obvious either. I knew other British Asians who didn't want to have anything to do with these 'fundamentalists'. I felt I needed to address Muslims as much as I needed to address the wider public, and I needed to address them in a way that both exhibited identification and solidarity with them and said: *This is where I stand and this is where we should stand – and we should distinguish ourselves from some other Muslim positions*. So it was a critical stance, but I was expressing it as a Muslim.[11]

My biography, or my social location, as a brown Brit of Pakistani origins and Muslim background, is very present in my work – both in the questions I am engaged with, and also to some extent the answers. But I don't think of myself as *simply* speaking as a Muslim. When I speak, I speak as a *multicul-*

turalist above all. This is the intellectual commitment that I bring to public debate.

Should public intellectuals stand up for the marginalised or dispossessed?

I don't accept the argument that the role of intellectuals is to always support the weaker party. We should all attend to the state of the weaker party. But that is an issue of justice and fairness, it's not especially to do with political theory or sociology or being an intellectual.

The answer to your question comes back again to the Rushdie Affair. At that time, there were at least two prominent things motivating me: concern for the well-being of British society *and* concern for the well-being of British Muslims as a particular part of British society. I was trying to follow these two deep, personal commitments *equally*. It wasn't just Muslims and Salman Rushdie who were affected. British society was affected by this incident – and, in fact, this set of issues is not confined to one country.

Some people might say about me, 'He doesn't care about Britain, he just wants to look after the Muslim constituency'. I personally have never thought along those lines. I have an abiding concern for the well-being of British society, which doesn't mean that British society sometimes doesn't misunderstand where its well-being lies. When I try and engage with a broader British public, I am trying to get people to think about what is *really* good for British society. What is consistent with its beliefs and long-term character? Because, of course, British society has to work and adapt to include in a fair and just way what we might call the 'new British'. What I have been concerned about – in the Rushdie Affair and after – has not been the well-being of Muslims per se, but the well-being of Muslims who are part of British society and whose future is part of British society. The well-being of these parties is entangled, and the conflictual parts of the entanglement have to be worked out so that the well-being of each becomes interdependent and, if you like, integrated.

Does sharing an identity mean sharing solidarity?

My biography gives me insights and a sensibility that others don't have. I don't claim to be especially empathetic, but I can say that I know certain things, having been brought up as a Muslim, having been an Asian in Britain since I was a child, and going to a very white, working-class school with a lot of racist and other kinds of bullying. I think this was the basis for my career. I could see that the way that British society was beginning to politically conceptualize the issues around race in the 1970s and '80s just did not fit with my own sense of who I was. And I felt that I was actually the norm in Asian communities and not the exception. For example, like most British Asians I did not think I was black, nor, of course, white; and nor did I define myself against Britishness, but as making a new, distinctive claim on it. That gave me the basis for arguing against a kind of black-white racial dualism and towards ethnic pluralism – towards multicultural Britishness, where there are different ways of being British.

The emergence of religion as a live issue – in particular, the assertion of Muslim identity – was actually a bit of a surprise to me. When I first heard about the Rushdie Affair I thought, 'It's not right for Muslims to be getting so angry'. But *being* among Muslims made me realise that this really mattered to some Muslims, and they were unable to do what their sympathisers were asking them to do – which was basically to just forget about the novel entirely. I could see that these Muslims were headed for a confrontation, and this wasn't good for Muslims or for British society. And because I could identify with them I could understand not because I'm particularly empathetic, as I say, but because I belong to a certain social world.

You said above that the issues raised by the Rushdie controversy are not confined to one country. Could you expand on that?

Comparable issues to do with Muslims protesting how their religion, especially the Prophet Muhammad, is portrayed arose with the Danish cartoons affair and more recently the cartoons in *Charlie Hebdo*. In each case, an important question has been to look beyond the horrific violence and murder and to ask how, in a multicultural society, groups of people such as Muslims or Jews or blacks should and should not be portrayed. We need incitement to hatred legislation, but I think in the main, these issues should be dealt with through 'censure not censor' (see chapter 3 above and Modood 2006).[12] We should handle the offensive portrayal of racial and religious minorities through censuring rather than legal bans. When several prominent European newspapers and magazines republished the original Danish cartoons of Muhammad, no British newspaper or magazine did so, on the grounds that they were not in the business of giving gratuitous offence. This is the same British approach that, unlike France and many European countries, has not tried to make Holocaust denial a criminal offence but dealt with it through a culture of civility and censure.

Do you think that racism, and in particular Islamophobia, are growing problems in this country, and what can politics do to fight against this rise?

Most of the evidence suggests that racial discrimination, say in relation to jobs, persists. Ethnic minorities continue to make progress in terms of socio-economic mobility and participation in public life, but that's mainly because of the extra qualifications they achieve rather than because there is a level playing field. On the other hand, I think that racial prejudice is in relative decline if we look at the views of younger people compared to older people, and at friendship, dating, relationships, marriage and so on. Yet both in terms of employment and social life, suspicion of and hostility to Muslims continues to rise. Partly this is collective blame for jihadi terrorism, but it's also an antipathy to publicly asserted religious identities. This 'Muslim penalty' has to be much more publicly stated as a problem. Blanket condemnation of racism is not enough. We need positive national narratives which feature Muslims and Islam as aspects of what it is to be British. Politicians also need to work with Muslim communities to identify, isolate and defeat the processes leading to terrorism, rather than speak as if Muslims were the problem or that terrorism is a problem the Muslim community could solve on its own – or indeed that it could be solved without the full engagement of the Muslim communities, including conservative Muslims and critics of government foreign policies.

You said that you see yourself as a multiculturalist intellectual. Do you think multiculturalism is still the model we should be following in Britain?

Multiculturalism is the accommodation of minorities not just as individuals, but as people sharing, promoting and remaking their group identities within a common citizenship and the rethinking of a national story. No doubt this has sometimes been expressed too simply, both theoretically and politically, so we must learn from critics emphasising community cohesion, or the fluidity and multiplicity of identities, or what is called 'interculturalism'. But these are really modifications of multiculturalism, not alternatives to it. This is clear as soon as you pose the question, What is it that anti-multiculturalist countries like France or Germany have achieved that Britain has failed to achieve? In fact by virtually any measure you care to pick – discrimination and victimisation, social mobility, presence in and participation in public life, rethinking national identity in a more inclusive way, inter-ethnic friendships, interfaith dialogue and cooperation and so on – the position of non-European-origin minorities in Britain is better than in most or all other European countries. So, to paraphrase Churchill, British multiculturalism may be the worst model, except for all the others. In the last few years I have been particularly sympathetic to voices on the centre-left (like Jon Cruddas, John Denham and Sunder Katwala) emphasising that the cultural identities and anxieties of the majority need to be part of a communitarian One Nation politics. I think that is right, but it is important that such a politics should not be cast as anti-multiculturalist but should include what might be called a 'critically evolving multiculturalism'.[13]

NOTES

1. *Encyclopaedia Britannica* defines a 'sophist' as 'certain Greek lecturers, writers, and teachers in the 5th and 4th centuries BCE, most of whom traveled about the Greek-speaking world giving instruction in a wide range of subjects in return for fees', https://www.britannica.com/topic/Sophist-philosophy, last accessed 01/03/2019.

2. At this stage Rawls had moved away from the methodology of his most famous work (Rawls 1971) – namely, the Veil of Ignorance, as described earlier.

3. When published in March 1989, five weeks after Khomeini's infamous fatwa, it was way ahead of the debate to which it contributed. Besides his own publications, Parekh used his office as part-time Deputy Director of the Commission for Racial Equality at the time to

convene three workshops on the topic, the publications from which, too, considerably raised the level of intellectual engagement.

4. This also at least partly gives political multiculturalism the character of a bottoms-up mobilisation, paralleling other kinds of identity politics like feminism or gay pride, as I display in relation to Britain (Modood 2005). Bloemraad (2015, 11), however, has argued that that multicultural discourse and policy in Canada, Australia, and Sweden was elite driven.

5. Oddly enough, while the cited article has been viewed and cited in numbers that are satisfying to its authors, and the article was published together with four responses and a rejoinder, it is not too unusual for the article, which engages with the interculturalist critique of multiculturalism, to be read as an endorsement of that critique, when it is, of course, a multiculturalist riposte to that critique. For an attempt to be absolutely clear on this point, see my two contributions to the Levreau and Loobuyuk symposium (Levreau and Loobuyuk 2017–2018).

6. In its British version, the critique is less likely to be expressed in terms of 'interculturalism' and more in terms of a positive focus on 'multiculture' or 'conviviality' or 'everyday multiculturalism'. I have subsumed it under what I refer to as 'cosmopolitanism'. Under 'cosmopolitanism' I bring together the interculturalist emphasis on cultural encounters and everyday interaction in localities, schools, clubs, public spaces; the multiple and fluid character of identity; the emphasis on the transnational and on globalisation and the 'problematising' of the national (Modood 2012).

7. Loobuyck, too, uses the macro-micro distinction to distinguish between interculturalism and multiculturalism but he conflates it with a state-civil society distinction (Loobuyck 2016, 230) and does not see that multiculturalism is not confined to the state and extends to citizen-to-citizen relations (Modood 2007/2013, chapter 6). Contrary to another distinction he makes, multiculturalism is not just about justice and neglects the importance of belonging: on the contrary, belonging is more central to multicultural nationalism than either the liberal goal of furthering autonomy or the social democratic means of redistribution of resources (Levey 2018). Stokke and Lybaek (2018) offer a better combining of intercultural dialogue with the kind of political multiculturalism that I advocate, but they perhaps overstate the separation of multiculturalism at the level of political critique and mobilisation from multiculturalism at the level of the state. In my view, multiculturalists need to draw the state into public dialogues, not define it as something beyond the scope of the reach of dialogue and learning.

8. This is nicely brought out in his conversations with Ramin Jahanbegloo in which his review of the principal themes of his opus display how an engagement with contemporary politics is a guiding thread (Parekh and Jahanbegloo 2011).

9. A longer version of this interview was originally given and recorded in March 2015 and this considerably shortened and edited version appeared in the journal *Renewal* in its April, 2016, issue (Modood 2016a) and is reproduced here with kind permission of the editors of *Renewal*.

10. In an earlier interview I give more content to the idea of a public intellectual by reference to Bhikhu Parekh and Stuart Hall, who have inspired me and exemplify two different kinds of public intellectuals: the reformer and the critic respectively. See D. O. Martinez (2013), 'Intellectual Biography, Empirical Sociology and Normative Political Theory: An Interview with Tariq Modood', *Journal of Intercultural Studies*, *34*(6), 729–741.

11. Examples of my public or journalistic interventions in relation to the Rushdie Affair are collected in Modood 1992, 69–87.

12. The symposium that this piece is in is a good example of an intercultural debate between liberal, free-speech absolutists, such as Randall Hansen and Brendan O'Leary, and liberal inclusivists or multiculturalists, including Erik Bleich and Joe Carens (Modood et al. 2006), and relates to my earlier reference to Edward Said on free speech.

13. Further reading: Modood (2007/2013) and Modood (2019 forthcoming).

REFERENCES

Bloemraad, I. (2015). 'Theorizing and Analyzing Citizenship in Multicultural Societies'. *The Sociological Quarterly*, *56*(4), 591–606.

Burawoy, M. (2005). 'For Public Sociology'. *American Sociological Review*, 70(1), 4–28.
Council of Europe. (2008). 'Intercultural Dialogue: Living Together as Equals in Dignity'. White Paper, Committee of Ministers, Council of Europe, Strasbourg.
Gagnon, A. G. and Iacovino, R. (2006). *Federalism, Citizenship and Quebec*. Toronto: University of Toronto Press.
Gamble, A. (2015). 'Multiculturalism and the Public Sphere'. In Uberoi, V. and Modood, T. (eds.), *Multiculturalism Rethought*, 273–299. Edinburgh: Edinburgh University Press.
Hashemi, M. (2016). 'A Post-Secular Reading of Public Sociology'. *Social Compass*, 63(4): http://scp.sagepub.com/content/early/2016/09/21/0037768616663983.full.pdf+html [accessed 5/10/2016].
Hobbes, T. (1968). (1651). *Leviathan*, ed. C. B. Macpherson. London: Penguin.
Kenny, M. (2008). 'Britain's Anti-Intellectual Intellectuals: Thoughts on Stefan Collini's "Absent Minds"'. *Political Studies Review*, 6(1), 1–13.
Levey, G. B. (2018). 'The Bristol School of Multiculturalism'. *Ethnicities*, OnlineFirst: https://journals.sagepub.com/doi/10.1177/1468796818787413.
Levreau, F. and Loobuyuk, P. (eds.). (2017–2018). 'Multiculturalism-Interculturalism'. *Comparative Migration Studies*: https://comparativemigrationstudies.springeropen.com/multi culturalism-interculturalism [accessed 20/11/2018].
Locke, J. (1966). (1690). *Two Treatises of Civil Government*. London: Dent.
Loobuyck, P. (2016). 'Toward an Intercultural Sense of Belonging Together: Reflections on the Theoretical and Political Level'. In Meer, N., Modood, T. and Zapata-Barrero, R. (eds.), *Multiculturalism and Interculturalism: Debating the Dividing Lines*, 225–245. Edinburgh: Edinburgh University Press.
McLennan, G. (2007). 'Towards Postsecular Sociology?'. *Sociology*, 41(5), 857–870.
Meer, N. and Modood, T. (2012). 'How Does Interculturalism Contrast with Multiculturalism?'. *Journal of Intercultural Studies*, 33(2), 175–196.
Meer, N., Modood, T. and Zapata-Barrero, R. (eds.). (2016). *Multiculturalism and Interculturalism: Debating the Dividing Lines*. Edinburgh: Edinburgh University Press.
Modood, T. (1992). *Not Easy Being British: Colour, Culture and Citizenship*. Stoke-on Trent, UK: Runnymede Trust and Trentham.
Modood, T. (2005). *Multicultural Politics: Racism, Ethnicity, and Muslims in Britain*. Minneapolis and Edinburgh: University of Minnesota Press and University of Edinburgh Press.
Modood, T. (2006). 'The Liberal Dilemma: Integration or Vilification?'. *International Migration*, 44(5), 4–7.
Modood, T. (2007/2013). *Multiculturalism: A Civic Idea* (2nd ed., 2013). Cambridge: Polity Press.
Modood, T. (2009). 'Universities and Public Benefit'. *100: A Collection of Words and Images to Mark the Centenary of the University of Bristol*, 245–247. Bristol, UK: University of Bristol.
Modood, T. (2014). 'Multiculturalism, Interculturalisms and the Majority', Kohlberg Memorial Lecture. *Journal of Moral Education*, 43(3), 302–315.
Modood, T. (2016a). 'On Being a Public Intellectual, a Muslim and a Multiculturalist: Tariq Modood Interviewed by Simon Thompson'. *Renewal*, 24(2): 90–95.
Modood, T. (2016b). 'What Is Multiculturalism and What Can It Learn from Interculturalism?'. In 'Interculturalism versus Multiculturalism – The Cantle-Modood Debate'. *Ethnicities*, Online First.
Modood, T. (2019). 'Thinking About Public Intellectuals. Review of Michael C. Desch, ed., *Public Intellectuals in the Global Arena: Professors or Pundits?*' Notre Dame University Press, 2016. SCTIW Review, *Journal of the Society for Contemporary Thought and the Islamicate World*, January 29th, pp. 1-10: https://sctiw.org/wp-content/uploads/2019/01/171-Public-Intellectuals-in-the-Global-Arena-Tariq-Modood.pdf.
Modood, T. (2019 forthcoming). 'A Multicultural Nationalism?' *Brown Journal of World Affairs*, Spring/Summer Issue.
Modood, T., Hansen, R., Bleich, E., O'Leary, B. and Carens, J. (2006). 'The Danish Cartoon Affair: Free Speech, Racism, Islamism, and Integration'. *International Migration*, 44(5), 3–62.

Parekh, B. (1989). 'Between Holy Text and Moral Void'. *New Statesman and Society*, 24 March, 29–33.
Parekh, B. (2000/2006). *Rethinking Multiculturalism: Cultural Diversity and Political Theory* (2nd ed., 2006). Basingstoke, UK: Palgrave Macmillan.
Parekh, B. and Jahanbegloo, R. (2011). *Talking Politics: Bhikhu Parekh in Conversation with Ramin Jahanbegloo*. New Delhi: Oxford University Press.
Rawls, J. (1971). *A Theory of Justice*. Cambridge, MA: Harvard University Press.
Rawls, J. (1985). 'Justice as Fairness: Political Not Metaphysical'. *Philosophy and Public Affairs*, 223–251.
Rawls, J. (1987). 'The Idea of an Overlapping Consensus'. *Oxford Journal of Legal Studies*, 7(1), 1–25.
Rousseau, J. J. (1920). (1762). *The Social Contract: And Discourses*. London: J. M. Dent and Sons.
Said, E. W. (1996). *Representations of the Intellectual*. New York: Vintage.
Stokke, C. and Lybaek, L. (2018). 'Combining Intercultural Dialogue and Critical Multiculturalism'. *Ethnicities*, *18*(1), 70–85.
Taylor, C. (1994). 'The Politics of Recognition'. In Guttman, A. (ed.), *Multiculturalism: Examining the Politics of Recognition*, 25–74. Princeton, NJ: Princeton University Press.
Taylor, C. (2009). 'Foreword: What Is Secularism?' In Levey, G. B. and Modood, T. (eds.), *Secularism, Religion and Multicultural Citizenship*, 216–242. Cambridge: Cambridge University Press.
Tully, J. (1995). *Strange Multiplicity: Constitutionalism in an Age of Diversity*. Cambridge: Cambridge University Press.
Tully, J. (2008). *Public Philosophy in a New Key*, vol. 1. Cambridge: Cambridge University Press.
UNESCO. (2008). *Investing in Cultural Diversity and Intercultural Dialogue: World Report on Cultural Diversity*. Paris: UNESCO.
Walzer, M. (2002). *The Company of Critics: Social Criticism and Political Commitment in the Twentieth Century*. New York: Basic Books.
Wise, A. and Velayutham, S. (eds.). (2009). *Everyday Multiculturalism*. Basingstoke, UK: Palgrave Macmillan.
Young, I. M. (1990). *Justice and the Politics of Difference*. Princeton, NJ: Princeton University Press.

Index

accommodation. *See* multicultural accommodation; Muslim accommodation
l'affaire foulard, 167, 174n7
African Americans, 4–5, 37–38
agency, 156, 157
agora, 215
AKP. *See* Truth and Development Party
Alibhai-Brown, Yasmin, 93, 97
alienation of British Muslims, 12–13, 105, 190, 206, 207, 207–208
Alternative fur Deutschland, 78
anti-essentialism, 79
anti-Muslim hostility, 22, 154, 172, 175n15, 203; racism and, 138. *See also* Islamophobia
anti-racism, 22, 27n2; identarian, 4–5; 1970s minority politics and, 48
antisecularization, 204–205
anti-Semitism, 36–37, 64, 66, 73n3; anti-Zionism, 86, 122–123
Anti-Terrorism, Crime and Security Act, 131n2
Arbitration Act 1996, 142
Archbishop of Canterbury, 14, 25, 154
Arendt, Hannah, 226, 227
Asad, Talal, 84
Asians. *See* British Asians
assimilation, 40–43, 118; in France, 53–54
Atlantocentric racism, 33
Austria, 78

autonomy of politics, secularism and, 10, 195–197, 198
Ayatollah Khomeni, 146
Aziz, Mohammed A., 98

Bader, Veit, 183–184
Baldwin, James, 223
Bangladeshis, 52, 57n1, 57n2, 102
Bano, Samia, 142
BBC Television, 39, 93
Belgium, 9, 55, 56, 57n4, 127, 128, 132n5, 183, 198
beliefs, 164; of hate speech victims, 23–24, 62–65, 69–73, 73n2; literacy, 105–106; secular, 99, 109n18. *See also* Commission on Religion and Belief in British Public Life (CORAB); religion and religiosity
belonging: citizenship and, 1, 11, 15, 17, 63, 107, 136–137, 149, 201, 206, 220, 231n7; community/group, 223, 227; parties to a dialogue, 218–219
Benda, Julien, 221
Benedict XVI (Pope), 169
Benn, Tony, 10
Bhargava, Rajeev, 147–148, 150, 163, 173, 174n1, 210n9; Indian religious diversity and, 205; Laborde and, 206–207; on multiculturalism as problematic, 205–206; on secularism, 181–182, 191n7, 191n9, 197–198; on weak

establishment, 182, 192n15
biological determinism, 78
biological racism, 36, 37, 37–38, 42, 75
Bishop of Bradford, 191n14
black identity, 3–4; innocent black subject, 156; political blackness and, 48–49, 49, 57n1
Blair, Tony, 52, 125, 166
blasphemy, 61, 64; law, 52–53, 120, 131n2, 155, 166–167
Blum, Lawrence, 39
Bonnoti, Matteo, 27n1
BNP. *See* British National Party
bombings, London, 56, 57n5, 103
Bosnian Muslims, 77
bourka. *See* niqab
Bradford: Bishop of, 191n14; Honeyford Affair, the, 50; riots, 102; *The Satanic Verses* affair, 51, 191n14
Bradford Council of Mosques, 50, 130
Brah, Avtar, 39
Breivik, Anders, 209
Brexit, 21, 27n12
Bristol School of Multiculturalism, 21
Britain: Christian legacy of, 98; Danish cartoons censored in, 66, 120; multiculturalism in, 4–5, 27n3; postwar racism in, 77; religious identity census in, 100–101, 110n21; state-religion separation in U.S. *vs.*, 125. *See also* specific topics
British Asians, 4, 228; cultural racism and, 35–36; double racism suffered by, 34; Dobbernack, Jan, 27n1; Hindus and, 101, 102; misrecognition of British Muslims and, 43; second-generation, 44; South Asians and, 34, 38–39, 48, 110n24; upward mobility and, 22
British Christians: friction between Muslims and, 53; House of Lords inclusion of non-, 150; percentage, 101; percentage of British, 101; prejudice against Muslims of, 132n3
British Humanist Association/UK Humanists, 100, 109n18, 175n10
British identity (Britishness): Cameron on, 175n12; Christianity and, 98–99, 169–171, 175n12; CMEB and, 96–97; commission reports on, 107, 107–108;

minority religious identities and, 102, 110n27–110n29; racially coded, 95
British Muslims, 57n3; Christianity supported by, 169, 175n11; Christian *vs.* mainstream media and, 175n15; equality successes of, 56; friction between Christians and, 53; government-supported groups formed by, 57n3; lack of ethnic group status for, 47–48; misrecognition of British Asians and, 43; multiculturalist approach to, 13; negative traits in othering of, 83; political blackness and, 48–49, 49, 57n1; poll on optimism in, 206–207; population percentage, 101; religious identity salience for, 101, 102; responses to *The Satanic Verses*/Danish cartoons, 63, 66–67; Rushdie and, 51, 57n2; schools of, 52; secularism and, 122; separation of state and religion as alienating, 12–13, 105, 190, 206, 207, 207–208; state, Church of England and, 12; terrorism and, 98. *See also* anti-Muslim hostility; Islamophobia; Muslim accommodation; Muslim assertiveness
British National Party (BNP), 34, 38–39, 71
British Social Attitudes (BSA) survey, 100–101, 110n21
Brubaker, Rogers, 79
BSA. *See* British Social Attitudes
Burawoy, Michael, 224
Bush, George W., 125
Butler-Sloss, Elisabeth, 90, 97

Cameron, David, 54, 160n3, 175n12, 207
Camus, Albert, 222
Canada, multiculturalism in, 4. *See also* Quebec
Carens, Joe, 4, 231n12
cartoons, in *Charlie Hebdo*, 229. *See also* Danish cartoons, of Muhammad
Catholic Church, in France, 167
Catholics, 57n4, 62, 63, 101, 102–103, 110n21, 129, 130, 132n4, 152–153, 183–184, 201
CBMI. *See* Commission on British Muslims and Islamophobia

censorship, hate speech censure *vs.*, 65–69
census: BSA and, 100–101; religion question in, 121, 166, 169
Charlie Hebdo, 229
Chirac, Jacques, 124, 167
Christian-secular-diversity triangle, 98–99, 106
Christianity: British identity and, 98–99, 169–171, 175n12; generational difference in identifying with, 102; 'muscular' liberalism and, 169–171; Muslim accommodation and, 189–190; Muslims in Christian media, 175n15; Muslim support of, 169, 175n11; non-denominational worship in schools, 157; non-traditional forms of, 164; religious instruction in schools and, 15; secularism, compromise and, 146, 146–147. *See also* British Christians; establishment, Anglican
Church of England, 14, 54, 148, 169; Laborde and, 12, 27n8; SRCs and, 183
church-state separation. *See* state-religion separation
citizenship (citizenship equality): multilogues, 136, 156; positive accommodation and, 12; religion and equality in liberal, 123–124; religious identity component of, 2. *See also* multicultural citizenship
CMEB. *See* Commission on Multi-Ethnic Britain
COIE. *See* Commission on Integration and Cohesion
Collingwood, R. G., 158
colour racism, 33, 34, 47, 76; cultural and, 93; decline of, 38; in two-step racism, 34–35
Commission for Racial Equality, 70, 93, 98
Commission on British Muslims and Islamophobia (CBMI), 75–76
Commission on Integration and Cohesion (COIE), 90–91
Commission on Multi-Ethnic Britain (CMEB) (Parekh Report), 89, 90, 95, 96–97; Britishness and, 107–108; CORAB continuity with, 98; criticism of, 93; discrimination law recommended by, 103; false reading of, 95–96; members of, 93; misunderstanding of, 93; public criticism of, 90; reception and influence, 96, 109n13; recommendations acted on, 109n13; religion-based recommendations of, 94; remit and summary of, 92; Rushdie Affair and, 93–94; unusual features of, 93
Commission on Religion and Belief in British Public Life (CORAB), 16, 89, 90; belief and religion literacy recommendation, 105–106; on British identity, 107, 107–108; census and BSA survey used by, 100–101, 110n21; chair, 97; 'ethno-religious' and, 94, 102–103, 106, 110n27; membership, 98, 109n20; public criticism of, 90–91; reception of, 110n23; recommendations, 97, 105–107, 109n17; religious diversity and significance in light of, 101–107, 110n23; secularism and, 99, 100, 109n18; terms of reference, 97–98
commission reports, on ethnic groups and religion, 89–91, 109n8; on British identity and diversity, 107–108; CMEB/Parekh Report, 90–91; membership, 108n4, 109n9; overview, 89–91, 107–108, 108n4; personnel continuity, 109n9; Swann Report of 1985, 89, 90, 91–92, 108n5
conversion, 40–41, 169
Copson, Andrew, 100
CORAB. *See* Commission on Religion and Belief in British Public Life
corporatism, 129, 167
cosmopolitanism, 231n6
Council of Europe, 220
Council of Religions, Belgian, 128, 132n4
Crime and Disorder Act, 69, 131n2
crisis of secularism, 163–166, 174n1; pluralising option and, 172–173
cultural essentialism, colour racism and, 35
culturalism, 35
cultural majoritarianism, 143
cultural racism, 37–40; anti-Semitism and, 36–37; assimilation and, 40–43; biological aspect of, 36; colour racism

and, 34, 76, 93; concept of, 34; in
contemporary Britain, 34–35;
culturalism and, 35; Islamophobia as, 2,
23, 76–78, 122

Danish cartoons, of Muhammad, 72–73,
120, 170–171; Norwood poster and,
71–72; responses to *The Satanic Verses*
vs., 63, 66–67
Davie, Grace, 149
Dawkins, Richard, 158
Debré law, 184
Declaration of Independence, U.S.,
151–152
Denham, John, 96
Denmark, 56, 169, 170–171, 175n13. *See
also* Danish cartoons, of Muhammad
dialogue: intercultural, 219–221,
231n5–231n7; interfaith, 220;
Islamophobia, contrast, 85–86; macro-
micro distinction in, 220, 231n7;
multiculturalism, 7, 15–16, 96, 105,
128, 136–137, 139, 156, 169, 191n14;
multiculturalist use of, 217–219, 231n4;
in political theory, 21, 27n11, 215,
215–217
difference: blindness, 12, 201; classic
liberal response to, 118; education,
106–107; equality as recognition of,
8–9, 118, 118–122; generational, 102
discrimination: CMEB recommended
legislation against, 103; indicators of
racial, 49; laws against religious, 166;
legal, 47; religious, 119, 166;
workplace, 120–121
diversity, 205; British identity and,
107–108; commission reports focus on,
107–108; Davie on religious, 149;
immigration and, 25, 51, 89; racialized
ethno-religious, 47; religion
significance in religious, 101–107;
Western Europe challenge of, 1
double racism, 34
dress codes, Muslim, 103. *See also* hijab
(headscarf)
drop-out rates, school, 153
Dworkin, Ronald, 182, 191n13

EDL. *See* English Defence League

education: difference, 106–107; drop-out
rates, among British Pakistani males,
153; of sensibility, 66; Swann report
and, 89, 90, 91–92, 108n5. *See also*
schools; state-funded faith schools
Education Act of 1944, 184
English Defence League (EDL), 38, 209
equality: difference-affirming, 118–122;
equalising upwards/downwards, 99,
119; identity and, 4–5; identity politics
and, 118, 118–122, 122; King and, 3;
moderate secularism for multicultural,
127–131; multiculturalist concern with
difference and, 8–9; Muslim
accommodation and, 118–122; Muslim
successful agenda for, 56; politics of
recognition and, 117; two conceptions
of, 118. *See also* religious equality
Equality Act of 2010, 99, 103
Equality and Human Rights Commission,
93
eristic dialogue, 215
essentialism: anti-, 79; cultural, 35
establishment, Anglican, 150; British
Muslim view of, 207; social meaning
of, 13; SRCs and versions of, 180; as
symbolic, 183, 206; weak or modest,
182–184, 192n15, 200
d'Estaing, Giscard, 169
ethnic cleansing, race and, 77, 103
ethnic groups: British Muslims denied
status of, 47–48; dominant group
shaping of, 81; Honeyford Affair and
Pakistani, 23, 50; interaction emphasis
and, 81–82; Jews and Sikhs recognition
as, 47–48, 49; laws recognizing certain,
47; *Mandala v. Lee* and, 49–50; migrant
waves and, 89; monitoring, 121; most
disadvantaged, 52, 57n1; political
blackness and, 49, 57n1; Somalis
compared to Muslim, 57n1; surveys of
minority, 156. *See also* commission
reports, on ethnic groups and religion
ethnicity (ethnic identity): combining
religion and, 5, 154; Muslim, 6–7; need
for recognition, 7; race, religion and,
174n7; religious identity replacing, 102,
110n25

ethno-religious groups, 6, 9, 82, 154; CORAB on, 103, 106; crisis of secularism, 164; diversity, 15–16, 47, 143, 174n5, 201; laws and policies of 1960s regarding, 47; multiculturalist recognition of, 5, 10–12, 11, 22, 25, 154, 165, 180, 190–191n1, 200–201, 203, 205; Muslims and, 6–7, 24, 56; othering, 81; race and equality for, 5, 7, 23, 43, 48, 50, 51, 76–77, 78

Europe, secularism comparison for, 53–56, 146–147

European Convention on Human Rights, 99, 103

European Court of Human Rights, 56

European Union Constitution, debate over, 169

Faith Communities Consultative Council, 55, 149–150

feminism, 21–22, 83–84

Fortuyn, Pim, 170

Fourth National Survey of Ethnic Minorities, 156

France: assimilation approach in, 53–54; Danish cartoons published in, 66; niqab (face veil) banned in, 56; North African Muslims in, 41; racist political party in, 42; radical secularism (laïcité) in, 3, 167; state-funded faith schools in, 174n8, 184; state recognition of Islam in, 167; state-religion separation in, 125–126

Fredrickson, G. M., 34, 39, 40–41, 42, 44; on assimilation, 41

freedom of speech (freedom of expression), 51, 65, 68; absolutism, 218–219; Mill on, 61–62, 65

Freedom Party, in Austria, 78

French Interior Ministers, 129

Le Front National, 42, 78

Galeotti, Anna, 11

Gamble, Andrew, 224–225

Germany, 55, 56, 78, 169; Danish cartoons published in, 66; state-religion separation in, 125–126

Greater London Assembly, 93

Grillo, Ralph, 109n8

Guardian, 96

Habermas, Jürgen, 163, 174n1, 210n3

Hall, Stuart, 38, 79, 93, 156

Harries, Richard Douglas, 109n20

hate speech (incitement to hatred), 120, 166; censor/censure and, 65–69; education of sensibility and, 66; feelings of victim in addressing, 23–24, 62–65, 69–73, 73n2; freedom of speech and, 61–62; group subjectivity and, 23–24; immediate violence aspect of, 62, 63; institutional self-restraint and, 65; legislation, 63–65, 68–69, 73n4–73n5; racial hatred and, 61

Hayes, David, 136

headscarf debate. *See* hijab

Hepple, Bob, 93

hijab (headscarf), 13, 83–84, 171; *l'affaire foulard* and, 167, 174n7; state paternalism and, 208

Hitler, Adolph, 73n3, 171

Hobbes, Thomas, 216

Holocaust denial, 61, 62, 73n1

Home Office Citizenship Survey, 154

Honeyford, Ray, 23, 50

Honeyford Affair, 23, 50

humanism, 99, 100, 109n18, 109n20

humanities subjects, education and, 106

identarian anti-racism, 4–5

identities: agency and, 156, 157; black identity, 3–4; choice and givenness elements of, 185–186; fluidity of, 5; group, 7, 23–24, 79; hybrid and multiple, 44; identity-less self and, 216–217, 218; identity movements, 4–5, 117; majority and minority, 8–9; Muslim, 6; necessary fictions of, 79; political blackness and, 48–49, 49, 57n1; relational nature of, 8; religious and non-religious sources of, 5–7; solidarity and shared, 228–229; Turkish, 9. *See also* British identity; ethno-religious groups, in Britain; Jews and Jewish identity; national identity; religious identity

identity politics (politics of difference), 200; cultural turn in studies of, 145;

equality viewed by new, 118, 122; religious equality and, 123–124
identity recognition: endorsement differentiated from, 11; faith communities and, 204; mediated, 11; terms of inclusion and, 26
ideological secularism, 131, 146
iftar, 11–12
Ignatieff, Michael, 71
imams, state training of, 152, 199
immigration: diversity and, 25, 51, 89; religious belief decline and, 164, 174n3; religious identity and, 102–103, 110n24; waves, 89
incitement to hatred. *See* hate speech
inclusivity: additive not subtractive, 15, 209. *See also* equality; belonging
India, 147, 204, 205, 207–208
inherentism, 39–40, 78
Inner Cities Religious Council, 149
institutional racism, Miles on, 42
institutional self-restraint, 65
intercultural dialogue: multiculturalism and, 219–221, 231n5–231n7; political theory and, 21, 27n11; *The Satanic Verses* and, 218–219
IRA, 152–153
Iraq War, 56–57n1, 97, 125, 132n6
Islam: Benedict XVI on, 169; corporatist form of recognizing, 129, 167; ecclesiastical authority and, 140; founding texts of, 139; French state recognition of, 167; institutional integration of, 127–128; racial and moderate secularism examples in, 146; recognition, 129–131; symbol of pig in, 72; Turkish government department of, 152, 159n1; vilayat-i-faqih, 146
Islamkonfrenz, 55, 167
Islamophobia: anti-essentialism and, 79; critique of othering and, 80–83; cultural anxiety and, 104–105; as cultural racism, 2, 23, 76–78, 122; denial of, 75; group interaction in theorizing, 81–82; liberalism and, 171–172, 175n14; multiculturalism and, 45; Muslim-non-Muslim dialogue and, 84–85; normative framework for studying, 83–85; propositions and study of, 76;
racialization and, 78–79; racial stereotypes as, 103; reasonable criticism distinguished from, 85–86; rise in, 22, 229–230; study of, 75–86; term origin and usage, 75–76; UNESCO definition of, 24; U.S., 209
Islamophobia: A Challenge for Us All (CBMI), 75–76

Jansen, Yolanda, 204–205, 210n8
Jenkins, Roy, 91
Jews and Jewish identity: acknowledgement of race and, 76–77; anti-religious, 102–103; ethnic group recognition of Sikhs and, 47–48, 49; need for recognition, 7; racialization of, 103, 110n29; religious and non-religious sources of, 5–7; state relations with, 130
jihadi terrorism, 229
John Paul II (Pope), 169
Jones, Peter, 11
Joppke, Christian, 193n34
Jyllands-Posten, 63, 72, 170–171

Kessler, Ed, 98
King, Martin Luther, Jr., 3, 117
Kivisto, Peter, 22
Kymlicka, Will, 16, 26, 179, 202–203, 204

Laborde, Cécile, 7, 182, 191n5; Bhargava and, 206–207; Church of England and, 12, 27n8; Jansen and, 210n8; Muslim alienation and, 12, 27n5; secularism advocated by, 207; on symbolic establishment, 183, 206
laïcité. *See* radical secularism
Lawrence, Stephen, 90
LDC. *See* liberal democratic constitutionalism
Leverhulme Programme, Bristol-UCL, x, 96, 109n14
legal positivism, 139
legislation: CMEB recommended anti-discrimination, 103; on hate speech, 63–65, 73n4–73n5; Waldron on hate speech, 69–71, 73. *See also* specific laws

legislature, U.K., Church of England and, 14, 27n8
Levey, Geoffrey, 21, 27n1, 108n1
liberal democratic constitutionalism (LDC), 2, 14, 100, 180, 187–189, 190, 196
Liberal Democrats, Church of England and, 54
liberalism: difference response of, 118; liberal citizenship and identity politics, 123–124; liberal theory, multiculturalism and, 44–45; multicultural accommodation and nationalism, 8; 'muscular', 169–172, 175n14; Muslim practices critique by, 83–85; non-procedural, 192n28; secularism and, 9–11, 27n4; SRCs, multiculturalism and, 179–180, 185–190. *See also* liberal democratic constitutionalism (LDC)
Locke, John, 216
London: bombings, 56, 57n5, 103; Olympic Games in, 96–97, 109n15

Macpherson Report, 90
Madeley, John, 148–149
majoritarianism, 143
majority identity, 8, 155, 200, 218, 230; composite, 8; national identity, 14, 208
majority precedence, 14–15, 16
Malcolm X (El-Hajj Malik el-Shabazz), 4, 223
Mandala v. Lee, 45, 49–50
Marr, Andrew, 93
Marx, Karl, 208
MAT. *See* Muslim Arbitration Tribunal
MCB. *See* Muslim Council of Britain
McLennan, Gregor, 225
Meer, Nasar, 27n1, 220
Mein Kampf (Hitler), 171
#MeToo movement, 73n2
Merkel, Angela, 55, 167
Miles, Robert, 40, 42
Mill, John Stuart, 61–62, 65
minorities: anti-racism politics of 1970s and, 48; British identity and, 102, 110n27–110n29; intercultural dialogue and, 21, 27n11; as projections of dominant groups, 78; survey of ethnic, 156; voice of, 13
minority faiths: accommodation of, 104; CORAB and, 101, 110n23; equalising upwards and, 119; equality and, 119–120; second-generation, 102; state-supported majority religion and, 12, 27n6
minority identity recognition: criterion of inclusivity, 155; multicultural accommodation and, 7; multilogues and, 156; religious identity and, 152–153
misrecognition, 9, 43, 75, 78, 121, 192n28
Moderate Islamist Party, 159n1
moderate secularism: establishment and, 180, 182–184, 191n13; multicultural equality through, 127–131; multiculturalist, 13–17; Muslim accommodation and, 148, 198; Muslim assertiveness, radical and, 166–167, 174n7; neutrality and, 203; pluralising or abandoning, 172–173; problem not solution view of, 205–209; radical distinguished from, 145, 146–147; state-supported religion in, 10, 151–159; variations, 200; Weber and, 18; in Western Europe, 3, 27n2, 197–200, 210n6
Mogra, Ibrahim (Sheikh), 54, 207
Mosque and Community Affairs, 54
Motor-Cycle Crash Helmets (Religious Exemption) Act of 1976, 49–50
Muhammad (The Prophet). *See* Danish cartoons, of Muhammad; *The Satanic Verses* affair
multicultural accommodation: antisecularization vs., 204–205; difference, equality and, 8–9; ethno-religious identity and, 6–7; liberal nationalism and, 8; of minorities (minority faiths), 104, 204–205; minority faiths and, 104; moderate secularism for equality and, 127–131; multiculturalism and, 230; positive accommodation and, 12; praxis-based, 103; religion and, 3–9; secularism and, 9–13, 53–56; in workplace, 109n17
multicultural citizenship, 25; radical secular incompatibility with, 186;

religion and, 137–138; Shari'a controversy and, 135–143
multiculturalism: antisecularization *vs.* accommodation in, 204–205; Bristol School of, 21; in Britain, 4–5, 27n3; Cameron policy ideas on, 160n3; corporatist form of, 129, 167; criticism of, 136; definition of, 1; dialogue in, 217–219, 231n4; feminism and, 21–22; Hayes on radical, 136; hybrid methods and, 17–23; identity, British, 4–5, 27n3; interculturalism and, 219–221, 231n5–231n7; in liberal theory, 44–45; London bombings and, 56, 57n5; moderate secularism and, 13–17, 172–173; multicultural accommodation and, 230; Muslim accommodation and, 202; Muslim assertiveness impact on, 131; need for unity and polarity in, 136; neutrality impossibility in, 9–12, 27n4; pluralistic integration and, 91–92, 127; political use of, 21; religion as part of, 149, 202–204; religious education and, 14; secularism and, 1, 43–45, 195; Shari'a councils as practical, 140–141; SRCs, liberalism and, 179–180, 185–190; state policy of, 43–44; Swann Report impact on concept of, 91; in Western Europe, 200–202
multiculturalist challenge, 1–2; group identities and, 7
multicultural nationalism, 16–17, 231n7
multilogues, citizenship, 136, 156
multiplex privileging, 10–12, 159, 188, 189, 190; establishment, 190
Muslim accommodation: blasphemy law and, 120, 131n2; Christianity and, 189–190; equality demands specific for, 118–122; European context of secularism and, 53–56, 56; Islam recognition and, 129–131; moderate secularism and, 148, 202; multiculturalism and, 202; practice-based religions and, 103; secularism and, 53–56, 124–127; SRCs and, 128–131
Muslim Arbitration Tribunal (MAT), 141–142

Muslim assertiveness: crisis of secularism and, 164–166; equality agenda success, 56; moderate and radical secularist response to, 166–167, 174n7; multiculturalism impacted by, 131; religious equality demands in, 121–122
Muslim Council of Britain (MCB), 52, 53, 54, 57n3, 130; New Labour and, 132n5, 166–167
Muslims: Bosnian, 77; dress codes and, 103; feminism critique of, 83–84; racial stereotypes of male, 40; reasonable criticism of, 85–86; survey on Christians prejudice against, 132n3; terrorism and, 98, 103–105. *See also* British Muslims; Muslim accommodation; Muslim assertiveness
Muslims, in Western Europe: alienation of, 12, 27n5; identity recognition and, 11; identity understanding of, 6; prioritizing religious identity and, 2

national identity, 169–171; CMEB on, 95, 106, 107–108; German, 169. *See also* belonging and citizenship
nationalism (national culture): multicultural, 16–17; problem of 'thinning', 16
Nazis, 36
Netherlands, 128, 132n5, 165, 171
neutrality, state: liberal goal of, 9–12, 27n4; moderate secularism and, 203; multiculturalism impossibility of, 9–12, 27n4; religion and state, 9–12, 27n4; SRCs and, 186–188, 187, 190. *See also* multiplex privileging
new ethnicities, 154
New Labour government: Brexit and, 21, 27n12; CMEB and, 96; MCB and, 52, 53, 132n6, 166–167; multiculturalist, 7
9/11 attacks, impact of, 71, 72, 73n5, 98, 103, 131n2
niqab (face veil), 13, 56, 167
normativity (norms): framework for studying Islamophobia, 83–85; social science and, 19–23
North African Muslims, in France, 41
Northern Ireland, 36, 42, 47, 62, 63, 64, 68, 94, 102–103, 120, 152, 165

Norwood v. Director of Public Prosecutions (DPP), 71–72

Oakeshott, Michael, 19, 158
Obama, Barack, 156
Olympic Games, in London, 96–97, 109n15
On Liberty (Mill), 61–62
operative public values, 81, 128
Orientalism, 84
Orwell, George, 222
othering, 24; cultural racism and, 76–78; empirical inquiry and, 84; Islamophobia and critique of, 80–83; knowledge of other presupposed by, 80–83; normative framework in critique of, 83–85
Our Shared Future, 90
Ouseley, Herman, 93

Paki-bashing, 22
Pakistanis: Bangladeshis and, 52, 57n1; change to Muslim identity, 102; Honeyford Affair and, 23, 50; religiosity, school attendance among male, 153
Parekh, Bhikhu, 27n1, 90, 108n1–108n4, 128, 218–219, 225, 230n3; as CMEB chair, 92, 98; commission reports involvement of, 108n4, 109n9; on pluralistic integration, 91–92; racism viewed by, 92; *The Satanic Verses* and, 224; Taylor and, 220
Party for Freedom, 171
Le Pen, Marine, 78
Pew Survey, 154, 203
Phillips, Trevor, 93
pillarization, 165
Plato, 151, 215
pluralistic integration: moderate secularism and, 172–173; multicultural equality and, 127; of Parekh, 91–92; state-religion separation obstacle to, 137–138
policy, religion-based, 151–159; danger reason for, 152–153; identity reason for, 153–157; religion as truth reason for, 151–152; respect for religion and, 157–159, 160n3; utility reason for, 153
policy, welfare, 174n4

political blackness, 48–49, 49, 51, 57n1
political secularism. *See* secularism, political
political theory: contextualised, 19; dialogue in, 21, 27n11, 215–217, 230n1; hybrid of normative and empirical, 17–23; intercultural dialogue and, 21, 27n11; limits of, 9; multiculturalist dialogue and, 217–219, 231n4
politics of recognition: equality understood in terms of, 117; interculturalism and, 220
polygamy, 126
poverty, state-religion ties and, 153, 159n2
Presbyterian Church, 182
Prevention of Incitement to Hatred Act 1970, 73n4
Private Choice Test, 190
privileging, of religion, 188–189, 193n34–193n37
The Prophet. *See* Danish cartoons, of Muhammad; *The Satanic Verses* affair
Protestants, 132n5, 152
protestors, focus on grievance of, 67
PSI Fourth Survey, 132n3
public intellectual engagement, 26, 221–225; interview on, 226–230
public good, 2, 10, 14, 100, 106, 148, 153, 180, 198–199
public bad/harm and, 106, 198–199
public-private distinction, 123, 126, 127–128, 200
Public Order Act, 69, 131n2

Quebec, 173, 187, 218, 220

race, 95; as beyond biology and colour, 77; ethnic cleansing and, 77, 103; ethno-religious groups and, 76–77; racial dualism, 33; racial hatred, 61; racialization as more than, 78–79; reduction, 78–79; religion, ethnicity and, 174n7
Race Relations Act, 69
racial equality, religious and, 52–53
racialization, 78–79, 81–82; counterexamples and, 41–42, 80–81; of Jews, 103, 110n29; religious basis of,

37; of Western European Muslims, 2, 23, 43, 78–79
racial stereotypes, 40, 81–82, 103; exceptional counterexamples and, 41–42, 80–81
racism: anti-Muslim, 138; Atlantocentric, 33; biological, 36, 37, 37–38, 42, 75; CMEB conceptualisation of, 93; inherentism feature of, 39–40; institutional, 42; narrow definitions of race and, 33; Parekh on, 92; postwar, 77. *See also* colour racism; cultural racism; Islamophobia; anti-semitism
radicalization: group identity, 7; terrorism and, 199
radical secularism (*laïcité*), 3, 10, 25, 27n2, 121; in France, 3, 167, 184; incompatibility with multiculturalism, 186; moderate distinguished from, 145, 146–147; Muslim assertiveness and, 166–167, 174n7; state-religion ties in spite of, 55–56
Ramadan, Tariq, 12, 143, 144n10
Rawls, John, 44, 216–217, 218, 219, 230n2
RE. *See* religious education
reasonable person exercise, 13
Reconquista, 36, 41
religion and religiosity: ban on ostentatious dress/symbols of, 171; census question on, 121, 166, 169; combining ethnicity and, 5, 154; criticism of, 64; as danger, 152–153; decline in church attendance and, 164, 174n3; different countries secularism and, 125; in different forms of secularism, 124–127; equality and, 119–120; as ethnic feature of Britain, 154; humanism and, 99, 109n18, 109n20; increased public salience of, 105; literacy, 105–106; meaning variations, 103–104; moderate secularism and state-supported, 10; multicultural accommodation and, 3–9; multicultural citizenship and, 137–138; as part of multiculturalism, 202–204; plurality, 150; positive inclusion of religious groups, 120–122; post-immigration diversity and, 25; practice-based, 103; privatisation of, 125–126; privileging of, 159, 188–189, 193n34–193n37; protecting people/beliefs and, 63, 71; as public good, 106, 180–181, 198, 199; as public good and public bad, 106, 180–181, 198; public-private boundaries and, 122, 123–124, 124–127, 132n5, 197, 226; race, ethnicity and, 174n7; racialization based on, 37; religious diversity, 101–107, 149; respect for others', 157–159, 160n3; in schools, 14–16, 27n9; secular beliefs on par with, 99, 109n18; as secularism reference point, 196–197; secularist accommodation and, 9–13; state neutrality and, 9–12, 27n4; as truth, 151–152; as utility, 153. *See also* Commission on Religion and Belief in British Public Life; commission reports, on ethnic groups and religion; ethno-religious groups, in Britain; policy, religion-based; state-funded faith schools; state-supported religion
religious discrimination: demand for abolishing, 119; laws against, 166
religious education (RE), 14, 16
religious equality, 118–122; identity politics and, 123–124; Islam recognition and, 129–131; liberal citizenship implications of, 123–124; racial equality inclusion of, 52–53
religious identity, 153–157; among post-immigrant groups, 102–103, 110n24; census, 100–101, 110n21; citizenship equality and, 2; ethnic replaced by, 102, 110n25; inclusivity criterion, 155; Muslim salience of, 101, 102; non-religious included in, 102; political equality and, 226; South Asian community and, 110n24; survey on social class and, 154
religious instruction (RI), 14–16
religious intolerance, culturalism and, 35
RI. *See* religious instruction
Richardson, Robin, 86n1, 98, 108n1, 109n9, 109n11
riots, 102
Rousseau, Jacques, 216
Roy, Olivier, 157, 163

Royal Commission on the Reform of the House of Lords, 54, 128, 150
Royal Courts of Justice, 135
Runnymede Trust, 24, 75–76, 86n1, 90, 93. *See also* Commission on Multi-Ethnic Britain; Commission on Religion and Belief in British Public Life
Rushdie, Salman, 3, 24, 47. *See also The Satanic Verses* affair

Said, Edward, 21, 221–224
The Salisbury Review, 50
The Satanic Verses affair, 26, 40, 51, 52–53, 57n2, 75, 122; burning of, 191n14; censure and censor issue in, 229; CMEB in light of, 93–94; CORAB and, 98; crisis of secularism and, 165–166; education of sensibility and, 66; failure of campaign to ban, 166; intercultural dialogue and, 218–219; most hurtful aspect of, 67; public intellectual engagement and, 227–228; response to Danish cartoons *vs.*, 63, 66–67; seriousness of incitement in, 66
Scarman Report, 90
schools: Christian non-denominational worship in, 157; drop-out rates, 153; religion in, 14–16, 27n9
secular bias, 121
secular Christian, 169–170
secular Jew, 169–170
secularism, political, 100; Asad and, 84; autonomy and, 10, 195–197, 198; Bhargava on, 181, 181–182, 191n7, 191n9, 197–198; British Muslim identity and, 122; Christianity and, 146, 146–147; Church of England constitutional privileges and, 14, 27n8; in comparative European context, 53–56; in contemporary Western Europe, 146–147; CORAB report and, 99, 100; core idea of, 195–197; country by country, 124–127; crisis of secularism and, 163–173; definition of, 10; dominance of non-accommodative, 158–159; dominant mode of Western Europe, 2; Hayes on radical, 136; hegemonic power of, 122; humanism and, 99, 109n18; ideological, 131, 146;

incitement to religious hatred law and, 120; liberalism and, 9–11, 27n4; mainstream, Western, 147–150; moderate distinguished from radical, 145, 146–147; multicultural accommodation, religion and, 9–13, 53–56; multiculturalism and, 1, 43–45, 195; Muslim accommodation and, 53–56, 124–127; Muslim challenge to, 165; philosophical understanding of, 99; 'post', 173; public-private boundaries and, 122, 124–127, 132n5, 226; religion as reference point in, 196–197; SRCs and, 180–185, 191n5, 191n7, 191n9, 191n13; state-religion separation and, 9; theory *vs.* practice, 179–180; welfare and, 174n4. *See also* moderate secularism; neutrality, state; radical secularism
selective assimilation, 42
self-restraint, institutional, 65
Shari'a councils, 135–136, 138; critical interpretism and, 139; legal positivism and, 139; practical multiculturalism and, 140–141; Ramadan response to talk on, 143, 144n10; retrospection on controversy over, 141–143; women's use of, 142–143
Sikhs (Sikh identity), 101, 102; ethnic group recognition of Jews and, 47–48, 49; multicultural accommodation of, 4; turban campaign of British, 23, 49–50, 51, 110n25
social contract, 216
social meaning: context and, 12–13; of establishment, 13
social science: normative character of, 19–23; Weber and, 18, 19
sociology, normative political theory and empirical, 17–23
Socrates, 215
solidarity, shared identity and, 228–229
Somali settlement, 57n1
Southall Black Sisters, 51
South Asians, 35–36; BNP targeting, 38–39; colour racism and, 34; political blackness and, 48; religious community identification among, 110n24
SRCs. *See* state-religion connections

state: Church of England recognized by, 12; CORAB on religious education support from, 106; difference education and, 106–107; historical-cultural character of, 187; imams training by, 152, 199; multiculturalism policies, 160n3; paternalism, 208; policy of multiculturalism, 43–44; religion interest of, 151. *See also* neutrality, state

state-funded faith schools, 106, 140, 156, 165; in France, 174n8, 184; non-Christian schools and, 52, 92

state-religion connections (SRCs), 2; Britain's policy of deepening, 54–55; Cameron 'Big Society' and, 160n3; definition of, 196; French *laïcité* and, 55–56; hijab debate and, 170; Jewish model for, 130; LDC and, 187–190, 191n1, 196; monarch crowning example of, 154; multiculturalist, liberalism and, 179–180; Muslim accommodation and, 128–131; Muslim school funding and, 52; in Netherlands, 128, 132n5; Netherlands example of, 128, 132n5, 165; pluralisation of, 54; pluralising existing, 190; public goods of religion necessitating, 199; reason typology for importance of, 151; secularism and, 180–185, 191n5, 191n7, 191n9, 191n13; state neutrality and, 186–188, 187, 190; welfare to needy and, 153, 160n3

state-religion separation: in France, 125–126; in Germany, 126; historical actuality and, 145, 150; lack of neutrality in liberal goal of, 9–12, 27n4; *laïcité* as not requiring, 55–56; Muslim alienation resulting from, 13; political secularism assumption of, 9; secularism as, 54; secularism variations in different countries version of, 124–127; U.S. wall of separation and, 121. *See also* secularism

state-supported religion: CORAB on education and, 106; minorities and, 12, 27n6; reason typology for benefits of, 151; religion-based policy and, 151–159

Steering Group of CORAB, 98
stereotypes. *See* racial stereotypes
Straw, Jack, 56, 95–96, 96
Der Stürmer, 66, 73n3
Sufi Muslim Council, 57n3
Sunni Islam, 129, 140
Suti Muslim Council, 57n3
Swann, Michael, 90
Swann Report (*Education for All: Report of the Committee of Inquiry in the Education of Children from Ethnic Minority Groups*), 89, 90, 91–92, 108n5
synopsis, 23–26

Taylor, Charles, 4, 11, 171, 192n28, 220; dialogical ethics of, 218
terrorism, 52, 98, 105, 131n2; Islamophobia and, 229–230; jihadi, 229
Thatcher, Margaret, 90
Theory of Justice (Rawls), 44
Thompson, Simon, 19, 26
Thompson, Simon, interview with, 225, 226–230
Trump, Donald, 78, 209
Truth and Development Party (AKP), 159n1
Tully, James, 218
turban-bomb cartoon. *See* Danish cartoons, of Muhammad
turban campaign, Sikh, 23, 49–50, 51, 110n25
Turkey, 152, 159n1, 169
Turks, as Belgium minority, 9

Uberoi, Varun, 27n1, 108n1
UK Action Committee on Islamic Action (UKACIA), 52
UKIP. *See* United Kingdom Independence Party
UNESCO, 24, 76, 220
United Kingdom (UK), migration into, 89
United Kingdom Independence Party (UKIP), 78, 167
United States (U.S.), 203, 208, 209; Declaration of Independence, 151–152; religious instruction banned in schools of, 14; secularism in USSR *vs.*, 195; state-religion separation in Britain *vs.*, 125; Supreme Court, 190, 195; wall of

separation, 121
U.S. *See* United States
USSR, 195, 196

the Veil of Ignorance, 216–217, 230n2
vilayat-i-faqih, 146
violence, incitement to hatred leading to, 62, 63

Waldron, Jeremy, 23–24, 69–71, 73
War on Terror, 142
Weber, Max, 14, 18, 19, 20
welfare, 174n4
Western Europe: diversity challenges facing, 1; dominant mode of political secularism in, 2; moderate secularism in, 3, 27n2, 197–200, 210n5; multiculturalism in, 200–202; Muslim racialisation in, 2, 23, 42–43, 78–79; Muslims in, 2, 6, 11, 12, 27n5; political theorists on secularism in, 197–198; secularism and accommodation comparison, 53–56; secularism in contemporary, 146–147; two movements in, 3, 27n2
Wilder, Geert, 171
Williams, Rowan, 135, 138, 141
Wittgenstein, L., 42, 79
Women Against Fundamentalists, 51
Woolf Institute, 97, 98
workplace: discrimination, 120–121; reasonable accommodation in, 109n17

Young, Iris, 117, 218
Yugoslavia, 103

About the Author

Tariq Modood is Professor of Sociology, Politics and Public Policy and the founding Director of the Centre for the Study of Ethnicity and Citizenship at the University of Bristol and the co-founder of the international journal *Ethnicities*. He has held over 40 grants and consultancies, has over 35 (co-)authored and (co-)edited books and reports and over 200 articles and chapters. He was a Robert Schuman Fellow at the European University Institute for part of 2013–2015, and a 'Thinker in Residence' at the Royal Academy of Flanders, Brussels, in 2017.

He is highly committed to public engagement. His work is frequently cited by policy-makers and practitioners and on several occasions has influenced policy. His impact case study, *'Influencing law, policy and public discourse on the accommodation of Muslims in Britain'* was one of three which collectively were ranked as 3rd in the UK by the Sociology 2013 REF.

He was awarded a MBE for services to social sciences and ethnic relations in 2001, was made a Fellow of the Academy of Social Sciences in 2004 and elected a Fellow of the British Academy in 2017. He served on the Commission on the Future of Multi-Ethnic Britain, the National Equality Panel, and the Commission on Religion and Belief in British Public Life.

His latest books include *Multiculturalism: A Civic Idea* (2nd edition, 2013); and as co-editor *Multiculturalism Rethought* (2015), *Multiculturalism and Interculturalism: Debating the Dividing Lines* (2016) and *The Problem of Religious Diversity: European Problems, Asian Challenges* (2017). His website is tariqmodood.com.